Chapter 1

The English legal system

1.1 The nature of law

Any system of law is basically a method of enforcing order and a reasonable standard of fair play. In any community, man-made rules will develop to control the relationships between individual members. At the same time, there must be some method of enforcing these rules, and ensuring that the system is flexible enough to respond to the need for change where and when it is necessary. Law is a very important influence in society. It can reflect a country's moral values, but the difficulty with a moral attitude to the law is that moral values change with time and place. A legal system enables persons to order their lives with a degree of certainty and, normally, in a manner which the community considers to be just and fair. The layman tends to avoid involvement in this process if possible. Criticism is made of the delay, expense and complexity of the system and sometimes this criticism is justified. However, it ought to be recognised that the law is able at times to provide a solution to human problems and difficulties which in itself is an achievement.

1.2 Civil and criminal law

As legal systems develop, two main categories tend to emerge, the objects of which are different. These are the criminal and the civil law. The object of the criminal law is to punish conduct of which the state disapproves and to act as a deterrent. Because of its nature, the criminal law is said to be part of the public law which governs the relationship between the state and the individual. It is the state (the prosecution) which is responsible for bringing a case against the

1

person considered to be responsible for the criminal act (the defendant or the accused). However, as we live in a monarchy, proceedings are brought in the name of the Crown which normally delegates to the police the task of bringing the case. In more complex cases, the Director of Public Prosecutions takes over this role.

The civil law is not concerned with punishment but essentially with compensation. It concerns itself with dealings between individual members of the state, whether private individuals, firms or companies. It attempts to resolve disputes and to give a remedy to the person wronged, normally financial in nature. In a civil case, the plaintiff brings the action against the defendant. Most of the civil law is known as private law because it only affects the individuals involved in the proceedings even though the state may have made the law regulating the conduct between those individuals.

Sometimes the same set of events gives rise to both criminal and civil proceedings. Road accidents are a good example. If a driver is alleged to have injured a pedestrian through his dangerous or careless driving, two types of issue arise. A prosecution in a criminal court may well be brought against the driver under the Road Traffic Acts, while the compensation aspects will be determined in a separate civil action brought by the injured party in a civil court. There are numerous other situations where this dual liability arises. Whether the case be criminal or civil, an appeal may normally be made to a higher court against the decision of the original court. In this case, the person bringing the appeal is known as the appellant, and the person against whom the appeal is brought is known as the respondent.

1.3 The common law

Most legal systems in Europe are based upon Roman law, but England and Wales are subject to the so-called common law. This dates from the unification of local customs which followed the Norman conquest of 1066. Up to that date, the laws and courts of England and Wales varied from area to area as there was no unified legal system. Each court operated in isolation. Moreover, there was no centralised institution exercising either administrative or judicial control over the legal system. The object of the Normans was to establish a national system of law which would be common to the whole country, a system which would apply to all persons alike,

Basic Construction and Surveying Law

Basic Construction and Surveying Law

DOUGLAS WOOD

BA, LLB, ACIArb

GRANADA

London Toronto Sydney New York

Granada Technical Books
Granada Publishing Ltd
8 Grafton Street, London W1X 3LA

First published in Great Britain by
Granada Publishing 1984

ISBN 0-246-11963-2

Printed and bound in Great Britain by
Mackays of Chatham Ltd

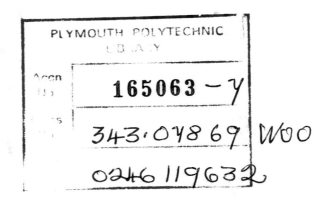

Contents

Preface

This book is aimed primarily at students studying law as an integral part of degree and diploma courses in estate management, construction and quantity surveying. Consequently, it is also appropriate for those preparing for the direct examinations of the Royal Institution of Chartered Surveyors, the Incorporated Society of Valuers and Auctioneers and the Institute of Housing. In addition, the text has been written for building students studying for the examinations in law subjects of the Chartered Institute of Building and for the Higher TEC Certificate and Diploma in Building Law and Contractual Procedures and Legislation.

The overall purpose has been to provide a text which is sufficiently detailed for professional students yet readable and practical enough for those studying at pre-professional level. It is not a specialist commentary. Those seeking detailed advice on matters such as building contracts, landlord and tenant or housing law must look elsewhere. Legal terminology has been kept to an essential minimum and footnotes have been discarded.

I wish to express my gratitude to John Snape for his initial suggestions relating to publication and to Jennifer Roberts who typed the manuscript and advised on various legal aspects.

I have endeavoured to state the law as it was on 1 January 1984.

Douglas Wood

wherever they were situated geographically and whatever their status in society. This law was based partly on the Norman law which they brought with them from France and partly on those English customs which they found to be widespread.

King William I set up the King's Council or *Curia Regis*. This was the central government of the kingdom which exercised administrative, law-making (legislative) and judge-like (judicial) functions without distinction. It consisted mainly of the King's 'tenants in chief', meaning those to whom the King had granted large tracts of land in return for some service, such as providing soldiers and horses. All land belonged to the Crown as it still does today, at least in theory.

As the creation of the common law was strictly on an *ad hoc* basis, each problem was settled as it arose. However, the Normans developed a strong central government and gradually the old local customs began to disappear, their place being taken by the King's court. From this court, special courts were instituted to deal with particular types of cases in which the King's justice was sought. These courts were able to compel the attendance of parties involved in the proceedings and of witnesses. They were also able to enforce their own decisions.

The practice also grew up of sending judges appointed by the King to act as Royal Commissioners throughout the country. These judges dealt with both civil and criminal matters wherever they arose. This process was developed in the reign of Henry II (1154-89), and eventually it led to the introduction of the assize system which existed until the Courts Act of 1971. As new courts developed, the *Curia Regis* diminished in importance. These courts included the Court of Exchequer, the Court of Common Pleas and the Court of King's Bench. Therefore, when the expression 'common law' is used, it means that body of law which was developed in these courts.

COMMON LAW PROCEDURE

From the reign of Henry II, civil actions in the common law courts had to be started by writ. This royal command had to be obtained from the King's Chancellor. For every civil case there was a separate writ and the plaintiff had to select the particular writ which he considered fitted the facts of the case. These original writs were simply documents containing an order from the King addressed to the defendant, the County Sheriff or the Lord of the Manor, normally requiring the defendant's attendance at the royal court to answer allegations against him. The different types of writ gave rise to different forms of action. This meant that the method of trial and the procedural rules which were applicable depended upon the nature of the writ used to start the case off. Much civil law was built up defining the circumstances in which the various writs could be brought.

1.4 Equity

By the end of the reign of Edward I (1272-1307) the deficiencies of the common law system were becoming apparent. The writ system had become very formalised. Writs were not available to cover every set of circumstances, and the general rule was that unless there was an appropriate writ there was no remedy. No action could succeed unless the correct court was chosen. In addition, technicalities tended to dominate common law procedure. These became very complex and an action might fail because of a slight error in the preparation of the documents required to start a case off (pleadings). Above all, the greatest problem in the common law courts was the lack of appropriate remedies, these being generally limited to an award of compensation in monetary form (damages).

Plaintiffs who were dissatisfied with the process of justice in the common law courts began to petition the King in an attempt to redress their grievances. By the end of the fourteenth century there were so many petitions that the King referred them to the Lord Chancellor. From this process, the courts of equity emerged, presided over by the Lord Chancellor. They granted remedies where they thought it equitable and just to do so. The judges in these courts were able to grant remedies which the common law courts could not. These Chancellor's courts, or courts of chancery, as they became known, provided an alternative set of courts to those of the common law. At common law the only remedy was damages, but equity offered new remedies, such as specific performance, injunction, and the right to withdraw from a contract. The main problem was that each court could only award its own particular remedy. Any plaintiff seeking both damages and an equitable remedy had to go first to the common law courts in order to obtain compensation and then to the courts of equity for an equitable remedy. As far as the available remedies were concerned, equity eventually became as formalised as the common law. Equity, however, has never been a complete system of law. Instead, it is a gloss or addition to the common law and it is unlikely that any new equitable concepts would be created today.

In the middle of the nineteenth century, a number of reforms were effected to the legal system resulting in the Judicature Acts of 1873 to 1875. These acts set up the system of courts which we have today. The existing court structures were reorganised while it was established that both common law and equity matters could be dealt with in the same court. The acts ordained that where the rules of common law and equity conflicted, the rules of equity were to prevail. Although the common law and equity were fused for administrative purposes, they still retained their own individual characteristics. If a plaintiff succeeds in winning his case the common law remedy of damages is available automatically. On the other hand, equitable remedies are in the discretion of the court. Equity is of particular importance in the development of land law, while in the law of contract the use of equitable remedies is important in the construction industry.

1.5 The sources of law

Before the common law system can be fully understood it is necessary to consider the ways in which English law developed and to find out where the law comes from. Most continental countries have a system whereby almost the whole of their law is contained in written codes, which are amended as the need arises. The Code Napoléon in France is a good example. On the other hand, English law has been developed from a number of sources, each arising as the situation required it. Most new law is produced by act of parliament to meet the complex requirements of contemporary society. However, the greater part of English law has developed from the rules and principles pronounced in the decisions of courts throughout the centuries. The other major source of law which is referred to is custom. This was originally a source of law of great importance. In fact this is where the common law originated. Its practical importance nowadays is slight but occasionally a case comes before the courts establishing a local custom.

1.6 Custom

A custom is a right or duty which has come to exist through the consent of the population. Traditionally a custom could either be general (applicable to the whole country) or local (applicable to a particular area). Nowadays, only local customs are of any importance as general customs have become incorporated into the common law. If a person wishes to prove the existence of a custom never previously recognised by the courts, such as a right of way, a number of tests have to be satisfied before it will become law.

TESTS OF RECOGNITION

Time immemorial
The custom must have existed since 'time immemorial'. This is fixed as 1189. As it is normally impossible for the person claiming the custom to show conclusively that it existed in 1189, it is enough to show that the local custom has existed for a substantial period. This was proved in *Mercer* v. *Denne* (1905) where is was established that fishermen had a right to dry their nets on a privately-owned beach. The owner was restrained from building on the beach because to have done so would have interfered with their 'rights'. However, this presumption can be challenged if it can be shown that the custom could not have been exercised at some time since 1189. In *Simpson* v. *Wells* (1872) a custom of holding a stall on a highway was shown not to have been authorised before the fourteenth century.

Continuity
This custom must have been continuously in operation, but it need not have been exercised throughout the required period as long as the right existed. It seems that a customary right cannot be lost by disuse but only by act of parliament. In *Wyld* v. *Silver* (1962) the inhabitants of a parish were entitled, by act of parliament, to hold an annual fair on a particular piece of land. Although no such fair had been held within living memory the parishioners were able to obtain an order preventing the landowner from building on it.

Exercised as a right (nec vi, nec clam, nec precario)
The basis of a custom is that it is exercised by consent. Therefore, if it is exercised with force or in secret there can be no custom.

In particular, if the so-called custom is exercised by permission it cannot be as of right and therefore it is impossible to establish it as a local custom. In *Mills* v. *Colchester Corporation* (1867) a claim to a custom entitling the plaintiff to an annual licence to fish for oysters failed as the existence of a licence prevented the fishing from being as of right.

Reasonableness and certainty

The courts will not recognise any custom which is unreasonable. In addition the custom must be certain. This means that the area of application of the custom must be certain while the persons who are to benefit from it must be capable of proper identification. In *Wilson* v. *Willes* (1806) a claim to a local custom to take turf failed because the extent of this so-called 'right' could not be identified.

In addition to the above tests, the custom must be consistent with previously established customs and it must not conflict with statute law or any basic principle of the common law.

Examples of local customs appearing before the courts are few. However, from time to time, such rights are recognised despite the law's reluctance to do so where the custom has not been established before. The cases normally concern rights in land. In *New Windsor Corporation* v. *Mellor* (1975) a local authority was prevented from utilising land where it was proved that for many centuries the land had been used for recreational purposes by the local inhabitants. Similar issues arose in *Egerton* v. *Harding* (1968), a case involving the custom to fence alongside common land.

Case law

HISTORY

Case law is the essence of the common law. The greater part of English law consists of rules and principles stated by judges throughout the centuries. When a judge makes a decision on a particular aspect of the law, this will be recorded and other judges are obliged to follow this decision in subsequent cases. Therefore, when a judge is dealing with a case he must first look back to previous cases which have involved similar facts in the same area of law to see how these cases have been dealt with.

LAW REPORTS

The importance of case law as a source of law depends upon the existence of law reports. Important cases which establish new principles of law are published in law reports. The report contains details of the facts of the case, together with the decision of the judge and the reasons given. The history of law reporting began with Year Books. These were manuscripts which mentioned cases which had been dealt with in a particular locality. After the demise of the Year Books, the practice arose whereby a number of private reports were separately published. These were often compiled by lawyers for their own personal use. The standard and quality varied greatly. Good examples included those by Coke, Blackstone and Burrow, who all established a reputation for reporting cases accurately. Many of the cases reported between the disappearance of the Year Books and 1865 have been collected and reprinted for the sake of convenience and are referred to by judges in the course of their decisions.

Modern law reporting dates from 1865 with the creation of the Council of Law Reporting. This was followed in 1870 by the Incorporated Council of Law Reporting which issues four series of reports: Appeal cases (AC), Queen's Bench (QB), Chancery (Ch) and Family (Fam). Construction industry disputes appear in the first three of these. In addition, the Council also publishes the Weekly Law Reports (WLR). Although the courts prefer traditionally to use the more official reports, there are a number which are commercially produced. The All England Reports (All ER) are amongst the best known. The Local Government Reports (LGR) often include important building and engineering cases while recently a new series of reports was introduced to deal with cases affecting the construction industry. These are Building Law Reports (BLR), which attempt to include cases which have not been previously reported. *The Times* carries daily reports of leading cases, while professional publications such as *Estates Gazette* publish reports of interest to their readers. When a case is reported, after the names of the parties there is normally given the name of the reports and the page where the case is to be found. For example, *Dutton* v. *Bognor Regis UDC* [1972] 1 QB 373 means that the first volume of the Queen's Bench reports for 1972 must be consulted and on page 373 details of the case are reported.

JUDICIAL PRECEDENT

After the reorganisation of the courts implemented by the Judicature Acts (1873-75) and the emergence of good law reporting in the later part of the nineteenth century, judicial precedent became a fully-established source of law. By this doctrine of *stare decisis* (to stand upon decisions) as it is sometimes known, whenever a judge reaches a decision on a particular point, that decision will bind judges in later cases dealing with a similar issue. However, not every judicial decision makes a precedent as some courts are more important than others and not every case is important enough to make new law.

HOW THE SYSTEM WORKS

The principle forming the reason for a decision is called the *ratio decidendi*. This is the binding precedent which must be followed in future cases. During the course of its decision a court may make other remarks of a more general nature about the law which are not strictly relevant to the decision. These are known as *obiter dicta* and are said to be of persuasive authority. The importance of distinguishing between the two lies in the fact that it is only the *ratio* which is binding on a later court and not the *dicta*. However, in the higher level courts, things said 'by the way' (*obiter dicta*) are frequently of very persuasive authority even though they are not legally binding.

This doctrine of judicial precedent is applied on an hierarchical basis. Basically, the lower courts are bound by the decisions of the higher courts. Therefore, the High Court will be bound by a decision of the Court of Appeal and the Court of Appeal will be bound by a decision of the House of Lords, which is the supreme appeal court in both civil and criminal matters. Decisions of this court are binding on all lower courts. In addition, some courts are bound by their own previous decisions. Since 1966, the House of Lords has been able to depart from its previous decisions. Instances of this have been rare. The decision in *Herrington* v. *British Rail Board* (1972) is a good example. The County Court and the Magistrates Court at the bottom of the court hierarchy are known as inferior courts. They are bound by the decisions of the superior courts but are not subject themselves to the rules of precedent or bound by their own decisions.

AVOIDING PRECEDENT

Despite the importance of precedent in English law, a court will sometimes refuse to follow an earlier decision if it thinks application of the old precedent would in the circumstances cause injustice.

So if there are grounds for distinguishing a case from an earlier decision the latter will not be followed. In addition, a court may not agree with the earlier decision of a lower court and may overrule it. Similar criteria apply where the decision of a lower court is reversed on appeal or where a higher court disapproves of a previous decision. Before the precedent has a binding effect, it must be shown to be a decision of a court in the English hierarchy. American or Australian decisions, for example, are not binding, although foreign cases are increasingly referred to in English courts. In addition, a decision of the Judicial Committee of the Privy Council is not binding. A factor which has had an effect on case law is the growth of European Community law which has directly made the United Kingdom subject to the laws of the Common Market. By joining the EEC, parliament accepted that in the interpretation of the various treaties between the member states of the Community, the supreme court would be the European Court of Justice.

THE ADVANTAGES OF PRECEDENT

Certainty

It is usually suggested that precedent gives at least some degree of certainty and consistency to the law so that the probable outcome of a case can be predicted:

Flexibility

The flexible aspect of the doctrine is its ability to provide an answer to legal problems. Where appropriate, a judge is able to avoid an unsatisfactory precedent by distinguishing or overruling.

Detail

Case law has many detailed rules. The law reports provide full information relating to decided cases and it is argued that a code could never furnish similar precision.

Practical aspects

It is more useful to have a precedent than to argue a case on each occasion that a legal issue arises. Critics suggest that it is necessary to wait until an actual dispute arises before the law is known.

THE DISADVANTAGES OF PRECEDENT

Rigidity
The system gives a judge limited scope for manoeuvre. At least parliament can legislate for a change.

Technicalities
The sophisticated methods of avoiding a precedent tend to confuse the law and produce a degree of uncertainty.

Bulk
Because of the volume of cases, it is increasingly difficult to refer to every appropriate authority. Sometimes cases go unreported but they still remain precedents.

1.8 Legislation

This is the most important source of law in the United Kingdom today. A statute or act of parliament is the quickest and clearest method of changing or adding to the law. Such an act overrules any existing custom, case law or earlier act with which it is in conflict, and the only external factor which can possibly affect this parliament-made law is the EEC. This supremacy of legislation over all other sources of law is known as the sovereignty of parliament. The effect of this is that the legality of parliament to make a specific law cannot be challenged. This is to be contrasted with the position in the United States of America where the supreme court may question legislation on the basis that it is unconstitutional.

THE MAKING OF A STATUTE

In this country, parliament consists of two different legislative institutions known as the House of Commons and the House of Lords. Ideas for new laws are put forward by both the government and by private members of parliament, though the former are by far the more numerous today. The idea is put into technical language in a bill. Government bills are prepared by civil servants called parliamentary draftsmen. Normally, a bill has to pass through several stages in both the Commons and the Lords before it receives the Royal Assent (the Queen's approval) and becomes an act. It is then printed, and copies may be purchased from Her Majesty's Stationery Office. Traditionally, when a bill becomes law, the act comes into operation on 1 January of the following year. However, with the bulk and complexity of contemporary legislation, much statute law is now brought into operation section by section over a period of time. Once it becomes law, the act remains in force unless and until it is repealed.

TYPES OF ACTS

Public acts
This is an act which affects the community generally. It is the most common type of act which is promulgated.

Private acts
These do not alter the general law but confer special or local powers. They are often promoted by local authorities.

Consolidating acts
This is a statute which gathers together several acts on one area of law and re-enacts them so that all the statute law on a particular topic can be found in the same act. This is periodically done with tax legislation, while other examples include planning law, and the law relating to highways.

Codifying acts
This arises where the whole of the law on a particular topic is enacted in one statute. It includes all previous case law, established customs, and legislation. The law of most continental countries is codified, but in the United Kingdom and other common law countries there is little codification. The classic example of codification in English law is the Sale of Goods Act 1893 (now SGA 1979) which reduced all the law on the subject into a single code.

STATUTORY INTERPRETATION

As explained previously, the courts cannot challenge the validity of an act of parliament because of the concept of parliamentary sovereignty. However, the meaning of a particular act or a section of it is normally a matter for the courts to decide. Specific rules have been formulated to deal with the interpretation of statutes by the courts. Many acts include an interpretation section dealing with the words and phrases used in it. A good example of this is section 205 and the Law of Property Act 1925. Parliament has also helped the courts to some extent by passing the Interpretation

Act 1978 which defines many expressions used in legislation, unless a contrary intention is apparent. The theoretical test of the courts is to 'interpret the will of parliament' as expressed in the statute. To help the judges in that task of interpretation, the courts have developed a number of rules. It is for the judge to decide which is the appropriate rule in a particular case.

The Literal Rule

This provides that if the words of the statute are clear and unambiguous they will be applied as they stand.

The Golden Rule

Where application of the literal rule results in an absurdity, the meaning to be given is that which expresses best the intention of parliament from reading the act as a whole.

The Mischief Rule

Here the court attempts to find out the mischief which the act is attempting to remedy and interprets the statute accordingly: *Heydon's* case (1584).

The ejusdem generis *('of the same kind') Rule*

Although not of general application, it is a practice in some acts to state that they have application to a particular list of items and then to state that the statute also applies to 'similar things', without listing those matters.

In addition, there are other presumptions which guide a judge. Normally, an act will not operate retrospectively (affect situations before the act became law). Nor is the Crown generally affected by a statute. The judges also look to the title of the act and the preamble which sets out the purpose of the statute.

DELEGATED LEGISLATION

On occasions, parliament passes on responsibility for enacting legislation to others. In this way, the framework of an act can be laid down while the delegated body can fill in the detail required. This legislation often appears in the form of rules, regulations and orders while the legislators range from government ministers to local authorities. In the construction industry this is very important. Examples include the building regulations, many aspects of planning law, and safety legislation.

EXAMPLES OF DELEGATED LEGISLATION

Orders in council
Normally used in times of national emergency, this is a method of legislating quickly. The government implements the order by a meeting of the Privy Council.

Ministerial orders
Sometimes known as statutory instruments, these have become of increasing importance as a source of law. Their object is to fill out the details of legislation. Since 1946, these rules must be published or 'laid' before parliament before they become effective.

By-laws
Local authorities and other statutory bodies have power to introduce legislation concerned with local or specialised matters. All local authority by-laws are derived from statute. Confirmation of the by-law by the appropriate minister is required.

Regulations of professional bodies
These regulate the conduct of their members and provide for sanctions where appropriate. Examples include the powers of the Law Society and those of the British Medical Association in respect of solicitors and doctors.

THE ADVANTAGES OF DELEGATED LEGISLATION

Speed
In an emergency, parliament may not have time to deal with every problem which arises.

Volume of legislation
It saves time for parliament to deal with general aspects of policy and then to delegate the detail to the sub-legislators.

Flexibility
A flexible legislative process confers obvious advantages. The rules can be quickly altered and amended as necessary.

Technicality of subject matter
Much statute law nowadays, such as public health and factory legislation, is technical in nature and better dealt with by experts than by members of parliament.

THE DISADVANTAGES OF DELEGATED LEGISLATION

Bulk
Over two thousand statutory instruments come into force each year, each one making new law.

Lack of control by Parliament
With the widespread use of delegated legislation, law-making moves out of the control of the elected representatives of the people and more into the hands of the civil servants.

Lack of consultation
Because delegated legislation need not even be mentioned in parliament, there is a danger of insufficient publicity and consultation with interested parties.

CONTROL OF DELEGATED LEGISLATION
Control over delegated legislation is exercised by parliament and by the courts.

By parliament
Committees of the House of Commons review statutory instruments and decide whether any of them should be brought to the attention of parliament. Moreover, the enabling act (the individual act which grants power to make particular regulations) sometimes requires that the instrument be 'laid before' (brought to the notice of) parliament. Appropriate government ministers are answerable to parliament in respect of regulations made by their own departments, while by-laws must normally be confirmed by a government department before they become law. Parliament also has the overall safeguard in that it may withdraw the delegated power if it so wishes.

By the courts
Although the courts cannot challenge the validity of an act of parliament, they can challenge delegated legislation on the basis that the sub-legislator has exceeded the powers which parliament has conferred upon him. In this case, the statutory instrument will be held to be *ultra vires* (beyond the power) and the rules rendered void. Many statutes, those dealing with compulsory purchase of land and planning law for example, contain provisions whereby delegated legislation can be challenged on the basis that it is

ultra vires. In addition, before certain types of delegated legislation are effected, a public enquiry is held so that the view of the public may be made known on the particular issues and representations may be made.

1.9 European Community law

The European Economic Community (EEC) was set up by the first Treaty of Rome in 1957. By the European Communities Act in 1972, the United Kingdom became a full member of the Community, thereby diluting its sovereign powers and accepting the supremacy of European Community law over its own national and domestic system of law. In the event of a conflict between Community law and a state's domestic law, the Community law prevails. Therefore, EEC law has become a very important source of law in the United Kingdom.

COMMUNITY INSTITUTIONS

The Commission
This is the executive body of the Community which is responsible for policy. It initiates and drafts most Community legislation and in some cases has power to enact legislation itself.

The Council of Ministers
The Council is the legislative body of the Community, but normally it may only act on proposals put forward by the Commission.

The Assembly
Normally referred to as the European parliament, it acts mainly as an advisory or consultative body.

The Court of Justice
In passing the European Communities Act in 1972, parliament accepted that in the interpretation of the various treaties between the member states of the Community, the supreme court for deciding disputes would be the European Court of Justice in Luxembourg. Its decisions must be accepted by the courts of member states and there is no right of appeal. The court currently consists of eleven judges. They are assisted by Advocates General who prepare conclusions to the cases submitted to the court. As in most continental

legal systems much greater emphasis is placed upon written submissions and pleadings, and unlike in the United Kingdom, dissenting
judgments are not expressed.

THE SOURCES OF COMMUNITY LAW

The Treaties
These are the primary sources of Community law, based upon the
Treaty of Paris (1951) which set up the European Coal and Steel
Community together with the two treaties of Rome (1957) which
established the European Economic Community and the European
Atomic Energy Community. Subsequent treaties have been added
to these, together with trading agreements between the Community
and other states.

Community legislation
Both the Commission and the Council of Ministers have law-making
powers delegated to them. Hence they are able to enact secondary
legislation in a number of ways.

Regulations are of general application in all member states and, in
theory, are binding without the need for further legislation.

Decisions are of more specific application in that they may be
addressed to an individual member state or company and have
binding effect only on that particular body.

Directives are used where there is a need to modify existing domestic
legislation. They are addressed to individual member countries
who may implement them as they so wish. Those countries served
with directives are bound by them.

Recommendations and *opinions* simply express the view of the
Council and Commission on policies generally and have no binding
effect. Therefore they are not a secondary source of law.

Apart from parliament being obliged to give up its sovereignty
as far as Community matters are concerned, European Community
law has also had an effect on case law. Where the House of Lords
deals with a case requiring an interpretation of a European treaty,
it must be submitted to the European Court for a ruling. The

decision of the European Court must be accepted by the member state and enforced in its own domestic courts.

As the Community has been mainly concerned with business and economic matters, most of the changes which have come about so far have been in company and commercial law. For example, certain principles of English company law were immediately amended on our joining the Community while certain sections of the Companies Act 1980 are the direct result of Community secondary legislation. The law relating to taxation, and to some extent industrial relations will also be affected. For the time being there will be little change in our court system, while the criminal law, contract, tort and property law will remain much the same as before.

1.10 Books of authority

Occasionally, judges refer to legal textbooks for assistance. At one time, this practice was rarely used but now in common with continental systems it is used more frequently. The texts which are used with most authority are those of considerable antiquity, such as the works of Bracton, Coke and Blackstone. Modern textbooks are not treated as works of authority but are cited as persuasive argument. Examples are Cheshire's *Modern Law of Real Property*, Woodfall on *Landlord and Tenant* and Hudson's *Building Contracts*.

1.11 Law reform and the Law Commission

It is important that any legal system should be continually assessed in order that its principles do not become out of date. Statute law is the principal method by which the law is changed, but there are also pressure groups who enquire into the state of the law, and, where appropriate, make proposals for amendment. In addition to professional bodies such as the Law Society and the Bar Council, external organisations such as the National Council for Civil Liberties together with lawyers' political groups such as the Society of Conservative Lawyers and the Haldane Society (a group of lawyers interested in legal reform) seek to influence the present state of the legal system. There are also a number of standing committees of lawyers who advise the Lord Chancellor on matters of law reform. Sometimes the government appoints a Royal Commission to look into a particular topic. The Beeching Commission, which led to the Courts Act 1971 and a fundamental change in the system of courts, is an example of this.

The Law Commission Act 1965 established the Law Commission. This is a permanent organisation consisting of lawyers appointed by the Lord Chancellor to recommend changes which should be made in the law. It is an advisory body, and its recommendations only become law if they are adopted by parliament, but it can claim considerable success in bringing about law reform, including many changes in the criminal law. Examples of statutes which have been the result of the Commission's work include the Animals Act 1971 and the Supply of Goods (Implied Terms) Act 1973, both of which made the law more appropriate to prevailing conditions in society. One area which they have examined is the law of trespass, which is in an unsatisfactory state. A long-term aim is to embody the whole of the law of contract into statute form.

Sometimes the law is changed by act of parliament to reverse an unpopular decision of the House of Lords. The enactment of the Trade Disputes Act 1965 is one example. Recently, the House of Lords has had a look once more at the problem of limitation periods (the length of time you have in which to bring a case) in respect of defective buildings. Many lawyers considered that, since the decision in *Anns* v. *Merton London Borough Council* (1978), it was established law that the right to bring a claim in respect of an action in tort relating to a defective building commenced when the defect was discovered or ought reasonably to have been discovered. Recently in the case of *Pirelli General Cable Works Ltd* v. *Oscar Faber & Partners* (1983) the Lords took the view that an action in tort alleging negligent design of a building runs from the date the damage comes into existence, and the fact that only later was it discovered, or even could be discovered, does not alter the period. This problem has been referred by the Lord Chancellor to the Law Reform Committee for consideration.

Chapter 2

The administration of the law

2.1 The Criminal Courts

THE MAGISTRATES' COURT

Almost all criminal cases start off in the Magistrates' Court and over 95 per cent finish there as well. Every town of any size has at least one such court. This court is usually composed of lay magistrates or justices of the peace as they are sometimes known. These are part-time judges, not formally trained in the law, who decide the innocence or guilt of the defendant on the facts put before them. At the moment there are about 20,000 lay magistrates. On matters of law, procedure and sentencing, they are advised by a clerk to the court who is either a barrister or a solicitor. The court must be composed of at least two magistrates but usually numbers three so that, in the event of a conflict of opinion, a majority decision will be given. Justices are appointed by the Lord Chancellor on the recommendation of local advisory committees, and since 1966 all newly appointed magistrates have had to undergo some initial training. The retiring age is 70. In London and the larger provincial cities, stipendiary magistrates supplement the work of justices of the peace. These are paid, full-time, magistrates, being either solicitors or barristers. They generally sit in the busier courts where the volume of work is greater and more complex. They sit alone, having the powers equivalent to a bench of lay magistrates. In court a magistrate is addressed as 'Your Worship'.

Criminal offences fall into two main categories. These are classified as either summary or indictable offences. Summary offences tend to be minor matters such as drunkenness, common assault and the vast majority of motoring offences. Matters of this type constitute the bulk of the work of the Magistrates' Court. They comprise those offences where there is normally no right of trial by jury. The maximum penalty which the court can impose is to fine the defendant £1,000 or send him to prison for up to six months. If the defendant has been convicted of two or more offences at the same time, the maximum is twelve months. Many summary offences are now dealt with in the absence of the defendant.

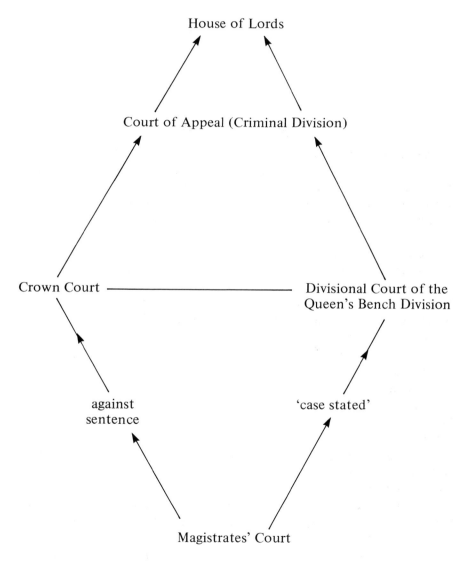

Fig. 2.1 Structure of the criminal courts

Indictable offences are so called because they may only be tried 'on indictment' which means by the Crown Court before judge and jury. These cases are commenced in the Magistrates' Court so that the magistrates may hear the prosecution evidence and decide whether to commit the accused for trial to the Crown Court. The prosecution has to establish a prima facie case, that is, a case in which there is some evidence in support of the charge, and which will stand unless it is displaced. These are known as committal proceedings.

In addition to hearing summary offences and committal proceedings, magistrates hear a large number of indictable offences. If the defendant elects for this form of trial, instead of appearing before a jury in the Crown Court, he may be sent to the Crown Court for consideration of a more severe sentence than can be imposed in the lower court.

Special conditions apply where the accused is a juvenile (under 17). Proceedings must take place separately from the adult court, and the public are not admitted. Reporting restrictions are also enforced. Normally magistrates dealing with these cases must have had training in dealing with juvenile offenders and the panel must include at least one woman.

Appeals

The Crown Court: The accused may appeal against sentence or conviction where appropriate.

The Divisional Court of the Queen's Bench Division: Any party to the proceedings (including the prosecution) may appeal on a point of law by way of 'case stated'.

THE CROWN COURT

The practice established by Henry II of sending judges into the provinces to try cases lasted for hundreds of years. The assize system, as it was known, existed alongside another system for dealing with criminal cases known as quarter sessions. The Courts Act 1971 abolished these courts and established the Crown Court as the single first instance criminal court above the Magistrates' Court.

The Central Criminal Court (the Old Bailey) is the Crown Court for the Greater London area. It must be remembered that a defendant does not come straight to the Crown Court but first has to be committed from the Magistrates' Court. England and Wales are divided into six circuits, and the Crown Court sits at various towns throughout each circuit. To take into account the volume of work dealt with by each court, cases may be transferred from one centre to another if necessary.

Not all Crown Courts are of the same importance, there being three different levels or tiers of courts. The first tier courts are the most important and they deal with the more important criminal cases. The judges in first tier courts are High Court judges, sometimes known as puisne judges, and circuit judges. Civil cases are also dealt with here. The second and third tier courts deal only with criminal cases. Circuit judges or recorders (part-time judges) normally hear cases in these courts, but High Court judges can hear cases in the second tier courts.

In addition to this classification of courts, Crown Court offences are also categorised into four groups indicating the level of judge who may try a particular offence. Since the implementation of the Courts Act 1971, lay magistrates have been empowered to sit with the judge in the Crown Court. In fact, they must form part of the Crown Court where it hears appeals from Magistrates' Courts, and when it is sentencing persons who have been committed for sentence by the Magistrates' Court. Apart from these circumstances, Crown Court cases are heard by a judge to decide the law and a jury to decide the facts.

Appeals
The Court of Appeal (Criminal Division): The accused may appeal against sentence or conviction where appropriate. Permission of the Court of Appeal is sometimes required. The prosecution may also appeal against an acquittal on a point of law in a Crown Court trial. This involves an application by the Attorney-General. The result does not affect the acquittal.

The Divisional Court of the Queen's Bench Division: An appeal by way of 'case stated' may be made from the Crown Court to this court.

The two courts described above are known as courts of first instance. This means that they are courts where a case is originally heard. The courts which are to be considered next are so-called appellate courts dealing solely with appeals from lower courts.

THE DIVISIONAL COURT OF THE QUEEN'S BENCH
DIVISION OF THE HIGH COURT

The powers of the Divisional Court to deal with criminal proceedings are limited. Criminal appeals are heard in this court by way of 'case stated' from the Magistrates' Court and the Crown Court. The Divisional Court consists of three High Court judges, and sits in London. Appeals to this court cannot be founded on disputes of fact, but only on questions of law. The lower court draws up a statement of the facts found to be proved, the decision made, and the reasons for it. Either the prosecution or the accused may appeal. The Divisional Court may affirm, reverse or vary the original decision, or remit the decision to the inferior court for further consideration. This usually takes place where an error has been made which requires the magistrates to hear or rehear evidence.

Appeals

The House of Lords: Either party may appeal to the House of Lords, but only where a point of law of general public importance is involved. Permission to appeal must be obtained.

THE COURT OF APPEAL (CRIMINAL DIVISION)

The Court of Criminal Appeal was set up in 1907, and in 1966 the name was changed to the Criminal Division of the Court of Appeal. The court is composed of Lord Justices of Appeal who often sit with High Court judges of the Queen's Bench Division. The Lord Chief Justice is the head of this court. The court sits only at the Royal Courts of Justice in London. Its main business is to hear appeals against conviction in the Crown Court and also appeals against sentence where an accused has been sent to the Crown Court for this purpose. Appeals against sentence may only be made by leave of the court. The court has power to quash (dismiss) the original decision, decrease the sentence, or order a new trial.

Appeals

The House of Lords: Either the prosecution or the defence may appeal to the House of Lords. However, it is necessary to show that the appeal involves a point of law of such general importance that either the Court of Appeal or the House of Lords considers it appropriate to be heard by the Lords.

THE HOUSE OF LORDS

The House of Lords occupies an unusual position in English law. This is because it has both legislative and judicial functions. As a law-making body, it constitutes one of the Houses of Parliament, and generally before a bill can become law it has to pass through a number of stages in this chamber and then receive the Royal Assent. As a court of law, it is the final court of appeal in civil and criminal cases for the whole of the United Kingdom. Originally, appeals were heard by all members of the House of Lords, but since the second half of the nineteenth century, lay peers have played no part in the judicial business of the House.

On the criminal side, the House hears appeals from the Court of Appeal (Criminal Division) and also from the Divisional Court of the Queen's Bench of the High Court. Permission to bring the case must be given by these courts or by the House of Lords itself through its Appeal Committee. Either the Court of Appeal, or the Divisional Court, if appropriate, must certify that a point of law of general public importance is involved. The prosecution or the accused may appeal. The House of Lords is presided over by the Lord Chancellor, who is a member of the government. Appeals are heard by Lords of Appeal in Ordinary, the so-called *law lords*. These are life peers, who in practice are the highest ranking judges in the United Kingdom. They are normally appointed after sitting as Lord Justices of Appeal in the Court of Appeal. As the House is also the highest civil court of appeal for Scotland and Northern Ireland, and the highest criminal court of appeal for Northern Ireland, two or three of the law lords are appointed from these parts of the United Kingdom. At least three judges must hear the case, but usually the appeal is heard by five judges who deliver their opinions in the form of speeches. The appeal is heard in a committee room of the House of Lords at Westminster. Because the issues involved are concerned with points of law from the highest ranking court in the United Kingdom, judgments from the House of Lords are almost always reported because each one either adds a new principle to the law or clarifies an existing point.

2.2 The Civil Courts

THE MAGISTRATES' COURT

The Magistrates' Court is basically a criminal court but it does have some civil jurisdiction. The most important aspect of this is in connection with so-called 'domestic proceedings'. These are family law matters and include applications for custody of children, affiliation and maintenance orders, separation and adoption proceedings. As in the case of juvenile courts, the public is usually excluded, there are rules as to the composition of the 'bench' and strict limitations are imposed on press reports. There is no power to hear divorce cases.

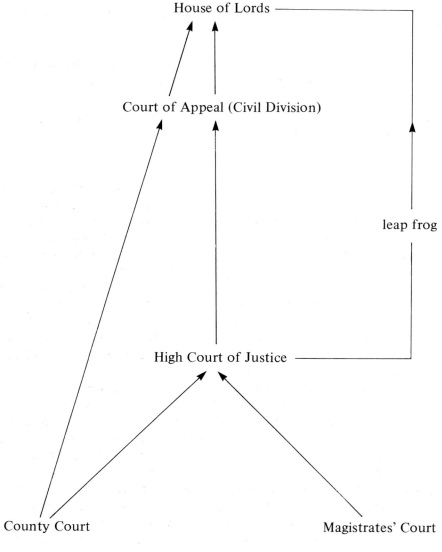

Fig. 2.2 Structure of the civil courts

Magistrates are also responsible for the granting or refusal of the statutory licences required for businesses which sell alcohol to the public and also for betting, gambling and film licences. There is also a varied jurisdiction to recover civil debts such as income tax, rates, electricity and gas charges.

Appeals

The Crown Court: This is appropriate in licensing and debt collecting cases.

The Divisional Court of the Queen's Bench Division: Where appropriate, the 'case stated' procedure will apply on a point of law.

The Divisional Court of the Family Division: This applies in the case of 'domestic proceedings'.

THE COUNTY COURT

The County Courts were established in 1846 to deal with minor civil cases cheaply and on a local basis. The County Court is the major first instance court in civil matters and its jurisdiction is exclusively civil. In England and Wales there are some 400 County Courts divided into 63 circuits. Each circuit has its own judge and in the major cities more than one judge is normally attached to each court. County Courts are staffed by circuit judges who travel about on their respective circuits to hear cases. These judges spend the balance of their time hearing criminal cases in the Crown Court. In addition to the judge, each court has a registrar. The registrar is a solicitor, who is responsible for the administration of the court. He is assisted by a clerical staff of civil servants.

In addition to his administrative duties, the registrar is allowed in certain circumstances to act as a judge. Registrars have the right to hear claims involving less than £500 and for higher amounts if the parties both agree. An appeal from the finding of a registrar goes to the judge. The registrar also frequently acts as an arbitrator in defended actions where the claim is for less than £500. If the disputed amount exceeds that sum, the matter can still be referred to arbitration if both parties agree or the judge makes an appropriate order. The arbitrator's decision can be enforced in the same way as that of a court of law. Such proceedings are of an informal nature and normally each party pays his own costs.

In recent years, there has been an attempt to encourage the layman to use the County Court without the aid of a solicitor where small amounts are involved and there are no difficult points of law. If a case is within the limits of the County Court jurisdiction, certain rules apply to dissuade the parties from bringing the case in the High Court where the jurisdiction is concurrent. The most important of these is that a successful party to civil proceedings in the High Court will only be allowed his costs on the lower County Court scale if he could have brought the proceedings in the County Court. Normally in the County Court the judge sits alone without a jury. Solicitors, in addition to barristers, have the right to appear in this court.

Jurisdiction

The jurisdiction of the County Court is set out in the County Court Act 1959 as amended. The technical rules governing the procedures in the court are to be found in the annual *County Court Practice* or 'Green Book'. Cases have to be started off in the actual County Court for the district in which the defendant lives, carries on business, or where the reason for the action took place. If the plaintiff is attempting to obtain possession of land, the place of trial depends upon where the land is situated. In most cases, the jurisdiction of the court is restricted by the size of the claim. The limits vary from time to time. At the moment, the following constitutes the bulk of County Court work:

(a) Actions in contract and tort not exceeding £5,000. (Libel or slander are excluded unless the parties agree.)
(b) Actions concerning the possession or ownership of land where the rateable value does not exceed £1,000.
(c) Equity matters involving sums up to £30,000. This includes such matters as trusts and mortgages.
(d) Probate disputes, where the deceased person's estate is valued at less than £30,000.
(e) The winding up of companies with a paid-up capital of less than £120,000.
(f) Certain family law matters concerned with adoption, guardianship and legitimacy of children.
(g) Issues arising under the Rent Acts, landlord and tenant, housing and consumer credit matters.

(h) Some courts also deal with the following matters:
  - (i) undefended divorce petitions and proceedings ancillary to them;
  - (ii) Admiralty matters;
  - (iii) bankruptcy matters (this does not apply to London);
  - (iv) cases brought under the Race Relations Acts.

Appeals

The Court of Appeal: Subject to certain conditions, an appeal from a circuit judge in the County Court lies directly to the Court of Appeal.

The Divisional Court of the Chancery Division: Where the County Court has bankruptcy jurisdiction, appeal lies to this branch of the Divisional Court.

THE HIGH COURT OF JUSTICE

The High Court was established by the Judicature Act 1873-75 replacing the Common Law and Chancery Courts which existed previously.

The work of the High Court on the civil side is divided into three divisions, each of which has a separate jurisdiction. The court is staffed by High Court judges, known as puisne judges, and generally speaking they have jurisdiction to hear civil cases which involve some complexity or large sums of money. However, as previously mentioned in connection with the County Court, where there is concurrent jurisdiction, plaintiffs are encouraged to bring their cases in the lower court where it is more appropriate. Administrative matters in the High Court are dealt with by registrars, as in the County Court. In the Queen's Bench and Chancery Divisions, they are known as masters.

In London, cases are dealt with at the Royal Courts of Justice in the Strand. Since the Courts Act 1971, High Court civil cases in the provinces have been heard at 26 first tier centres. These are situated at the major Crown Courts. Therefore, serious criminal cases, and High Court civil cases in the provinces are normally heard in the same building. The majority of chancery matters are still heard in London and there are only a few other centres where such matters are heard. High Court civil cases can be commenced in the provinces without the need to go to London. This is done by filing the appropriate documents at District Registries which exist in the larger cities in England and Wales.

The Queen's Bench Division is the largest of the three divisions. This court has the residual task of dealing with all matters not covered by the other divisions. It is presided over by the Lord Chief Justice and staffed by High Court judges. A large number of judges are needed because the Division also staffs the Crown Court where the judges exercise both civil and criminal jurisdiction. The majority of actions brought are claims in contract and tort outside the County Court limits. Cases involving the construction industry are normally dealt with in this court. The normal practice is for the judge to hear the case alone without a jury. Where a person's character is in dispute, a jury is empanelled (formed) to sit with the judge. Two highly regarded specialist courts, the Commercial Court and the Admiralty Court sit within this Division.

The Chancery Division, in the same way that the jurisdiction of the old Common Law Courts is now to be found in the Queen's Bench, has inherited the Chancellor's Court of Equity. This Division is the smallest of the three and its nominal head is the Lord Chancellor. However, in practice the senior judge is known as the Vice Chancellor. Its jurisdiction involves the sale of land, mortgages, trusts, planning, company and revenue matters. It is therefore an important court for anyone connected with the surveying profession.

The Family Division, established in 1970, deals with all aspects of family law. Defended divorce cases have to be heard in this court. The senior judge is the President. For administrative reasons, non-contentious probate matters (matters relating to wills where there is no dispute) are dealt with in this Division.

Appeals
The Court of Appeal (Civil Division): There is an appeal to this Court from any of the three Divisions of the High Court on matters of law and of fact.

The House of Lords: By the Administration of Justice Act 1969, it is possible in some cases to by-pass the Court of Appeal and to 'leap frog' directly to the House of Lords. The parties to the dispute must agree to this course of action. The original trial judge has to grant a certificate that the matter should go directly to the Lords and that it involves a matter of statutory interpretation, or the first instance judge considers himself bound by a previous decision of a superior court. In addition, the House of Lords itself must grant leave. Examples of this procedure are rare because of the qualifying conditions. In *National Carriers Ltd* v. *Panalpina Ltd* (1981) these conditions were satisfied where the problem of a lease being subject to contractual rules relating to frustration were discussed.

The Offical Referees Court

As it is part of the High Court and its rules of procedure and evidence tend to follow High Court practice, some mention ought to be made of this court. Disputes relating to building contracts and schedules of dilapidations are often referred to this court. Before the Courts Act 1971, the judges who constituted these courts were known as official referees. Since then, designated circuit judges have discharged official referee business, although the original expression continues to be used. Normally these cases are heard at the law courts in London, but they may be heard on any of the five circuits other than the South Eastern. Some of the procedures used in this court are similar to those used in arbitration proceedings.

Appeals

The Court of Appeal (Civil Division): On a point of law, appeal lies to the Court of Appeal (Civil Division). No leave is required. The right to appeal on a question of fact is narrow and is limited to a charge of fraud or breach of professional duty.

The Divisional Court of the Queen's Bench Division

In addition to their original jurisdiction, judges of the Queen's Bench hear appeals in the appropriate Divisional Court. This normally consists of the Lord Chief Justice and two other puisne judges. Appeals are heard from certain tribunals and the court also possesses what is known as supervisory jurisdiction. This is the power to control tribunals and inferior courts of law. It is effected by the use of the so-called *prerogative orders*. The court also hears applications for the writ of *habeas corpus*.

The Divisional Court of the Chancery Division

This court hears appeals from the County Court on bankruptcy matters. Normally two judges hear the case.

The Divisional Court of the Family Division

Appeals from the decisions of lower courts hearing domestic and family matters are heard in this court. Again, the matter is normally heard by two judges. As in the other divisional courts, the case is not reheard but centres on legal argument.

Appeals
The Court of Appeal: An appeal will lie from the Divisional Court to the Court of Appeal. Leave of the Divisional Court or the Court of Appeal is required.

THE COURT OF APPEAL (CIVIL DIVISION)

Appeals from the High Court and the County Court are heard in this court. The appeal may be on a question of law or fact. There is also a right of appeal to this court from certain tribunals including the Lands Tribunal on a point of law. In practice, the court is presided over by the Master of the Rolls and staffed by Lords Justices of Appeal. Each court will normally comprise of three judges. Several divisions of the court sit at the same time.

Appeal
The House of Lords: Leave must have been granted by that court or by the Court of Appeal.

THE HOUSE OF LORDS

The majority of cases reaching the Court of Appeal are civil matters. Appeals are heard from the Court of Appeal, and from the High Court in those rare situations where the Court of Appeal is 'leap frogged'. The constitution of the court is the same as in criminal matters.

2.3 Tribunals, inquiries and arbitration

TRIBUNALS

A major characteristic of the English legal system since the end of the Second World War has been the growth in importance of tribunals. A defect of the traditional court system is that it is not suitable for dealing with the settlement of every type of dispute. A system has to be formulated whereby disputes dealing with specialist topics can be dealt with by experts instead of by judges in courts of law. Moreover the increasing role of government in economic and social matters has brought about a proliferation of disputes between private individuals and government departments.   Acts of parliament have set up tribunals to provide, as a supplement to the court system, a speedy and cheap method of settling disputes with less formality than in a court of law. There is a diversity of functions amongst these administrative tribunals, and they vary from immigration appeals and tax assessments to employment matters and disputes concerning tenanted farms. There are in fact well over 2,000 different tribunals in existence, of more than 50 types.

Many tribunals have legally qualified chairmen but frequently members may also be qualified in their own particular capacity. Surveyors, for example, sit on Rent Tribunals. Appointments are made for a fixed term but are frequently renewed. Composition varies from one to another. Most tribunals are made up of three members, with a lawyer chairman and two lay representatives. The government department regulating the matter in dispute will normally have responsibility for the appointments. In many cases before tribunals, legal representation is not necessary. On matters of fact, there is usually no appeal from the decision of a tribunal. By the Tribunals and Inquiries Act 1971 an appeal on a point of law is possible to the High Court. Tribunals must now give reasons for their decisions. In 1957 the Franks Committee reported upon the workings of tribunals and concluded that there was a need for review and supervision of the system. Consequently the Tribunals and Inquiries Act 1958 established a Council on Tribunals to fulfil this purpose. The council has to report to parliament each year on these matters.

SPECIFIC TRIBUNALS

The Lands Tribunal
This tribunal was established by the Lands Tribunal Act 1949 to settle disputes involving the valuation of land on compulsory acquisition. The dispute will normally involve the property owner and the local authority. Other jurisdiction includes applications relating to the variation or discharge of restrictive covenants under the Law of Property Act 1925. However, most of the tribunal's time is spent on rating appeals from Local Valuation Courts. The tribunal consists of a lawyer, who acts as president, and other members who are either leading barristers or chartered surveyors of great experience. Administration is the responsibility of the registrar. Only one member sits to decide each dispute, but he is not confined to hearing cases in London and will travel wherever work demands. Legal aid is available.

Appeal lies to the Court of Appeal (Civil Division). In procedure and atmosphere the Lands Tribunal is somewhat more formal than most other tribunals.

The Agricultural Lands Tribunal

The eight Agricultural Lands Tribunals are organised on a regional basis. They are staffed by a lawyer chairman and two lay representatives. Nominations are considered from the Country Landowners' Association and the National Farmers' Union. This tribunal is primarily concerned with tenant farms. It considers disputes relating to notices to quit tenanted farms and compensation for improvements. On average 400-500 cases per year have been dealt with in the last few years.

The Rating Valuation Court

This is a busy tribunal established in 1948 to replace local assessment committees. It hears appeals from rating valuations with a further right of appeal from the Valuation Court to the Lands Tribunal. The court is a local one and has no power to award costs. Hearings are comparatively informal and are open to the public. The court must sit 'as often as may be necessary' and is composed of a chairman and one or two other members of the local valuation panel. The panel itself consists of local businessmen and members of the local authority. On matters of law, they are guided by the clerk of the court who is a paid official. The court also deals with water rates.

Rent Assessment Committees

As they deal with disputes between landlords and tenants in the private sector, these committees are not, strictly speaking, tribunals. However, they operate on similar lines to administrative tribunals. Their major task is to fix rents in respect of residential property which comes within the scope of the Rent Acts. These tribunals also have power to deal with *security of tenure*. This is the right of a person to stay in possession of property once the original agreement has come to an end. Some of these powers have recently been transferred to the County Court. Members of the committee are appointed by the Secretary of State at the Department of the Environment. The normal composition is a legally qualified chairman, together with surveyors and laymen possessing local knowledge. The Assessment Committees are established on a county basis.

Members may visit the relevant property if necessary. Legal representation is allowed, while there is a right of appeal on fact only to the Divisional Court.

Domestic tribunals

Not all tribunals are administrative tribunals. In addition, there are domestic tribunals which have been established to resolve disputes within professional bodies and to exercise disciplinary control over their members. Doctors, lawyers, surveyors and architects are, amongst others, subject to such rules. Trade associations and trade unions have similar machinery to ensure common standards and to maintain discipline.

INQUIRIES

These are fact-finding bodies, instigated by government departments. Their object is to test public opinion and to obtain the fullest information relating to a proposed project. The procedure involved is normally laid down by statute. Most 'public' or 'local' inquiries are concerned with planning or compulsory purchase matters. Inspectors appointed by the appropriate government department are sent to the locality where the matter has arisen. At the public hearing, interested parties are able to express their views before the so-called 'person appointed'. Rules of procedure are laid down by statutory instrument relating to persons entitled to appear, legal representation, inspection of the site and notification of the decision. Traditionally, the inspector reported his findings to the minister, who after deliberation, came to a decision. Nowadays, the inspector himself will often give the decision. Where the inspector reports back to the minister, the recommendations which he makes are normally followed. Reasons must be given for the decision if required. Sometimes, a distinction is made between those situations where the law requires that the minister must hold an inquiry and where he has a choice. These are known as *statutory* and *discretionary* inquiries respectively.

ARBITRATION

Where disputes arise of a specialist nature the parties sometimes agree to nominate a third party to settle the matter. This process is known as arbitration. It is a procedure which is appropriate where the issues involved are primarily of fact, and a degree of technical expertise is required. Advantages claimed for the system include speed, cheapness (sometimes) and informality. One important aspect of such proceedings is that the hearing is held in private, at a time and place suitable to the requirements of the parties. Most disputes referred to arbitration are of a commercial nature. However, arbitration is frequently used in the construction industry and there is a growing tendency to settle disputes relating to the rent payable on commercial and industrial property in this way. The principal law on the subject is to be found in the Arbitration Act 1950, which governs all arbitration agreements made in writing.

The agreement to submit a matter to arbitration often takes place when the dispute arises, although sometimes contracts and property agreements provide that, in the event of a dispute arising, the matter will be determined in this way. In this case a professional body, such as the Royal Institution of Chartered Surveyors or the Royal Institute of British Architects, may appoint the arbitrator. Normally an arbitration agreement will be entered into in writing. Arbitration agreements are often to be found in one of the clauses in standard forms of contract. Sometimes the parties will have no choice but to refer the matter to arbitration because statute requires it. Disputes as to street works come into this category. In a similar way, a court will sometimes refer proceedings to arbitration where this is appropriate. Conversely, an arbitrator's award may be a condition precedent to the dispute being referred to court.

It is common practice for a preliminary meeting to be held to agree time and place of hearing, attendance of witnesses, legal representation where appropriate, and any issues of the proceedings upon which the parties have a common position. Both claimant and respondent (plaintiff and defendant) will usually have submitted pleadings outlining the basis of their case while the arbitrator may order discovery (production) of relevant documents. Sometimes a so-called *Scott's Schedule* is used in these proceedings by the arbitrator to summarise the conflicting views of the parties. Procedure is similar to a court of law, but tends to be less formal. If a point of law arises during the course of the proceedings, the arbitrator may attempt to deal with it himself or take legal advice. An alternative is for the arbitrator to state a special case and seek the opinion of the High Court. This results in the proceedings being adjourned until the court has given its decision. Because of the possible misuse of this procedure by parties wishing to delay the outcome of the dispute, the Arbitration Act 1979 gave the parties a right to contract out of the special case application. A far narrower right of appeal is now allowed relating to a point of law arising from the arbitrator's award. The decision of an arbitrator is known as his award. If the award is defective in any way, application may be made for it to be referred back to the arbitrator so that he can amend it. If the defect is very serious, the decision becomes null and void, and it is set aside.

As in a court of law, the decision may be made at the end of the proceedings or the arbitrator may 'reserve his award' in which case it is given at a later date. The award is final and binding on all parties concerned. If the dispute involves a particular property the arbitrator should make an appropriate inspection before giving his award. On receipt of his fees the award is normally given by the arbitrator. Costs tend to follow the same rules as in court — the loser pays the winner's costs.

As mentioned previously, small claims in the County Court may be referred by the registrar to arbitration. This is where the sum involved is less than £500. Arbitration awards are enforceable in the same way as a judgment of a court of law.

2.4 Court procedure

This is governed by the nature of the dispute. Just as the choice of court is dependent upon the type of proceedings at issue, there is a considerable difference between criminal and civil procedure. In the criminal courts, much depends upon whether the accused is being tried on indictment or is subject to summary proceedings. Choice of court on the civil side is determined primarily by the complexity of the issues involved and the sum of money in dispute. One fundamental distinction lies in the obligation of proving facts. This is the so-called *burden of proof*. In a civil case it is up to the plaintiff to prove the factual issues on the balance of probabilities. A more stringent test applies in criminal actions in that the prosecution must prove the facts at issue beyond all reasonable doubt.

Another factor characteristic of court proceedings in this country is the so-called *accusatorial* or *adversarial* system. This means that the parties to a dispute or criminal proceedings have primary responsibility for finding and presenting evidence. The judge does not investigate the facts as such but listens to the case as it is presented by each of the two adversaries. This is to be contrasted with the *inquisitorial* system in force in some continental countries whereby the judge searches for facts, listens to witnesses, examines documents and orders that evidence be taken, after which he makes further investigations if he considers them necessary.

CRIMINAL PROCEEDINGS

Summary offences

These are commenced by the police laying information before a justice of the peace so that a summons can be issued against the defendant. The summons will require the defendant to appear at a Magistrates' Court at a time and date specified. The accused will appear in person but may be legally represented by solicitor and/or counsel. There are instances where the case can be dealt with in the absence of the accused. The majority of motoring offences come into this category.

At the hearing itself, the basis of the charge will be read and the defendant will be asked if he pleads guilty or not guilty. If he pleads guilty he will be dealt with immediately. If the defendant pleads not guilty the prosecution will outline the facts of the case. A senior police officer often conducts the prosecution case, although in more complicated cases the area police prosecuting solicitor will take over that role. In some parts of the country, the police may instruct a firm of solicitors to prosecute on their behalf.

The prosecutor will call his witnesses who are open to examination by the other side. It is open to the defendant at the end of the prosecution case to claim that the case against him has not been made out and that there is no case to answer. If the magistrates uphold this submission the case against the accused is dismissed.

If no such submission is made, or it is made unsuccessfully, the defence will then call their own witnesses who are open to cross examination from the other side. It is then up to the magistrates to decide whether or not to convict. If so, sentencing will take place forthwith. In the case of an acquittal, the accused will be discharged. In the event of any difficulty in respect of a point of law the assistance of the legally qualified clerk may be required. Appeals may be made to the Crown Court or the Divisional Court of the Queen's Bench Division where appropriate.

Indictable offences

These are the more serious offences. After a summons or a warrant has been issued for the arrest of the accused he will be brought before the magistrates who will inquire as to whether or not there is a prima facie case against the defendant to put him on trial at the Crown Court. The proceedings may be an oral hearing or, if the defendant agrees, a gathering up of written statements which may be passed on unread to the trial court. The prosecution must produce all its evidence.

If the accused is committed for trial he will be sent to the Crown Court where he will be asked if he pleads guilty or not guilty. If he pleads guilty, he will be sentenced by the judge after the facts of the case have been outlined and any mitigating circumstances put on the defendant's behalf.

If the plea is one of not guilty the court will swear in twelve men and women to act as jurors who are responsible for deciding on the facts of the case whether or not the accused is guilty or not guilty. At this stage, the prosecution will open its case and call witnesses who may be cross examined by the defence. The defence will then present its case calling witnesses who may in turn be cross examined by the prosecution.

After the respective parties have summarised their cases and made final speeches, the judge will sum up the case for the benefit of the jury. At this stage, the judge puts forward the conflicting arguments for the prosecution and the defence, leaving the jury to decide on the facts whether the accused is guilty or not guilty. Any questions of law which arise during the course of the trial are matters for the judge.

If possible the jury should come to a unanimous decision but, since the passing of the Criminal Justice Act in 1967, it is possible for the judge to accept a majority decision provided there are no more than two persons in the minority. The jury must have been out for at least two hours before a majority verdict can be accepted.

If the jury returns a verdict of not guilty, the accused will be released immediately. If there is a finding of guilt, sentencing will take place after a plea in mitigation has been made. If the jury are unable to agree on their verdict, there has to be a retrial before a different judge and jury.

CIVIL PROCEEDINGS

Where the parties to a civil dispute choose litigation instead of arbitration, they will have the choice of commencing proceedings in the County Court or the High Court. The choice of court will depend primarily on the complexity of the case and the amount of money involved. In most civil actions of any consequence there will usually have been considerable correspondence and bargaining between the parties before the action is commenced. In the High Court there is frequent delay between the action being commenced and the case being actually heard. The vast majority of civil actions never come to trial, but are settled at the door of the court. The high cost of litigation acts as an incentive to come to this conclusion.

The County Court

The procedure for bringing a claim in the County Court is to be found in the so-called 'Green Book' or *County Court Practice*. The claim is essentially one for damages, so the plaintiff will file at the appropriate County Court a request for a summons to be issued stating the name and address of the defendant and the sum claimed. In addition, a statement of claim will be filed setting out the circumstances in which the action arises. In return, a plaint note, giving details of the time limit within which the claim must be answered by the defendant will be given to the plaintiff.

It may be that the defendant has a defence to the claim or wishes to make a counter-claim. A counter-claim is one which the defendant has against the plaintiff which need not be connected with the plaintiff's action, but which can be conveniently dealt with at the same time. If the plaintiff sues for money owed, the defendant may counter-claim for a quite separate debt owed to him by the plaintiff. Alternatively, the defendant may have a right of *set-off*. This arises out of the same facts as the plaintiff's action and operates as a defence. So, if the plaintiff sues the defendant for goods sold and delivered, the defendant may plead that the goods were not fit for the purpose for which they were bought.

The registrar will fix a date for '*pretrial review*'. If the defendant has filed no defence or admission of liability, judgment may be entered for the plaintiff. If there is a defence, the matter will go forward to trial and at the review the registrar will fix a time and date for trial and deal with related matters.

The trial itself will normally be conducted by a circuit judge sitting in his capacity as a County Court judge. If the matter involves less than £500, the registrar will deal with the matter himself. The parties may be represented by a solicitor or counsel if they so wish. If the parties agree, a claim involving less than £500 may be submitted to arbitration in which case the registrar will usually act as arbitrator.

The High Court

Procedure in the High Court depends upon the Division in which the case is brought. Most construction industry disputes are commenced in the Queen's Bench Division, while disputes involving the title to land will be heard in the Chancery Division. Actions in the Queen's Bench Division are usually begun by issuing a writ against the defendant. This will be accompanied by a statement of claim setting out the basis of the plaintiff's case. A copy of the writ must be served on each defendant. This may be done by post or personally to the defendant's address.

After service of the writ, the defendant must show his intention to defend the action by entering an appearance. If the defendant fails to acknowledge service as required by the writ, he is taken to have admitted the claim in full and the plaintiff can apply for judgment in his favour. Where the defendant requires more information than the writ supplies, he may make a request for further and better particulars of specific matters mentioned in the writ.

Assuming the defendant contests the action, he must file a defence. This may be met with a reply from the plaintiff. Moreover, the defendant may wish to counter-claim or claim a set-off. This exchange of pleadings which takes place between the issue of the writ and the trial is known as *interlocutory proceedings*. The idea of this exchange of documents is to eradicate irrelevant matters and to state precisely the issues in dispute.

Order 14 of the *Rules of the Supreme Court* (the 'White Book' which governs procedure in the High Court) makes provision for a plaintiff to obtain judgment in the Queen's Bench Division without the expense and delay of a trial if he can prove to the satisfaction of the court that his case is unanswerable. Such a procedure is only used where there is no substantial dispute as to the facts.

Within one month of the close of pleadings the plaintiff takes out a summons for directions which is heard by a master, or in the provinces normally by a district registrar. The aim of the summons is to deal with all interlocutory matters at the same time and to receive instructions as to the conduct of the proceedings. At the summons itself the legal representatives of the parties will attend and deal with matters such as discovery of documents and interrogatories.

Each party is entitled to see all documents held by his opponent, unless they are privileged, while either side can be asked to answer questions relevant to the proceedings. This establishes the areas of conflict and saves time and trouble in preparing for trial. In court proceedings, experts' reports, and if necessary subsequent replies, are exchanged in advance of the hearing. The place and mode of trial will then be decided upon by the master or registrar.

At the trial itself, counsel will make an opening address on behalf of the plaintiff outlining the issues involved making reference to relevant documents. After opening, counsel for the plaintiff will examine his witnesses, who are open to cross examination from the other side. The plaintiff's representative may then re-examine the witness if he so wishes.

The defendant's counsel will then make his initial address and call evidence to substantiate his case. Cross examination and re-examination of the defence witnesses may take place. After the defendant's representative has summarised his case and made his submissions as to the law, the plaintiff's advocate will have the last word and conclude the proceedings with his speech. In many actions, the judge will deliver his judgment immediately thereafter, although he may reserve his judgment to a later date. He will then deal with ancillary matters raised by counsel, such as costs or leave to appeal.

The successful party is entitled to judgment and he must decide which is the most suitable method of enforcing it. Costs *'follow the event'* unless the judge pronounces otherwise. This means that the loser must pay the winner's costs. Costs may be *taxed*. This is a procedure for examining, and altering where necessary, amounts payable by a party in an action. This will be conducted by a taxing master or by a district registrar.

Where the judgment is to pay money, the county sheriff is authorised to enter the defendant's house and remove goods to the value of the debt, together with interest and costs if the defendant does not pay the debt. Alternatively, the plaintiff may apply for a charging order on any land, stock, shares or money of the defendant. Where appropriate, a receiver may be appointed to receive any rents or profits which are due.

A further alternative is that the plaintiff may recover a debt owed to the defendant by a third party, often a bank, by applying for a garnishee order to freeze the debt. Where the defendant has no capital, but is in full employment, an attachment of earnings order may be made, provided he has defaulted in one or more of the instalments of the judgment debt he was ordered to pay. The order is made only in the County Court, which has the power to enforce judgments of the High Court. Another option is that the plaintiff may serve on the defendant a notice that if he does not pay the debt (at least £200) within a specified time he has committed an act of bankruptcy.

Where the principal question involved is the construction of a statute, deed, contract, will or other document, and where there is unlikely to be any substantial dispute as to the facts, proceedings should normally be begun by originating summons. Such a summons is heard in the Chancery Division. Witnesses rarely appear where this procedure is used. At the hearing the plaintiff will open the case and read the affidavits which have been prepared. Each defendant then addresses the court. However, each defendant normally addresses the court once only.

EVIDENCE

Evidence is concerned with those rules which govern the presentation of facts and proof in proceedings before a court. One vital difference between criminal and civil proceedings is the burden of proof. In a criminal case a higher standard is required and the guilt of the accused has to be proved beyond all reasonable doubt. In civil proceedings the facts of the dispute must be proved on the balance of probabilities. In general the burden lies on the party who substantially asserts the affirmative of the issue. However, it is possible for this burden to shift during the course of the proceedings.

Evidence is normally given by word of mouth or in writing. The giving of oral evidence is very much a common law concept while the giving of documentary evidence is more a characteristic of the courts of chancery. Apart from the written correspondence which has passed between the parties, documents include any plan, map, graph or drawing. Every material document is basically admissible in evidence against the writer *unless* it is marked '*without prejudice*'. In proceedings where the court wishes to make a site visit or inspect a building, this is termed real evidence. This usually takes the form of an inspection of a specific object by the court.

There are a number of different classifications of evidence. A common distinction is between direct evidence and circumstantial evidence which is inferred from the circumstances. Another distinction is between primary evidence such as an original document, and secondary evidence such as a copy of a document.

One problem which has faced the courts has been that of hearsay evidence. This is where evidence is given before a court or tribunal, but which is asserted evidence of some person who is not before the court. In criminal cases, the general rule is that such evidence is not admissible. First-hand hearsay evidence was made admissible in civil proceedings by the Civil Evidence Act 1968.

Chapter 3

The personnel of the law

3.1 The legal profession

A peculiarity of the English legal system is that it is divided into two branches which have different functions. Solicitors give advice on legal problems to the general public and conduct legal proceedings on their behalf, whereas the primary function of a barrister is to act as an advocate and to give advice to solicitors when requested. The expression 'lawyer' may be used to denote either a solicitor or barrister. Apart from general practice, salaried lawyers are to be found in commerce, industry, the civil service and educational institutions.

SOLICITORS

The Law Society is the body responsible for the control of the solicitor's profession. In order to practise as such, a person must have been admitted as a solicitor and have a current practising certificate. This can only be obtained by passing the professional examinations of the Law Society and being articled (apprenticed) to an established solicitor. Once qualified, if the solicitor enters general practice, he may deal with a wide spectrum of legal work. He may be involved in giving general advice, conveyancing (transferring the ownership of land), drafting wills, appearing in the Magistrates' or County Court, handling divorces or preparing cases for trial. On the other hand, he may quickly become a specialist dealing only with cases involving one or two particular areas of law, such as tax, town planning or shipping law. Much depends on the type of practice and the locality. Some solicitors prefer to practise on their own, while others work in partnerships of varying sizes.

There are certain restrictions upon the right of solicitors to appear as advocates in courts of law. A right of appearance is allowed in the County Court or in the Magistrates' Court but, if the matter proceeds to a superior court, the solicitor must usually instruct a barrister to appear on the client's behalf. This is known as *briefing counsel.* Written instructions will be sent to a barrister relating to the representation of a client in legal proceedings. This will include a narrative of the facts, copies of any documents, specifications and, where appropriate, plans.

In addition, a solicitor may take *counsel's opinion* whereby he obtains the views of a barrister on the law which applies to the client's case. Unlike a barrister, a solicitor may sue his client for non-payment of fees. Solicitors may also be liable to their clients if they have acted negligently in the conduct of their case. Any allegation of professional misconduct against a solicitor is dealt with by the Disciplinary Committee of the Law Society, and in appropriate cases a solicitor's name may be 'struck off' the professional roll.

LEGAL EXECUTIVE

Much of the routine work in solicitors' offices is carried out by unadmitted assistants known as legal executives. Many of them are skilled in conveyancing and litigation. Training and qualifications are governed by the Institute of Legal Executives. The initial qualification is associate membership of the institute; after a further qualifying period of five years and an examination, the associate may become a fellow.

BARRISTERS

The Bar is the senior branch of the legal profession. The main functions of counsel are to act as advocates in the superior courts where they have an exclusive right of audience, and to give their legal opinion on a particular set of circumstances in the form of counsel's opinion when so required.

The governing body of the profession is the Senate of the Inns of Court and the Bar. In order to practise as a barrister, a person must have been called to the Bar by one of the four Inns of Court (Lincoln's Inn, Gray's Inn, the Middle Temple and the Inner Temple), and have passed the appropriate examinations of the Council of Legal Education. Once these stages have been completed, the newly-called barrister must undergo a period of *pupillage* whereby he assists an experienced barrister who supervises the new entrant's work.

Practising barristers are self-employed. Partnerships are prohibited but for the sake of convenience a number of barristers share offices or chambers, each contributing towards the overheads of the establishment. Each set of chambers has a clerk who deals with administration and, except in legal aid cases, negotiates the brief fee. The majority of barristers practise from chambers in London but most cities and some large towns have sets of barristers' chambers. In the provinces, barristers' work tends to be varied and common law orientated, while the majority of specialists, especially in company, commercial and chancery matters, are to be found in London.

Like solicitors, barristers are not allowed to advertise. They may not deal directly with the general public; they receive work only from solicitors who nominate the barrister they require for a particular case or opinion.

The vast majority of barristers are known as *junior counsel*. After ten years or more of successful practice, a junior may apply to the Lord Chancellor to become a *Queen's Counsel*. If successful, the applicant is said to have *taken silk* which entitles the QC to wear a silk gown in court. *Leading counsel*, as these barristers are called, do not draft pleadings. Instead, their work is confined to appearing as advocates in the more important cases. At one time, whenever a Queen's Counsel appeared in court he had to be accompanied by a junior barrister. Where appropriate, leading counsel may appear on their own without assistance.

Unlike solicitors, counsel may not sue for their fees. As advocates, barristers are immune from claims against them based on professional negligence, as shown by *Rondel* v. *Worsley* (1969). This rule is based on public policy and would seem to extend to any work carried out in the conduct of litigation or where litigation is pending. This immunity extends to the drawing of pleadings, but it does not extend to advisory or drafting work, see *Saif Ali* v. *Sydney Mitchell & Co.* (1978) where it was held that a barrister may be liable in respect of pre-litigation advice.

3.2 The judiciary

Reference has been made already to the different functions of judges. One particular feature of the judicial system in the United Kingdom is that judges are generally appointed from the ranks of practising barristers. The Courts Act 1971 allowed solicitors to be appointed as recorders, and they may then become circuit judges, but as yet, solicitors are not eligible for appointment to the High Court bench. This system of appointing judges only from practising lawyers contrasts with most legal systems elsewhere where judges are civil servants who are recruited as such normally after qualification as a lawyer.

In the United Kingdom, judges of the High Court, circuit judges and recorders are recommended for appointment by the Lord Chancellor. Superior judges, such as the Lords of Appeal in Ordinary, the Lord Chief Justice and the Master of the Rolls (see below), are recommended for appointment by the Prime Minister. These senior judges are subject to the power of removal only by the Queen on an address presented by both houses of parliament. The normal retirement age is 75, but circuit judges must retire at 72 unless requested to stay on for a further three years. Their salaries and pensions are paid directly from the Consolidated Fund.

The judicial offices are described below.

THE LORD CHANCELLOR

Abbreviated to LC in the Law Reports. This is the principal legal office in the United Kingdom. The appointment is made by the Crown on the Prime Minister's advice. The appointment is a political one and the Lord Chancellor is a member of the Cabinet and Speaker of the House of Lords. The Lord Chancellor can be removed from office at any time and his appointment will be revoked automatically on a change of government. The appointment is also judicial in character and, apart from his administrative tasks and appointment of judges, he is the senior judge of the House of Lords, the Court of Appeal and the Chancery Division.

THE LORD CHIEF JUSTICE

Abbreviated to LCJ. The Lord Chief Justice ranks next to the Lord Chancellor in the legal hierarchy. Although in theory he presides over the Queen's Bench Division of the High Court, his principal duties are as head of the Court of Appeal (Criminal Division) and the Divisional Court of the Queen's Bench Division.

THE MASTER OF THE ROLLS

Abbreviated to MR. The judge who presides over the Court of Appeal (Civil Division) is known as the Master of the Rolls. He decides the composition of the various appellate courts and organises the distribution of work. The Master of the Rolls also admits newly-qualified solicitors to the roll of the court, thus enabling them to practise.

THE PRESIDENT OF THE FAMILY DIVISION OF THE HIGH COURT

Abbreviated as P. The Family Division was established in 1970, after a reorganisation of business in the High Court. The President is the senior judge who, in addition to hearing cases, is responsible for the organisation and distribution of business of the court.

THE VICE CHANCELLOR

Abbreviated as VC. Although the Lord Chancellor is the nominal head of the Chancery Division, the actual organisation and management of Chancery Division business rests with the Vice Chancellor.

THE LORDS OF APPEAL IN ORDINARY

Abbreviated as 'Lord' followed by surname and any additional title. These are the senior members of the judiciary, usually appointed from the Court of Appeal, who hear appeals in the House of Lords. *'Law lords'* take little part in the non-judicial work of the Lords.

THE LORD JUSTICES OF APPEAL

Abbreviated as LJ. This is the title given to the judges who sit in the Court of Appeal. They are appointed by the Queen from judges of the High Court. On appointment, they are made Privy Councillors. As they hear only appeal cases, their work, like that of the law lords, is confined to London.

HIGH COURT JUDGES

Abbreviated as J. High Court, or puisne judges as they are sometimes known, are appointed by the Crown after recommendation from the Lord Chancellor. Appointments are normally made from the ranks of practising Queen's Counsel. On appointment, the judge will be knighted and assigned to one of the three divisions of the High Court. The Queen's Bench Division accounts for approximately two-thirds of the judges. Judges of High Court status and above are addressed as 'my Lord' or 'Your Worship'.

CIRCUIT JUDGES

Referred to as 'Judge' followed by surname. The vast majority of trials which are heard in the Crown Court or the County Court are dealt with by circuit judges. Such judges are appointed by the Queen on the recommendation of the Lord Chancellor from barristers of at least ten years' standing. Judges are allocated to one of the six circuits or groups of centres which they visit. In court, circuit judges are addressed as 'Your Honour'.

RECORDERS

Referred to as Mr Recorder followed by surname. The Courts Act 1971 provided for the appointment of recorders on a temporary basis to try cases in the County Court and Crown Court. Recorders may also sit as County Court judges. They must be solicitors or barristers of at least ten years' standing. Recorders are addressed as 'Sir'.

3.3 The law officers

THE ATTORNEY GENERAL

Abbreviated as Att. Gen. This title is given to the chief law officer of the Crown and head of the English Bar. The appointment is a political one chosen by the Prime Minister, and the holder is a Queen's Counsel and member of parliament. His principal tasks are to advise the government on legal matters and to represent the Crown in civil and criminal proceedings. Certain prosecutions may only be commenced with his consent. The Attorney General can also sue on behalf of the public to enforce public rights. He may lend his name to such an action at the request of a private citizen and these proceedings are known as *relator actions*. However, if he refuses to consent to the bringing of such an action his refusal cannot be questioned in the courts.

THE SOLICITOR GENERAL

Abbreviated to Sol. Gen. The Attorney General's deputy is known as the Solicitor General. He is normally a member of parliament and a Queen's Counsel (never a solicitor). His duties are in general similar to those of the Attorney General. He normally succeeds to that post if it becomes vacant. The law officers are forbidden to engage in private practice but they receive a salary inclusive of fees.

THE DIRECTOR OF PUBLIC PROSECUTIONS

Abbreviated as DPP. The Director of Public Prosecutions is appointed by the Home Secretary, but is responsible to the Attorney General for the exercise of his powers. He must be a solicitor or barrister of at least ten years' standing. His task is to undertake proceedings in important and complex criminal cases. He also reports on complaints against the police which are referred to him. Some statutes require his consent before a prosecution may be brought.

3.4 Juries

One feature of the English legal system is trial by jury. A jury is a body of persons selected to give a verdict in a particular case. Although seldom used in civil actions nowadays, they are always used in criminal trials held on indictment at the Crown Court. In criminal cases juries consist of twelve men or women. In general, the jury decides facts and it is left to the judge to decide questions of law. Consequently, juries have no place in the appeal courts.

Any person on the electoral register aged between 18 and 65 who has been resident in the United Kingdom for at least five years since the age of thirteen, may be required to sit on a jury. Certain persons, such as lawyers and the police are not eligible, while others are disqualified.

Traditionally, the verdict of the jury had to be unanimous but nowadays, if certain conditions are satisfied, the court may accept a majority verdict where the majority is not less than ten to two.

3.5 The expert witness

Although not strictly legal personnel, some reference should be made to the role of the expert witness. Quite frequently surveyors and architects are called upon to act in this capacity. There is a wide variety of courts and tribunals in England and Wales wherein expert evidence is required. The High Court, the Lands Tribunal, County Courts, Local Valuation Courts, and proceedings before arbitrators are all good examples.

The task of the expert witness is to assist the court or tribunal to determine the issues. Although he will have been employed by one of the parties, his primary duty is to uphold the integrity of his own profession. Only on that basis will his evidence be credible in the eyes of the court or tribunal. He may be questioned directly as to what inferences he would draw from the facts presented and to his opinions on the various aspects. The basic requirement is that the person chosen should have both specialised knowledge and experience of the subject matter in dispute.

Ideally, the expert witness should prepare a proof of evidence outlining what he is prepared to say at the hearing. In addition to giving direct oral evidence, such a witness may refer normally to his own reports, specialist books and refresh his memory by reference to notes. Moreover he may put forward observations and calculations based on his own specialist knowledge. The number of expert witnesses depends upon the number of specialised issues involved. However, every effort is made to limit the number of expert witnesses which each side may call.

Chapter 4

Aspects of constitutional law

The expression 'constitution' is used to denote the manner in which a state or other body is organised. The constitution of most countries is to be found in a documentary form which states the fundamental rights and rules of the nation. From this stems the duties and powers of the government and those of the people. The United Kingdom does not have a written constitution. Instead it is based on a number of elements comprising statute, the common law and so-called *conventions*. These are understandings, tacitly agreed, resulting from long practice by which the conduct of Crown and parliament is regulated in the absence of formal legal rules. One example of an established convention is that the party with the majority in the House of Commons is entitled to have its leader made prime minister.

4.1 Parliamentary sovereignty

Legislation is the supreme source of legal authority. Generally speaking, parliament can pass acts of parliament on any topic and in any way it so wishes. However, parliament is only supreme for the period of its existence and it cannot bind its successors, or pass laws on matters outside its jurisdiction. Because of this concept of parliamentary sovereignty, judges in this country have no powers to hold an act invalid or to ignore it, however unreasonable or unconstitutional it may be considered to be. In this respect, England differs from many countries which have written constitutions. In the United States of America for example, the Supreme Court, which is the equivalent of the House of Lords when acting in a judicial capacity, has the power to declare legislation passed to be invalid, if it considers that it is inconsistent with the written constitution.

4.2 The separation of powers

It is traditional to separate the functions of government into three independent divisions. This is the doctrine of the *separation of powers* which has been interpreted to mean that executive, legislative and judicial powers shall be in separate hands. The executive function is exercised by government departments shared with other bodies such as local authorities. Parliament is the principal legislative body as its main function is to pass acts of parliament in the Queen's name. Again, powers are delegated to other bodies to enact subordinate legislation. The judges comprise the third organ of government.

In the United Kingdom, there is no distinct separation of powers. Instead there is a blend of all three aspects. The Lord Chancellor, for instance, is vested with all three functions, being a member of the cabinet, head of the judiciary and speaker of the House of Lords.

4.3 The Privy Council

This body was the most important source of executive power in the state until the eighteenth century. It now plays a much diminished role as a formal body which advises the sovereign on matters such as orders in council and royal proclamations. The council consists of cabinet ministers, archbishops, senior judges and other dignitaries who are appointed as a political honour. All members are appointed by the Queen on the advice of the Prime Minister.

The Lord President of the Council supervises the business of the meetings. The whole council is called together on the death of the sovereign. The Judicial Committee of the Privy Council has appellate jurisdiction to hear appeals from courts outside the United Kingdom.

4.4 National and local government

After a general election, the successful party with a majority in the House of Commons, will form a government. The Prime Minister will be chosen and a *cabinet* formed. This is a group of ministers, selected by and presided over by the Prime Minister, who are collectively responsible for the general character and policy of legislation. Ministers, sometimes called secretaries of state, are appointed by the Monarch on the recommendation of the Prime Minister to head the various government departments.

The number and variety of departments will vary depending upon the government in power. Central government departments are staffed by civil servants who are full-time professional men and women. Their major role is to implement new and existing law which has been passed by parliament. In addition, technical staff are appointed to these departments to carry out specialist aspects of work. The Department of the Environment is a good example of this in its use of surveyors and architects. Departments also act in an advisory capacity.

Nowadays considerable powers are passed down by central government to local authorities. This is government on a local basis, formulated on a pattern of elected bodies for defined areas which are given responsibility for the provision of services within those areas. Their powers and importance should not be underestimated, although there are often attempts by central government to reduce their influence. Large areas of responsibility such as housing, highways, planning and education are in the hands of local authorities.

The essence of local government is that elected members formulate the policies in a particular area and these policies are carried out by officers employed by the authority. The legal framework of local government which was formulated in the nineteenth century has now been altered by the Local Government Act 1972. For some time before the act was passed, it had been apparent that factors such as population changes and overlapping services had made the system outdated.

The effect of the Local Government Act, which came into being on 1 April 1974, was to recognise the county as the major administrative unit in local government. Within the county areas are district councils which are responsible for much of the day-to-day work of local government. The smallest administrative unit is the parish, or community council as it is known in Wales.

Six of the English counties are known as metropolitan counties. These comprise the large conurbations of the West Midlands, Greater Manchester, Tyne and Wear, South Yorkshire, West Yorkshire and Merseyside. The districts within these counties are metropolitan districts. These have constitutions similar to those of other districts, but have extended functions.

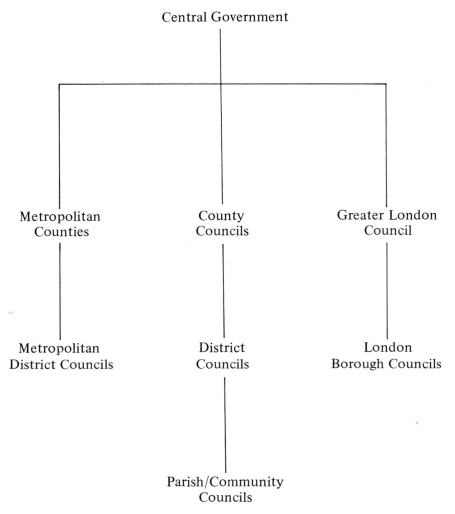

Fig. 4.1 Structure of local government since 1972

County Councils have responsibility for matters of policy and strategy. They deal with highways, the police and social services. District councils are more concerned with day-to-day considerations and deal with public health, housing and refuse collection. Parishes are concerned with matters in their locality relating to footpaths, litter bins and bus shelters.

Many functions are shared between counties and districts. Planning is a good example with the counties having responsibility for planning policy and the districts administering planning applications and enforcement provisions.

The structure of local government in London was not materially affected by the Local Government Act 1972. It was already significantly altered by the London Government Act 1963. The Greater London Council (GLC) is the major administrative unit having responsibility for such matters as planning policy, building control and main roads. Within the Greater London area are the London boroughs which deal with such matters as libraries, allotments, cemeteries and local roads. The GLC and the London boroughs share responsibility for areas such as planning and housing. Local government boundary commissions have been established to review local government boundaries and local electoral arrangements in England and Wales. The present government has indicated that it intends to abolish the GLC and the metropolitan counties.

CONTROL OF LOCAL AUTHORITIES

A local authority is a statutory body which enjoys *corporate personality*. This means that it is a person recognised by the law as having separate legal rights and duties. Each authority has elected members who formulate policies which are carried out by its officers. Normally these officers will be given specific areas of decision-making. Examples include district valuers, environmental health officers and education officers.

Local authority business is conducted through meetings, and rules are laid down as to their calling and conduct. Meetings are open to the public unless publicity about a particular matter is deemed to be prejudicial to the public interest because of the confidential nature of the business, or some other special reason.

Much of the work of local authorities is delegated to committees, who specialise in a particular matter, such as the planning committee. Most committees report to the council in full at a regular meeting. Membership of committees is fixed by the local authority.

It may be that a local authority does not wish to comply with a policy of central government. In that case can the council take its own course, or does it have to follow the central government line? To begin with, the powers of local authorities are defined by statute and if those powers are exceeded the authority is said to be acting *ultra vires*. The effect of this is to render the action of the local authority as being of no legal effect.

There are two major types of control of authorities. The most effective, which come directly from central government, are financial in nature and relate to restrictions on borrowing and the withholding of grants. Sometimes a district audit of local authority accounts takes place. In addition, in certain situations, the courts will interfere with a decision of a local authority which is wrong and rectify it. This is effected by the use of certain orders of the High Court, known as the *prerogative orders*. These orders are of three types. *Mandamus* orders the authority to carry out some public duty, while *prohibition* and *certiorari* are concerned with putting right an error made by an inferior court or body. Alternatively, the High Court may be asked for a declaration as to the law on a particular point, and, where appropriate, will grant an injunction to prevent a particular act being committed.

4.5 Statutory undertakers

These bodies, which are authorised to carry out transport, gas, electricity and other public obligations are known as *statutory undertakers*. Responsibility for these enterprises rests with public corporations. These are business corporations created by act of parliament. Members of these corporations are normally appointed by the relevant minister and annual accounts must be placed before parliament.

These bodies enjoy corporate personality, but, unlike a private company, a public corporation has no shareholders. Instead, it raises capital by means of loans. Each industry is required to make a profit and, in addition, to accumulate reserves for future capital development. Many undertakers tend to operate through area boards or authorities.

Electricity, for example, is produced by the Central Electricity Generating Board (CEGB) and distributed by twelve area boards which also sell appliances and undertake contracting work. The Water Act 1973 placed the water authorities under the control of the National Water Council. In 1983, the regional water authorities set up the Water Authorities Association as a trade association and the National Water Council was abolished. The water authorities are now autonomous bodies responsible for water supply, conservation, sewerage and recreational facilities. Since 1973, British Gas has been controlled by the British Gas Corporation, having previous been run by the Gas Council and area boards. These bodies are primarily controlled by parliament. Certain of these bodies have consultative councils to protect consumer interests: the National and Regional Gas Consumers' Councils are examples.

Chapter 5

The law of contract and agency

5.1 General principles

The law of contract is frequently the first 'case law' subject to which students are introduced when they commence their legal studies. The main reason for this is that contracts affect the general public more than most areas of law. Buying goods in a shop, a drink in a public house or paying the fare on a bus or train, are all examples of legally enforceable contracts. In addition, much of the civil side of the English legal system is based essentially on contractual principles and therefore an initial consideration of this area of law provides a good basis for future studies.

For the valuation surveyor, contract law is of the utmost importance. When land is transferred, the contract is the most important stage of the transaction. It is essential for a surveyor to be able to determine when a valid contract has come into existence. Many areas of law which affect the landed profession have a large contractual element in them, such as compulsory purchase and the assessment of compensation when interests in land are acquired. For the quantity surveyor, contract law is the most important legal subject which he studies. His principal requirement is an understanding of the forms of contract used in the construction industry where he carries out certain tasks and is referred to.

It is an everyday occurrence for each person in his own individual capacity to enter contracts, while in the business and professional world the multiplicity of agreements entered into often leads to disputes which need to be settled by one method or another.

60

5.2 The nature of contract

A contract is a legally binding agreement made between two or more persons. Ask the average person to define a contract and he will probably reply that it is an agreement. This is true, but before a valid contract can emerge there must be this extra legally binding element to show that the parties intend to adhere to the agreement made. Therefore, if the contract is broken by one side, the other person must be able to take the contract breaker to court if he so wishes. The essence of a contract in English law is that of a bargain and each side or party to the contract must contribute something to it for it to be valid.

5.3 Classes of contract

Regardless of the sum of money involved or the complexity of a particular agreement the normal rules of contract will remain the same. Obviously, if a large sum of money is involved or the matter is a complex one, there are advantages in having the contract drawn up by solicitors.

As a general rule, the parties to a contract may insert whatever provisions they wish into a contract. It is only recently that the law has placed restrictions on the extent to which contracting parties may exclude their liabilities.

SIMPLE CONTRACTS

As a general rule, a contract need not be in writing. Most contracts are made by word of mouth or informally in writing. These are known as simple contracts and they may also be implied from the circumstances. A major problem with an oral contract lies in proving the terms if the matter comes to trial.

CONTRACTS UNDER SEAL

Some contracts must be formally made by a deed. This means that they must be in writing and signed. Formerly, such documents required a seal also, but now a document purporting to be a deed is held to be one, even without a seal. These contracts are sometimes known as speciality contracts and, as an exception to the normal rule, they do not require consideration (see 5.6). Probably the best examples are conveyances of land and leases of more than three years. The fact that a contract is under seal has important consequences in connection with limitation periods (see under 5.16).

CONTRACTS WHICH MUST BE IN WRITING OR EVIDENCED IN WRITING

Certain contracts which do not need to be made under seal must nevertheless either be in writing or evidenced in writing before they can be enforced. A good example of the latter is a contract for the sale or other disposition of land under section 40 of the Law of Property Act 1925. This has been held to include the sale of building materials recovered from the demolition of a house.

STANDARD FORM CONTRACTS

A familiar characteristic of contemporary business life is the use of the standard form of contract. Certain transactions are governed entirely by standard terms which are predetermined. An obvious example is where one of the parties enjoys a monopolist position. For instance, a passenger of British Rail is not in a position to argue over the price of a rail ticket or the terms under which he will be carried. The situation is similar where there are few suppliers. Therefore it is not usual for a customer to negotiate over the terms of a hire purchase agreement or a mortgage. Instead, the customer contracts on a standard form prepared in advance by the company. Such contracts have done a great deal in recent years to make a mockery of the concept of freedom of contract whereby a person is free to contract or not at his own wish and the selection of subject matter, terms and parties are a matter of choice.

There are in fact two basic types of standard form of contract. One is the so-called 'adhesion' variety whereby no opportunity exists for any negotiations because a person must abide by the contents or not contract with that particular organisation at all on a 'take it or leave it' basis. The other is the 'incomplete' standard form in which the main terms of the contract are set out but the parties are free to negotiate matters such as dates of completion and fees. In the construction industry it is commonplace in the more important types of contract to use a standard form which is geared to the particular situation. Similar rules apply in civil engineering work.

5.4 The essential elements of a valid contract

In any contract there are three essential elements:
(a)   agreement, or the outward appearance of agreement;
(b)   consideration or else being under seal;
(c)   the intention to create legal relations.

5.5 Agreement

Before an agreement can be recognised at law there must normally
be a valid offer and an acceptance of that offer. However, there
are many contracts where it is impossible to identify an offer. The
real test is whether the parties have accepted obligations to one
another. The person who makes the offer is known as the offeror
and the person who accepts the offer is known as the offeree.

RULES AS TO OFFER

1.   The offer must be complete and final
Some contracts are too vague to be enforced and the courts will
normally hold that no contract has come into existence. In *Bushwall
Properties* v. *Vortex Properties* (1976) the purchase price of a piece
of land was to be paid by instalments. On payment of each instalment, a 'proportionate part' of the land was to be conveyed. It was
decided that the contract was void for uncertainty as it was not
clear as to how the proportionate parts were to be ascertained,
whether by price, area or other means.

2.   An offer must be distinguished from an invitation to treat
An invitation to treat is a starting point in negotiations which may
or may not result in an offer being made. Marked prices on articles
for sale in shop windows will normally amount to invitations to
treat and not to formal offers. In addition, catalogues and circulars
which offer goods for sale are generally in this category. In *Fisher*
v. *Bell* (1961) it was held that the display of a flick knife in a shop
window was simply an invitation to treat. In *Pharmaceutical Society
of Great Britain* v. *Boots Cash Chemists (Southern) Ltd* (1953) the
question arose as to when and where a sale had taken place in a
self-service store. It was decided that the sale had taken place at
the cashier's desk, and that the display of drugs on the counter was

simply an invitation to treat. The offer was made by the customer taking the drugs to the cashier, and the acceptance took place when the cashier accepted the customer's money. In *Gibson* v. *Manchester City Council* (1979) it was held that a statement made in a letter by the defendants that the council 'may be prepared to sell' and inviting the respondent 'to make formal application to buy' a council house, was simply an invitation to treat and therefore there was no binding contract.

A tender is normally an invitation to treat. Therefore, any request by a local authority to contractors to tender is not an offer, see *Spencer* v. *Harding* (1870). The tender is itself an offer, see *Great Northern Railway Co.* v. *Witham* (1873). Calculation of a price list is also an invitation to treat and not a formal offer.

As far as advertisements are concerned, it is usually a question of intention which decides whether these are offers or invitations to treat. The advertising of an auction sale is not an offer, see *Harris* v. *Nickerson* (1873). Those who bid at an auction make an offer which the auctioneers are free to accept or reject. As will be seen, an offer can be withdrawn at any time before the auctioneer accepts. On the other hand, advertisements are sometimes offers. For instance, advertisements for rewards are normally offers since the party who offers the reward does not intend any further negotiation to take place. The case of *Carlill* v. *Carbolic Smoke Ball Co. Ltd* (1873) is an illustration of where the courts were able to find that an advertisement constituted an offer. In *Crowshaw* v. *Pritchard* (1899) an offer was held to be in existence where a builder supplied an 'estimate' for work based on drawings and specifications supplied by the employer.

3.   A statement of price on its own does not normally constitute an offer

In *Clifton* v. *Palumbo* (1944) the plaintiff wrote, 'I am prepared to offer you my Lytham estate for £600,000.' The Court of Appeal considered that this was not an offer in any real sense as it amounted to no more than a statement of price as a guide to the defendant of the sort of terms on which the plaintiff might agree to sell his estate. A similar result was reached in *Harvey* v. *Facey* (1893) where the expression 'lowest cash price £900' was held to be simply a price guide. However, an agreement as to price may constitute a valid provision in a contract which is subsequently entered into, see

Bigg v. *Boyd Gibbins Ltd* (1971).

4. An offer must be communicated to the offeree
The offeree must be given the opportunity to accept or reject the offer. In *Taylor* v. *Laird* (1856) the captain of a ship resigned his post during the course of a voyage, but later helped to bring the ship home. It was decided that, since he had not communicated his offer to do the work, giving the owner the opportunity to accept or reject the offer, there was no contract.

5. An offer may be made to a specific person or to the community at large
As a general rule, where an offer is made to a particular person, or group of persons, no valid acceptance may be made, other than by a person to whom an offer has been made, see *Boulton* v. *Jones* (1857). It is possible to make an offer to the community at large and in that case any person who receives notice of the offer may accept or reject it. In *Carlill* v. *Carbolic Smoke Ball Co.* (1893) the defendant company advertised in a newspaper as follows: '£100 reward will be paid by the company to any persons who contract influenza, colds or other diseases after having used the ball three times daily for two weeks according to the directions supplied'. Mrs Carlill bought a smoke ball and used it as required but she caught influenza. She claimed £100 from the company. It was held that the advertisement was an offer made to the community at large and a contract was entered into with that part of the public, including Mrs Carlill who came forward and performed the conditions as to use on the basis of the advertisement.

Such a contract is known as a unilateral contract and it arises where a promise is made in return for an act. The promise becomes legally binding when the act is actually performed. This is to be contrasted with a bilateral contract of a-promise-for-a-promise where the agreement becomes effective at the moment when the promises are exchanged.

6. An offer may be withdrawn only up to the time of acceptance
This is the basic rule and where an offer is withdrawn it is said to be revoked. An offer may be revoked at any time before acceptance,

but revocation must be communicated to the offeree and once a valid acceptance has been made, the offeror is bound by the terms of the offer. Notice of revocation can be made by the offeror himself or by some other reliable source, see *Dickinson* v. *Dodds* (1876). An offer cannot be revoked after acceptance.

7.　*Revocation of an offer is only effective upon actual notice of its reaching the offeree*

This is the basic rule and where revocation is communicated by post it takes effect from the moment it is received by the offeree and not from the time of posting. The case of *Byrne* v. *Van Tienhoven* (1880) is a good illustration of this rule:

1 October: T posted an offer in Cardiff to B in the United States.
8 October: T posted a revocation of that offer.
11 October: B sent a telegram accepting the offer of 1 October
20 October: B received the revocation dated 8 October.

It was held that the revocation of 8 October was ineffective since it did not reach Byrne until after acceptance had been made.

8.　*An offer remains open until it is accepted, rejected, revoked or it lapses*

An offer normally lapses and becomes incapable of acceptance by passage of time. This occurs where there is a specific time limit within which acceptance may be made and that time has passed. It also occurs where no time limit is specified and there has been no acceptance within a reasonable period. The length of time is dependent upon the circumstances of the case and the question of reasonableness may vary depending upon the nature of the contract. The death of the offeror or the offeree also causes the offer to lapse.

9.　*The effect of rejection of an offer*

An offer may be rejected, but once an offeree has rejected an offer, he cannot go back and purport to accept it. Rejection may be express or implied. It is implied where there has been a counter-offer or where acceptance has been conditional. If the offeree inserts fresh terms into the contract, this will operate as a rejection of an offer.

RULES AS TO ACCEPTANCE

Acceptance of an offer is subject to the following rules.

1.   An acceptance must be unqualified

In *Tinn* v. *Hoffman & Co. Ltd* (1873) an offer to sell 1,200 tons of iron was met with a request for 800 tons. It was held that this amounted to a qualification of the offer and there was no contract.

This rule means that the acceptance must correspond exactly with the terms of the offer and to be valid they must correspond in every detail. In *Peter Lind Ltd* v. *Mersey Docks and Harbour Board* (1972) alternative tenders were submitted for the construction of a freight terminal. The offeree accepted 'your tender' without specifying which one and consequently there was no contract.

2.   Counter-offers

The insertion of new terms (see under 5.15) into the agreement amounts to a counter-offer by the person who makes it, rather than being a valid acceptance. Its legal effect is to reject the original offer. In *Hyde* v. *Wrench* (1840) an offer was made to sell a farm for £1,000. A counter-offer of £950 was made and refused, whereupon the buyer tried to accept the original offer of £1,000. It was decided that the seller could refuse this because the original offer had been rejected. However, an inquiry as to whether the offeror will vary the terms of his original offer will not constitute a counter-offer, see *Stevenson* v. *McLean* (1880).

3.   Tentative assents

These are not binding. Where an acceptance is made 'subject to contract', the addition of these words prevents the agreement becoming binding until such formal contract is completed or exchanged. In *Chillingworth* v. *Esche* (1924) no contract had come into existence where property was sold 'subject to a proper contract to be prepared by the vendor's solicitors'. However, a provisional agreement may be binding.

4.   Silence as a form of acceptance

An offeror cannot stipulate that he will take silence to be acceptance and thus bind the offeree. In *Felthouse* v. *Bindley* (1862) the plaintiff offered to buy X's horse for £30 and said that he would presume his offer to be accepted unless he heard to the contrary. X did not reply. It was held that no contract had been formed.

5.   Manner of acceptance

Normally acceptance may be communicated in any manner whatsoever. However, if the offeror stipulates a particular method of acceptance, it must be carried out in that manner. In *Manchester Diocesan Council for Education* v. *Commercial and General Investments Ltd* (1969) it was stated that the principle may be relaxed if it can be shown that a different method of acceptance places the other party in just as satisfactory a position. As a general rule, acceptance has no effect unless and until it is communicated to the offeror. There are two important exceptions to this rule:

Where acceptance is made by post: In this case, acceptance takes effect from the moment that the letter of acceptance is properly posted. (Contrast this rule with that as to revocation of an offer.) This rule applies even though acceptance is delayed or lost in the post, as long as there is sufficient evidence of posting, see *Henthorn* v. *Fraser* (1892). The consequence of this principle is that revocation of an offer received after a letter of acceptance has been posted is ineffective. Handing letters to a postman authorised to deliver letters is not a proper acceptance of posting. The letter is posted when it is put into the control of the Post Office in the normal manner, or given to a Post Office employee entitled to receive letters, see *Re London & Northern Bank* (1900). This rule can be excluded if the parties so wish. This was the result in *Holwell Securities* v. *Hughes* (1974), where an option to purchase land required actual communication.

Performance by the offeree: In certain cases the offeror may have included in his offer a term or provision providing that performance by the offeree shall be sufficient acceptance and that communication is not necessary. The conduct, however, must be unequivocal, see *Davies* v. *William Old Ltd* (1969).

6.   Instantaneous communication

In *Entores* v. *Miles Far East Corporation* (1955) the question arose as to where a contract is made in the case of instantaneous communication such as telephone or telex. The contract is made where the acceptance is received, while communication is inoperative unless it reaches the other party.

Retrospective acceptance

It was decided in *Trollope & Colls Ltd* v. *Atomic Power Construction Ltd* (1962) that an acceptance may have a retrospective effect and therefore apply to work done before the contract was agreed.

5.6 Consideration

This is the second essential element of a valid contract and, unless the contract is under seal, consideration must be present; otherwise, the contract is unenforceable. In English law a contract is essentially a bargain and some advantage or benefit must pass between the parties to the contract. A bare promise is not binding. If a customer buys food in a shop, the consideration is the gain to the shop of the customer's money, and on the other hand the advantage of the goods to the customer. Each side has parted with something and received a benefit in return. The most common form of consideration is payment of money, the provision of goods or the performance of services, but it may also consist of any benefit which accrues to one party or is to the detriment of the other.

Sometimes consideration is known as value. Where the consideration is an act, it is known as 'executed' consideration, but where it is a promise to act it is known as 'executory' consideration.

RULES

1. *Consideration must be real*

This means that there must be some consideration.

2. *The consideration need not be adequate*

This simply means that the consideration must have some value but the courts will not interfere with a bargain which has been made between the parties in the absence of fraud or other bad faith. In *Chappell & Co.* v. *Nestle* (1960) the wrappers from three bars of chocolate were held to constitute good consideration. In *Mountford* v. *Scott* (1975) a token payment of £1 securing an option to purchase a house for £10,000 was adequate consideration.

3.   *Consideration must not be past*

This means that something already done and completed by one person when the other person makes a promise to him cannot operate as consideration. This is because the second person has already had the benefit of what the other has done and there is nothing to exchange. If I paint my neighbour's house while he is away without asking him first, and upon his return he promises to pay me £500 for doing so, I have no remedy if he later refuses to pay. In *Re McArdle* (1951) a promise to pay the cost of repairing and decorating a property was made after the work was completed. Therefore the consideration was past and there was no legal obligation to pay.

In certain cases this rule is modified, as where there is an implied promise to pay at the outset of a transaction, despite the fact that payment does not take place until the transaction is completed. Examples include a journey by taxi and where a passenger on a bus is unable to pay his fare until he reaches his destination. There is also an exception made by statute in the case of a cheque, as cheques are frequently paid in connection with goods and services received and enjoyed in the past.

4.   *Only a party who has given consideration can bring an action for breach of contract*

A person who is only receiving a benefit under the contract and is not a party to it cannot commence proceedings. A, B and C enter an agreement under which A promises to do certain work if B will pay £50 to C. If A does the work but B does not pay, he can sue B, but C cannot bring proceedings because he gave no consideration and he is not a party to the contract.

5.   *Waiver*

This means to go without or forgo your rights. Where a debtor pays a lesser sum to his creditors than that which is due, the debtor is not discharged from his obligation to pay the balance. Therefore, the creditor can go back on the agreement and sue for the rest. This is known as the rule in *Pinnel*'s case (1602). However, there is a modification to this rule. If the creditor modifies the agreement by asking for payment in a different form (introducing a new element), compliance with this request will amount to consideration for the waiver and the creditor will have no further claim. In *D. & C. Builders* v. *Rees* (1966), the defendant owed £482 to the builders for work carried out but he refused to pay. The builders agreed to take a cheque for £300 in full satisfaction of the debt. It was held that the remaining £182 could be claimed since no new element had been introduced at the request of the creditor to modify the agreement.

6. Estoppel

At times the consideration rules operate unfairly. Because of this, the courts have developed the principle of estoppel which, in certain cases, prevents a person who has made a promise which has been acted upon from changing his mind at a later date if it would cause injustice to the other party to the contract. The rule is based primarily on conduct and first achieved importance in *Central London Property Trust Ltd* v. *High Trees House Ltd* (1947), the so-called *High Trees* case. This concerns the lease of a block of flats which turned out to be unprofitable because of the war. The landlord made a written promise to reduce the rent while the war lasted. After the war, the landlord changed his mind and started to charge the full rent again. It was decided that he could do this for the future, but the court said, *obiter*, that the landlord could not recover the full rent for the period between making his promise and the end of the war since the tenants had relied on the landlord's promise. This rule can only be used as a defence and not as a basis for starting off a case.

5.7 Intention to create legal relations

This is the third element of a valid contract, and, where no intention can be shown, there is no contract. Many agreements are never intended to be legally binding.

BUSINESS AGREEMENTS

In the case of business, building and commercial agreements, there is a presumption that the parties intend to create legal relations. However, this may be challenged (rebutted), if there is strong evidence from the contract that the parties do not intend to create legal relations, see *Milner & Sons* v. *Percy Bilton Ltd* (1966). In *Rose & Frank Ltd* v. *Crompton Bros* (1923) an agreement was expressed to be 'not subject to legal jurisdiction in the law courts'. It was held that there was no binding contract.

The parties to a contract are also not bound where the agreement is said to be 'binding in honour only', or something similar, see *Jones* v. *Vernons Pools* (1938) and *Appleson* v. *Littlewoods* (1939). In building contracts there is a presumption that a legal relationship is intended, but it is possible to insert a clause that the agreement shall not be binding in law. This will normally make the agreement unenforceable.

SOCIAL AND DOMESTIC AGREEMENTS

In agreements of this type, it is presumed that the parties do not intend legal relations to arise, but this may be rebutted by evidence to the contrary. If a friend fails to arrive for a meal or a husband is late when meeting his wife, there can be no action for breach of contract, even if a person complains that they have incurred expenses. In *Balfour* v. *Balfour* (1919) a man agreed to send his wife £30 per month while he was abroad. The Court of Appeal decided that there was no binding contract.

Although, in general, domestic agreements are not intended to be legally binding, this principle in turn may be rebutted. In *Simpkins* v. *Pays* (1955) a lodger and the members of the family with whom he lived agreed to go shares in a newspaper competition. It was held that when they sent in a winning entry, the prize money should be shared according to the agreement. In *Hussey* v. *Palmer* (1972) a mother-in-law who lived with her family paid for building work to be carried out on the family home. Although there was no enforceable contract, only a social agreement, the mother-in-law had an interest in the property equivalent in extent to her contribution.

It must be remembered, that although it is possible for the parties to make an agreement which excludes any intention to create legal relations, it is not possible to make an agreement excluding the jurisdiction of the law courts. It is always a decision for the courts to decide whether or not there is an intention to create legal relations.

5.8 Vitiating factors

We are now concerned with the second major area of the law of contract, the vitiating factors. This expression simply means those matters which affect a contract once it has been formed. The existence of vitiating factors (see 5.9-5.14) will make a contract either:

(a) void, where there will be no contract;
(b) voidable, where the contract exists but can be avoided;
(c) binding, where an enforceable contract exists.

5.9 Capacity to contract (or lack of it)

The law distinguishes between natural and artificial persons. Natural persons are human beings, while artificial persons are corporations. As far as natural persons are concerned, the general rule is that they have full capacity to contract, but there are exceptions in the case of minors, and drunken and insane persons. As far as corporations are concerned, they can only make contracts within the scope of their specific powers. Any contract entered into outside these powers is void.

MINORS (PERSONS UNDER THE AGE OF 18 YEARS)
The basic rule is that if a minor enters into a contract it is void. This has been established law since the Infants Relief Act 1874, which stated that all contracts entered into by infants for the repayment of money lent or for goods supplied (other than contracts for necessaries) shall be absolutely void. This will cover most contracts which a minor purports to enter. Until 1970, minors were known as infants. In *Leslie* v. *Shiell* (1913) a minor borrowed £400 from a firm of moneylenders by stating that he was of full age. The moneylenders attempted to recover the money but as the contract was void they could not do so.

Minors' voidable contracts
Where a person under the age of 18 enters into a contract of a continuing nature which may well last until after the minor reaches the age of 18, the contract may be voidable and the minor may avoid the contract either before or within a reasonable time of reaching the age of 18. However, if avoidance does not take place within a reasonable time, the contract will be binding on the minor. Examples of contracts within this category are those for the sale or purchase of land, taking a lease of property, buying shares in a company or carrying on business in partnership.

Contracts binding on minors
The following contracts are binding on minors:

Contracts for necessaries: These are goods suitable to the condition in life of such minor and to his actual requirements at the time of sale and delivery. A minor must pay a reasonable price for necessaries and whether or not such goods come within the definition depends upon the standard of living of the individual in question. Therefore, if a claim is brought by a shopkeeper against a minor in this respect the plaintiff must show that the minor needed the goods otherwise the claim will be unsuccessful. In *Nash* v. *Inman* (1908) such a claim failed in proceedings taken by a Savile Row tailor relating to an unpaid bill because the defendant had a sufficient supply of similar clothes.

Contracts for education and training: A person who has not reached the age of majority must pay a reasonable price for training where a price is agreed and he is bound by a contract of employment, apprenticeship and education which taken as a whole is for the minor's benefit. In *Doyle* v. *White City Stadium Ltd* (1935) a contract by which a boxer under the age of majority agreed to keep to the rules of the British Boxing Board of Control, was binding on him. A similar conclusion was reached in *Roberts* v. *Gray* (1913). However, it must be stressed that the contract exists for the minor's benefit and, if it does not, the court will not enforce it, as in *De Francesco* v. *Barnum* (1890) where the court considered the terms of the contract to be unreasonably harsh.

DRUNK AND INSANE PERSONS

A mental patient cannot validly enter contracts. If a person makes a contract while temporarily drunk or insane the contract is voidable if he can prove that he was so drunk or insane at the time so as to be incapable of understanding what he did, and the other party knew this. The contract must be avoided within a reasonable time of retaining sanity or sobriety.

5.10 Mistake

EFFECT ON AGREEMENT

The general rule is that a mistake by either or both parties to a contract does not prejudice its validity. There are circumstances, however, where the mistake is so important that it goes to the very root of the contract. Such a mistake is known as an *operative mistake*.

Fundamentally, these are mistakes as to the facts which affect the basis of the contract.

EXAMPLES OF OPERATIVE MISTAKE

Mistake as to the subject matter of the contract
If sufficiently serious this will render the contract void because the parties are at cross purposes. In *Raffles* v. *Wichelhaus* (1864) the defendant agreed to buy a cargo of cotton which was described as being on the SS *Peerless* from Bombay. In fact, there were two ships of that name sailing from Bombay with an interval of three months between them. The seller intended to put the cargo on the second ship while the buyer expected it on the first. It was decided that the contract was void.

A similar decision was reached in *Couturier* v. *Hastie* (1843-60) where, unknown to the parties to the contract, the cargo of wheat which formed the subject matter no longer existed. However, the circumstances in which the courts will hold that such a mistake avoids the contract are very limited in scope.

Mistake as to the identity of some other party
If it can be proved that the identity of the other party to the contract was a material factor when the contract was entered into, and that the plaintiff intended to deal only with a specific person and nobody else, the contract will be void, see *Ingram* v. *Little* (1961). However, this is often difficult to prove and in the majority of everyday contracts mistake as to identity will render the contract voidable instead of void. In *Lewis* v. *Averay* (1972) the plaintiff sold his car to a rogue who pretended to be Richard Greene, a film actor. The rogue paid by a 'bounced' cheque and then sold the car to the defendant. In proceedings which ensued it was held that the contract between the plaintiff and the rogue was voidable because the plaintiff could not prove that he was only willing to sell to Richard Greene and nobody else. This case follows the earlier decision of *Phillips* v. *Brooks* (1919).

Mistake as to the nature of the document signed
It may be that a party to a contract signs it believing that he is signing a document of a completely different nature. It is generally the case that a person is bound by the terms of any document which he signs even though he did not read or understand the contents, see *L'Estrange* v. *Graucob* (1943).

There are exceptions to this rule if the document was signed under a mistaken belief as to the nature of the document and the mistake was due to either:

(a)   the blindness, illiteracy or other disability of the person signing, as in *Thoroughgood*'s case (1584) and *Foster* v. *MacKinnon* (1869); or

(b)   where there is a trick or fraud as to the true nature of the document. In these circumstances, within narrow limits, the defence of *non est factum* may be raised, meaning 'it is not my deed'. To be successful, the person relying on the defence must prove:

    (i)   he was not negligent when signing;

   (ii)   the document was signed as a result of a fraudulent inducement;

  (iii)   that all reasonable precautions were taken when signing;

  (iv)   the document which was signed was fundamentally different from that which the party thought he was signing.

The difficulties inherent in raising this defence are well-illustrated by the case of *Saunders* v. *Anglia Building Society* (1971) where an old lady, thinking that she was transferring a lease to a relation signed a document passing the property to a rogue. However, she could not rely on the defence as she had not satisfied the conditions. The relatively recent case of *United Dominion Trust Ltd* v. *Western* (1976) illustrates the problems of satisfying the above conditions.

THE EFFECT OF EQUITY ON MISTAKE

In certain cases equity will intervene so as to affect a contract entered into by mistake. This only occurs where the mistake is not fundamental and usually applies where the parties have drawn a mistaken inference from the facts.

Rectification

In certain circumstances equity will rectify a contract so as to ensure that it accurately expresses what the parties had originally agreed. In *Craddock Bros* v. *Hunt* (1923) there was an oral agreement to sell some land. This was put into writing but by mistake the document missed out any reference to part of the land which had been paid for. It was held that the agreement would be rectified. See also *Roberts* v. *Leicestershire County Council* (1961) and *Thomas Bates & Sons Ltd* v. *Wyndham's (Lingerie) Ltd* (1981), where a provision relating to the appointment of an arbitrator to fix a rental in a lease was omitted due to a mistake and rectification was ordered.

Specific performance

This is an equitable remedy which is used to enforce a contract and is considered under 5.16. The court will not allow the order to be made where it would be unjust to the person who made the mistake.

In *Grist* v. *Bailey* (1966) the defendant agreed to sell a house to the plaintiff for £850. The price was low because Bailey believed that she had a tenant protected by the Rent Acts living in the property and could not give vacant possession. In fact, the tenant had died and Mrs Bailey only found this out after a valid contract for the sale of the property had been made, but before the transaction had been completed. The market value of the property was about £2,250 and she refused to sell. It was held that there was a common mistake and the courts refused to specifically endorse the agreement.

Setting aside

Where appropriate, the courts will set aside an agreement. In *Solle* v. *Butcher* (1950) the plaintiff rented a flat from the defendant at £250 per annum for seven years. The maximum rent payable was £140 per year under the Rent Acts and it was decided that the lease would be set aside.

5.11 Misrepresentation

A representation is a statement of fact, which is made by one person to another with the object of persuading the other party to enter a contract and which results in his actual contracting. If the representation turns out to be false or incorrect, it is a misrepresentation. A representation must be distinguished from a term of a contract (see under 5.15). In the case of construction works, negotiations will take place between the parties and statements may be made as to matters such as the site, provisions for sanitation, and methods of construction. If these statements are intended to be enforceable between the parties they will be representations and if they turn out to be false they will be misrepresentations.

To constitute a misrepresentation, the statement must normally be one of fact and not of opinion. For example, neither the client nor the person who has taken out quantities relating to a particular property implies to a contractor the correctness of bills of quantities. In *Bissett* v. *Wilkinson* (1927) the court took the view that a remark made that a parcel of land in New Zealand would support 2,000 sheep was only an expression of opinion and not a representation of fact. However, in *Esso Petroleum* v. *Mardon* (1976) the plaintiffs were liable, through their area manager, in respect of a forecast which had been given by him to a prospective tenant of a petrol station relating to the likely sales of petrol in a year. The defence of opinion was rejected since Esso were in a position to know the true position because of their special knowledge and skill. To attract liability, the statement must be made during negotiations and intended to operate as an inducement. In *Attwood* v. *Small* (1838) representations were made concerning a mine which was for sale. The purchaser paid his own surveyor to make a report. On receiving a favourable appraisal he purchased the mine but discovered that it was no longer of use since it had been 'worked out'. However, as the purchaser had not relied on the representations but instead on independent investigations he could not rescind.

REMEDIES
Misrepresentation is governed by the Misrepresentation Act 1967. The main distinction which is made is between fraudulent and innocent misrepresentation.

Fraudulent
This is where the person making the statement does not believe in its truth, or care whether it be true or false. In this case, damages may normally be claimed and the injured party may rescind the contract if he so wishes. Fraud was defined in *Derry* v. *Peek* (1889) as a false statement made knowingly, or without belief in its truth, or made recklessly not caring whether it be true or false. In *Pearson* v. *Dublin Corporation* (1907) respondents prepared plans without any belief in their conforming to specification. As a result, the work proved more expensive than anticipated and the appellant was entitled to damages.

Innocent
This is where the maker believes in the truth of his statement although

he has perhaps acted carelessly. In this case the contract may be rescinded. Damages may also be claimed unless the person making the statement honestly believed what he said and had reasonable grounds for doing so up to the time that the contract was made. Sometimes the expression 'negligent misrepresentation' is used to denote a false statement which the maker had no reasonable grounds for believing to be true.

Under the Misrepresentation Act, the court may in its discretion award damages in lieu of rescission. The right to rescind is an equitable remedy and will be lost if the person wishing to claim his rights has acted in an unsatisfactory manner in relation to the dispute. In such circumstances the plaintiff will only be entitled to the contract price. In *Leaf* v. *International Galleries* (1950) a plaintiff lost his right to rescind for innocent misrepresentation because he had delayed five years in bringing proceedings.

5.12 Illegality

Any contract containing an illegal element is void. The illegal aspect may be the contravention of a statute or it may be against public policy to allow certain types of contract to be enforced, such as defrauding the Inland Revenue or contracts involving the commission of a crime. Where a contractor enters a contract knowing that he is in contravention of a law and he completes the work, he will be unable to recover the contract price, see *Stevens* v. *Gourlay* (1859) where a contract was illegal because statute required buildings to be made of incombustible material and a contractor constructed a wooden building upon a wooden foundation.

However, if a contract appears to be perfectly valid at the outset and only becomes illegal while in the process of performance, the contractor may recover the price for his work depending upon the circumstances, see *Townshend Builders* v. *Cinema News* (1959). This is a case where the specifications for work to be undertaken were in contravention of a by-law but the final job was not. As the contract was not fundamentally illegal and the builder was not aware of the contravention until the work was well advanced he could claim payment.

5.13 Duress

This means coercion or force and the effect is to render the contract voidable.

5.14 Undue influence

In certain cases, the courts presume that a person entering a contract is doing so under the influence of some other person which prevents him from exercising a free and independent judgment. The effect of this is to render the contract voidable. Examples usually given include those between doctor and patient and solicitor and client. Recently the relationship between banker and customer was held to come within this category, see *Lloyds Bank* v. *Bundy* (1975).

5.15 Other factors relating to contracts

TERMS OF A CONTRACT

By this expression we mean the contents of a contract. Terms may be *express* or *implied*. Express terms are those mentioned and agreed by the parties at the date of contracting. This may be done in writing or by word of mouth. Where the parties have not come to express agreement on any particular point, the courts will sometimes imply terms to cover the position, imposing such obligations as in the view of the courts they would have reasonably agreed had they thought of the matter. Sometimes this arises in the form of a statute; the Sale of Goods Act 1979 is a good example.

A term will not be added just because it makes better sense of the agreement, see *Trollope & Colls* v. *N.W. Hospital Board* (1973) where the court refused to imply a term to make better sense of a building contract. There is a distinction between terms and representations (see 5.11 Misrepresentation). A term creates a contractual relationship and, if it is broken, a claim may be brought by the injured party. Remedies in respect of misrepresentation are governed by the Misrepresentation Act 1967.

Types of terms

Terms are normally implied into contracts for construction works. Examples include giving possession of the site within a reasonable time, executing the work with skill and care, and items such as implied fitness of materials. Often these matters are dealt with by express provisions stating the position of the parties. The traditional distinction between terms of a contract is to distinguish a *condition* from a *warranty*. This is important since there are different remedies if there is a breach of contract and things go wrong. There is no special test to determine into which class a term falls and each situation has to be decided on its own merits.

Conditions

These are terms of the contract but for which the injured party would not have entered the contract. Breach of condition allows the injured party to treat the contract as finished, whereupon he will be discharged from his obligations under the contract. In addition, he can sue the other party for damages. However, the contract is voidable and it is possible for the injured party to treat the breach of condition as a breach of warranty and to sue simply for damages.

Warranties

These are terms which are secondary or ancillary to the main purpose of the contract. Breach of warranty allows the injured party to claim damages but not to repudiate the contract. In other words, these are minor terms and if there is a breach of warranty the injured party is entitled to damages but cannot avoid the contract.

A number of recent cases have shown the difficulty of classifying terms in this way relying more on the consequences of the breach. In some cases, it has been shown that it is possible to have a term which is neither a condition nor a warranty. It would seem that the possibility of rescission in this case depends upon whether the term goes to the root of the agreement or not.

PRIVITY OF CONTRACT

This common law contract states that a contract cannot be enforced by or against a person who is not a party to it. This can cause particular problems in the construction industry where many parties are involved. In *Tweddle* v. *Atkinson* (1861) a young couple were about to marry. The husband's father and the bride's father agreed between themselves that each would make payments to the couple. The husband sought to enforce the contract when the bride's father failed to pay but it was decided that he could not recover.

A good example of the rule in practice occurs where a clause in a building contract which enables the employer to pay money directly to a sub-contractor may be used by the employer but cannot be enforced by the sub-contractor as he is not a party to the contract. There are certain exceptions to this rule, primarily in connection with agency and contracts of insurance.

EXCLUSION CLAUSES

It is common practice, when parties contract, for one party to insert a clause excluding or limiting his liability to another. Such clauses are frequently used by suppliers of goods and services in an attempt to limit or exclude liability for items such as defective materials and work. The courts have always disliked exclusion clauses and tend to lean against them when interpreting them.

The basic rule is that no new term can be imposed into a contract after it has been made except with the consent of both parties. Also, the clause must be displayed before or at the time the contract is made. Moreover, it must be clear that the clause was installed to form part of the contract and that it actually does so. By the Unfair Contract Terms Act 1977 and the Sale of Goods Act 1979, it is impossible to avoid liability for causing death or personal injury, while in other cases it depends on the reasonableness of the exemption. If the contract has been fundamentally breached, whereby one party has essentially diverted from his obligations under the agreement, no exclusion clause will protect him unless it can be shown unequivocally that the exemption should apply to a fundamental breach.

PART PERFORMANCE

Before it can be enforced, a contract for the sale of land must be evidenced in writing by a note or memorandum containing details of the transaction. However, if certain conditions are satisfied, a defendant who has acquiesced in the plaintiff's performance of a contract is barred from pleading absence of writing and the contract can be enforced. This is known as the equitable remedy of part performance. Before the doctrine can apply the following points must be satisfied.

(a) The act must be exclusively referable to the contract. In *Maddison* v. *Alderson* (1883) an employer made a promise by word of mouth to his housekeeper that instead of paying her wages as he had done in the past, he would leave her by will a life estate in a particular property. The court decided that this was not a sufficient act of part performance. In the later case of *Wakeham* v. *MacKenzie* (1968) the giving up by a housekeeper of her former home and moving into her employer's residence was sufficient to enable a successful claim to the house to be made on death.

(b)   The act must be of real performance. This means that the act must not be simply an act in preparation for the performance. Therefore simply viewing or visiting the land, measuring up or making a valuation are not sufficient acts.

(c)   The act must be such that it would be fraudulent to allow the defendant to attempt to rely on the absence of written evidence.

Examples of sufficient acts of part performance have included the carrying out of repairs and alterations on premises to be let, see *Rawlinson* v. *Ames* (1925), the erection of new buildings on land, and the taking possession of land by one party with the consent of the other. At one time it was thought that the payment of money, representing the purchase price or rental of a property could not be a sufficient act of part performance. This proposition is now of doubtful authority, see *Steadman* v. *Steadman* (1974).

5.16 Discharge and remedies for breach of contract

This is the last major area to consider and in some ways it is the most important.

DISCHARGE

Where a contract is at an end, it is said to be discharged. The basic rule is that on discharge the parties are freed from their obligations. Discharge must normally take place by some act of the parties as the contract does not end automatically. Discharge takes place in the following ways:

(a)   performance;
(b)   agreement;
(c)   frustration;
(d)   breach.

PERFORMANCE

The rule is that each party must perform completely and precisely what he has bargained to do. A person who claims to be discharged from his obligations on the ground of performance must show that the work has been completed in full. A building or engineering contract will be discharged by performance when the contractor has completed all the work, and the employer has paid all sums due. If there are any hidden defects, the contract has not been performed.

The old common law rule is well illustrated by *Cutter* v. *Powell* (1795) where the defendant agreed to pay Cutter a sum of money for performing duties as a seaman on a ship during a ten-week voyage. Cutter died and his wife attempted to recover some of the money under the contract. It was decided that because Mr Cutter had not performed his ten-week contract no action could succeed. Again, in *Sumpter* v. *Hedges* (1898) the plaintiff, a builder, agreed to construct two houses on the defendant's land for a sum of £566. He completed work to the value of £333 and then abandoned the work for lack of funds. The plaintiff was unable to recover for the work done as he had abandoned the contract. In order to avoid possible injustice and to prevent unfair manipulation of the common law rule, the courts have recognised certain exceptions where a person may claim a reasonable sum for the work he has done on a *quantum meruit* application, which means 'as much as it is worth'.

Exceptions are described below.

Divisible or severable contracts

Normally performance must be exact, but if a contract is divisible or severable, payment can be claimed for work done on completion of each stage. The rule only applies if the contract is severable. If the contract is an *entire* one which does not allow for sectional completion, the rule in *Cutter* v. *Powell* applies.

Substantial performance

This doctrine arises where performance under a contract, although not complete, is virtually exact. In this case, a claim may be made for the work completed. However, this is subject to a counter-claim in respect of the work not done by the other party. Normally the full contract price can be claimed subject to a deduction equal to the cost of putting right the defects. The idea behind the doctrine is to protect a contractor who has carried out the works in effect but where there remain defects or unfinished work of an insignificant nature.

In *Hoenig* v. *Isaacs* (1952) the plaintiff was employed to decorate a flat and also to provide furniture for it. The contract price was £750, of which £400 was paid on account and the balance on completion. Isaacs took possession of the flat, but complained of defects in the design and also of bad workmanship. Consequently, he refused to pay the balance. The court decided that Hoenig was not entitled to any further payments under the contract but he could claim on a *quantum meruit* basis for work done less the cost of remedying the defects.

If the defects are more serious and the work is carried out in a completely different manner from that originally envisaged and outside the original specifications, no action may be brought and a claim on a *quantum meruit* will not be available. Moreover, the doctrine does not apply where the work is not completed at all. In *Dakin* v. *Lee* (1916) the court stated that if a builder had done work under an entire contract, but the work has not been completed in accordance with the contract, he may claim on a *quantum meruit* unless the customer received no benefit from the work, the work done was entirely different from that which was contracted for, or the contractor has abandoned the work.

In *Bolton* v. *Mahadeva* (1972) the plaintiff agreed to install a central heating system for £650. The defendant refused to pay anything whatsoever, arguing that the system had been incorrectly installed. No claim for substantial performance was allowed because the defects were major and could not be rectified easily or at little expense. The test as to application of the doctrine seems to centre around whether or not the client has fundamentally received the benefit for which he entered into the contract initially.

Prevention of performance

Where the contractor is prevented by the client from performing what he agreed to do, he may either sue for damages or claim on a *quantum meruit* for work done. In *Roberts* v. *Bury Improvement*

Commissioners (1870) a contractor was held not to be in default where an architect neglected to supply him with the necessary plans thereby preventing completion by the contract date.

AGREEMENT

As contracts are created by agreement between the parties they may also be discharged in the same way. The parties may have made provision for discharge in their original contract or it may have come about by reason of a new agreement. In this case, the new agreement must be legal.

FRUSTRATION

This means impossibility. As a rule, contractual obligations are absolute in that a contract is not discharged simply because it is more difficult or expensive than expected to carry it out, see *Paradine* v. *Jane* (1647). However, as the law developed, it moved from this rigid position and now a contract may be discharged by frustration if supervening events make it impossible to carry out. In order to rely on this doctrine, it must be shown that the circumstances have changed to such an extent that the performance of the contractual obligations has become fundamentally different from that originally envisaged.

Examples of building and engineering contracts which have been frustrated are rare. A basic rule is that the fact that the work proves more difficult or expensive to perform will not frustrate the contract unless the difficulty arises from some fundamental change of circumstances. In *Davis Contractors Ltd* v. *Fareham UDC* (1956) contractors agreed to build 73 houses in 8 months. Mainly due to lack of skilled labour and shortage of materials, the 8 months extended to 22 months. Building costs in that period has risen considerably and the builders claimed that they should be entitled to claim on a *quantum meruit* for these costs. It was held that the contract was not frustrated, simply more difficult to carry out.

A similar result is to be found in *Thorn* v. *London Corporation* (1876) where a design for a new bridge proved impossible to construct. The contractor had taken the risk as to the method of completion and remained liable to carry out the work. The event causing the frustration must not have been one which the parties could have contemplated when making the contract and the event causing the frustration must not have been due to the conduct of the parties.

Specific examples of frustration
Where the subject matter of the contract has been destroyed: In *Taylor* v. *Caldwell* (1863) a building which was to be used for a series of concerts was accidentally destroyed by fire.

Death or serious injury could not be foreseen: In *Robinson* v. *Davison* (1871) a concert pianist was engaged to give a concert but became ill and was unable to perform.

Where a change in the law makes a contract illegal: In *Baily* v. *De Crespigny* (1869) statutory powers given to a railway company prevented the performance of a covenant in a lease.

Where there is government interference: In *Metropolitan Water Board* v. *Dick Kerr* (1918) contractors agreed with the plaintiffs to build a reservoir in wartime. After two years a government department acting under statutory powers ordered the defendants to cease work immediately. The contract was frustrated.

Leases are now subject to the frustration rules: In *National Carriers Ltd* v. *Panalpina (Northern) Ltd* (1980) the House of Lords decided that the doctrine of frustration does apply to leases although on the facts of this particular case the lease was not frustrated.

Effect of the doctrine
If a party successfully proves that the contract has become frustrated, the contract will automatically become void. Money paid before frustration becomes recoverable and no future payments need be paid. The court is permitted to allow the expenses of the other party. *The Law Reform (Frustrated Contracts) Act 1943* governs this area of the law.

BREACH
Where a person fails to do what he has agreed or does not do it properly, he is said to be in breach of contract and will be liable to pay damages to the injured party in order to compensate him for any loss. Any failure by a person who contracts to fulfil his obligations under the contract amounts to a breach. If the breach is sufficiently serious, the innocent party may treat the other person as having repudiated the whole contract. In each case, the issue as to whether the breach is to be taken as a repudiation depends upon

the importance of the breach in relation to the contract as a whole. Repudiation will assert itself in a building contract where execution of the works is so unsatisfactory as to affect the very basis of the contract.

REMEDIES

The main object of the civil law is compensation. Hence the general rule is that a plaintiff should be compensated for his loss. Damages, meaning compensation or money payable, fall into two categories:

(a)   unliquidated damages;
(b)   liquidated damages.

UNLIQUIDATED DAMAGES

This is where the parties to the contract make no pre-assessment of any damages payable in the event of a breach. The idea is to put the injured party in the same position as if the contract had been per-formed. It is against public policy to allow a plaintiff to be compen-sated for every consequence which might logically result from the defendant's breach or there would be no end to his potential liabi-lity. This is known as the *remoteness rule* and the same line of thinking applies in other areas of the law such as in the law of tort. The leading case on this principle is *Hadley* v. *Baxendale* (1845) where it was decided that the only losses recoverable are those which may fairly and reasonably be considered as arising naturally from the breach or be in the contemplation of both parties at the time when they made the contract.

In *Victoria Laundry* v. *Newman Industries* (1949) the plaintiffs ordered a new boiler for their business which arrived late. They were entitled to recover damages for normal loss of profits because the supplier should have anticipated this. However, they were not entitled to recover for further losses due to the demise of a profitable government contract caused by the late delivery, as the defendants were not aware of its existence. On the same basis, a different conclusion was reached in the *Heron 2* case (1969) where loss of profit could be recovered because it ought to have been foreseen by the parties to the contract that the market price of the ship's cargo would go down in the case of late delivery.

The injured party has a duty to mitigate or minimise his loss. This means that he must take all reasonable steps to reduce it. Therefore, an employee who is wrongly dismissed must attempt to find alternative employment, while a buyer of goods which are not delivered must try to buy as cheaply elsewhere; otherwise failure to do so will be taken into account when assessing damages. On the other hand, only reasonable steps to mitigate need be taken.

Classification of unliquidated damages

General damages: The measure of damages awarded is usually the actual monetary loss. These are known as general damages. The principle is that the innocent party should be restored to the position he would have been in had the other person performed his obligations.

Special damages: These are sometimes payable in respect of extra losses such as medical expenses.

Nominal damages: Where a technical breach of contract has taken place but no loss has been incurred, the breach is recognised by a token payment.

The traditional rule has been that damages should not take account of injured feelings. However, in *Jarvis* v. *Swan's Tours* (1973) damages were awarded where a holiday firm defaulted in its obligations causing misery and mental distress. A similar result was reached in *Heywood* v. *Wellers* (1976) where damages were awarded to the plaintiff in respect of misery and distress suffered when bringing an action in the law courts. There is no apparent authority as to recovery of such compensation in building cases.

Where a contractor does defective work in breach of contract damages will amount to the cost of reinstatement. Where a surveyor gives an incorrect report as to the state of a property, damages will be the difference in value between the property surveyed and what it is actually worth. Inflation and building costs often result in argument as to the date when repair costs should be assessed for the purpose of damages. In *Dodd Properties* v. *Canterbury County Council* (1979) the judge stated that the appropriate damages payable are the cost of repairs at the time when it is sensible to begin those repairs.

LIQUIDATED DAMAGES

In some cases the parties make an attempt in the original contract to assess in advance the damages which will be payable in the event of a breach. This so-called provision for liquidated damages will be valid if it is a genuine attempt to pre-estimate the likely loss.

Such a clause must be distinguished from a penalty clause. This is a provision which is inserted to frighten the potential defaulter and to compel actual performance of the contract. It is a threat and its effect is to render the contract void. Often building contracts or those for the sale of goods provide that in the event of late performance a specified sum shall be payable for each day of delay. The question as to whether a clause is a penalty or liquidated damages depends upon its construction and the surrounding circumstances.

Rules

(a) The name which the parties give to the clause is not conclusive and it is the task of the court to decide its category.

(b) The essence of liquidated damages is that the sum stated is a genuine pre-estimate of the probable loss, while the essence of a penalty is that it is a threat to carry out the contract.

(c) It is presumed to be a penalty clause if the sum stipulated is extravagant compared with the greatest possible loss. In *Re Newman* (1876) a building contract contained a provision that if the contract was not 'in all things duly performed', the contractors should pay £1,000 as 'liquidated damages'. This was considered by the court to be a penalty.

(d) It is a penalty if the breach consists of not paying a sum of money by a certain date and the sum fixed is greater that the sum originally to be paid. For example, X agrees to pay Y £1,000 on 1 June and if he fails to pay at the correct time he must pay £1,500 as 'liquidated damages'. Such an agreement will be void.

(e) There is a presumption that where a single sum is made payable on the happening of one or more events, some of which are serious and some of which are of little consequence the sum is a penalty. In *Law* v. *Redditch Local Board* (1892) the sum stated in a liquidated damages clause was to be paid in a single event only. Therefore, it was deemed to be a valid pre-estimate of the likely loss.

The case of *Dunlop Pneumatic Tyre Co. Ltd* v. *New Garage Ltd* (1915) is the leading case on this area of the law and from it the following conclusions may be made.

A liquidated damages clause is binding on the parties: In the event of a breach of contract, the sum fixed and no more or less can be claimed. No action for unliquidated damages can be pursued.

A penalty clause is void: In the event of breach the injured party may claim for unliquidated damages and the penalty clause is disregarded.

Interest on damages

The Law Reform (Miscellaneous Provision) Act 1934, now superseded by the Supreme Court Act 1981, provides that a court may allow interest on claims for damages in respect of the whole or part of the period between the date when the proceedings began and the date of the judgment (case proved). Sometimes interest is payable automatically as where there is express agreement between the parties.

EQUITABLE REMEDIES

Sometimes the court considers that a party to a contract is entitled to a remedy other than damages. In this case, an equitable remedy may be granted developed from the old rules of equity. These remedies cannot be claimed automatically as they are discretionary in nature. They will not be awarded where damages is an adequate remedy. The plaintiff's conduct is also taken into account. The case must be brought within a reasonable time while undue hardship must not be caused to the defendant. The 'maxims' of equity must be adhered to.

Specific performance

This is an order of the court directing a party to a contract to carry out his promise. It is normally only awarded where the subject matter of the contract is unique and nowadays it is mainly used as a remedy where contracts for the sale of land are broken. Apart from the normal rules as to the granting of equitable remedies, it will not be awarded to enforce a contract for personal services or to or against a minor. Where the contract is a building contract specific performance is not normally available because of the amount of supervision required to see that the order is being enforced and also because damages are usually an adequate remedy. Specific performance of a building contract will be awarded where:

(a)   the building work to be done is clearly specified in the contract preferably with drawings and bills of quantities;
(b)   the plaintiff has a special interest in having the work done which cannot be satisfied by damages;
(c)   the defendant is in possession of the land so therefore it is not feasible to employ another builder to carry out the work.

In *Wolverhampton Corporation* v. *Emmons* (1901) the defendant agreed to build new houses on land which he had acquired from the corporation. When he refused to build, the authority sought specific performance of the contract. This was granted because the three conditions outlined above had been satisfied.

Injunction

This is negative in nature and is an order of the court directing a person not to break his contract. Unlike specific performance, it applies to contracts for personal services. The usual rules as to equitable remedies apply. Many of the cases relate to artistic performers of various types: *Warner Brothers* v. *Nelson* (1937) and *Lumley* v. *Wagner* (1852).

Rescission

This is the right to have a contract set aside and where a contract is rescinded the parties are returned to their original positions. The right to rescind is an equitable remedy and the normal rules as to such remedies therefore apply. See *Leaf* v. *International Galleries* (1950) in connection with misrepresentation (5.11). If there is unreasonable delay in claiming the remedy the right may well be lost. The parties may rescind the contract by mutual agreement.

A claim on a quantum meruit

Where a person claims reasonable payment for work which he has done he is said to claim on a *quantum meruit*. This is a claim for as much as the work is worth. It is essentially a claim for reasonable remuneration as opposed to actual loss suffered. Such an order may be claimed in any contract where there is no express agreement as to how much the plaintiff is to be paid for his services. Such a claim is not available to a person who under a mistake considers he has a well-founded claim.

LIMITATION PERIODS

A claim must not be statute barred. This means that any action relating to a breach of contract must be brought within the appropriate time period. The law is now to be found in the Limitation Act 1980 which states that no action in simple contract may be brought after the expiration of 6 years from the date upon which the cause of action accrues. In the case of a contract under seal the period is 12 years. Time runs from the date the cause of action arose which means the date of the breach of contract. In the case of land, actions can be brought up to 12 years from the date of the cause of action.

There is an exception to the above rules in that where the right of action is concealed by fraud, the limitation period does not begin to run until the plaintiff discovers or should have discovered his right to claim. Although the 1980 Act does not generally apply to equitable remedies, one of the maxims of equity is that delay defeats the equities and therefore unless a remedy is sought reasonably promptly it will not be awarded.

5.17 Agency

An agent is a person who is appointed and authorised to act on behalf of another who is known as the principal. The agent's primary function is to create a contractual relationship between the principal and third parties. Where the agent contracts with such a party he is doing so on behalf of his principal. Therefore, the usual result is the creation of an enforceable contract between principal and third party with the agent dropping out of the transaction.

This relationship is a familiar characteristic of business life. Companies can only contract through agents such as their directors and managers while both employees and the self-employed can act in this capacity. Auctioneers, estate agents, architects and engineers are all examples of agents.

CREATION

Express authority
This is the usual method. An agent may be expressly appointed either by word of mouth or in writing. No particular form of appointment is required unless the agent is required to make contracts

under seal in which case the authority must be given by power of attorney. The principal must have contractual capacity when the agent acts but the capacity of the agent is of no consequence.

Implied authority

Where, by their conduct, the parties have acted in such a manner so as to infer the relationship of principal and agent it will be deemed to exist. This may occur where one party receives a commission, accepts goods or pays for items ordered by another person. In *Ryan* v. *Pilkington* (1959) an estate agent was instructed by owners of a property to find a purchaser. The estate agent accepted a deposit from a prospective purchaser 'as agent' of the owners. Although not expressly authorised to accept deposits, he was deemed to have acted as an agent. Consequently, the owner was liable for the deposit when misappropriated by the estate agent. Where a business is carried on in the form of a partnership each partner is prima facie the firm's agent and that of each other partner.

Necessity

Occasionally, the agency relationship arises through necessity. This will occur in an emergency where it is necessary to take immediate action to preserve property. In such a situation, although the person in possession of the property has no express authority to act, the agency position is implied. The following conditions must be satisfied.

(a   There must be a real emergency. The doctrine will not be applied simply because it is convenient to do so.
(b) It must be impossible to obtain the principal's instructions.
(c) The agent must act in good faith and in the interests of the parties concerned.

Ratification

If an agent has no authority to act on his principal's behalf in any particular set of circumstances, or he exceeds his authority, the principal is not bound. As an exception to this basic rule, the principal has the option of confirming or ratifying transactions which were made without his authority. The effect is to legitimise the agent's acts from the outset and the principal can adopt the transaction so as to obtain the benefit and undertake the obligations agreed. Certain conditions apply.

(a) The principal must have existed and had capacity to contract at the time when the agent acted.
(b) The agent must have been acting on behalf of his principal.
(c) Ratification must take place within a reasonable time.

Certain contracts cannot be ratified. Void contracts and forged documents come into this category.

THE AGENCY RELATIONSHIP

The existence of the relationship of principal and agent imposes certain duties and obligations upon both parties. Although primarily based on contract, there is also a fiduciary element of trust underlying the obligations between the parties.

DUTIES OF THE AGENT

Skill and care

An agent must exercise proper skill and care in the performance of his duties. If engaged in a profession, the standard expected is that of a reasonably experienced member of that profession. If the agent represents that he has special skills he must be able to apply them. Where he is employed to sell, he has a duty to obtain the best price possible. In *Keppel* v. *Wheeler* (1917) estate agents were liable where they omitted to inform their client that they had received a higher offer for his property. As a consequence of the trusting nature of the relationship, the agent must disclose anything coming to his knowledge which may affect the principal's position under the contract.

Accounts

An agent must account to his principal in respect of all transactions connected with the agency. Accounts should be rendered to the principal when requested. All sums received on the principal's behalf should be handed over to him. This applies even if the agreement under which the money was received was illegal. Moreover, the agent must not mix up the principal's property with his own.

Bribes

The agent must not take a secret profit from his position, nor must he take bribes. He is only entitled to his commission or other agreed remuneration. In *Mahesan* v. *Malaysia Officers Housing Society* (1979) both the amount of the bribe and secret profit were recovered by the principal where the agent had accepted money allowing a third party to make a secret profit. The agent is accountable to his principal in respect of any benefit received from the unauthorised use of his position. If this obligation is breached, the principal has the following remedies.

(a)   The agent may be dismissed without notice thereby terminating the contract.
(b)   The principal may recover the secret profit.
(c)   Payment of the agent's commission may be withheld.
(d)   The third party may be sued for damages.

Both the agent and the person paying the bribe may be guilty of a criminal offence.

Delegation
An agent cannot further delegate his duties to another except in the usual course of business by employing assistants and secretaries.

Good faith
This is the very essence of the agency relationship. As an agent owes a duty of disclosure he must not act for both sides in a transaction. In *Fullwood* v. *Hurley* (1928), without the knowledge of the respective parties, an agent acted for both sides in the sale and purchase of a hotel. Consequently, he was only entitled to commission from the vendor who initially engaged him.

Obedience
The agent is under a duty to obey the lawful instructions of his principal. If he does not do so, he is liable to him for losses incurred.

REMEDIES OF THE PRINCIPAL
In the event of a serious breach of the relationship, the principal can dismiss the agent. Where appropriate, he can obtain an account and payment of any secret profit. If, as usual, the agency is based on contract, an action for breach of contract may be brought. The principal can always refuse to pay the agent's commission.

DUTIES OF THE PRINCIPAL

Payment

Any agreed amount of commission may be claimed by the agent. He can only claim payment if there is an express or implied provision to that effect. If the agent is in breach of his fiduciary relationship he is not entitled to be paid. The amount depends upon the contract or the custom in a particular trade or business.

Indemnity

Obviously, the agent must be reimbursed for expenses properly incurred in carrying out his duties. He may lose his entitlement if he acts beyond the authority given to him or performs his duties negligently.

Lien

The agent has the right to retain possession of goods (a lien) where the principal has not paid him his proper remuneration or reimbursed him.

THE THIRD PARTY

The normal duty of an agent is to effect an enforceable contract between his principal and the third party. In the ordinary course of events the agent incurs no personal liability, simply acting as an intermediary. It is possible for a properly appointed agent to fail to disclose the capacity within which he is acting. Instead he may appear to a third party to be acting as a principal. In this circumstance the doctrine of undisclosed principal applies. In such a case, the third party may elect to sue either the principal or the agent, while the undisclosed principal can sue the third party on the contract subject to certain restrictions. The agent, as a contracting party, can also sue.

In the ordinary course of events, if an agent exceeds his powers he is liable to the third party for breach of warranty of authority. This applies if the third party suffers loss as a result of the agent's lack of authority and is unaware of the deficiency. Liability is strict and is not dependent upon the agent's state of mind. An estate agent has no implied authority to give a warranty that premises can be used for a specific purpose, see *Hill* v. *Harris* (1956) where such an agent was deemed to have no authority to warrant that premises used for boot and shoe making could be occupied for the confectionery and tobacco business. An auctioneer has implied authority to make statements concerning a particular property.

TERMINATION OF AGENCY

The agency relationship may be terminated by act of the parties or by operation of law. Examples include the following:

(a) mutual agreement, in which case the agent is discharged from further liability;
(b) complete performance of the contract;
(c) expiration of time where the agreement is for a fixed term;
(d) revocation of the agreement by the principal;
(e) frustration: impossibility of performance or supervening illegality will terminate the agreement;
(f) insanity of one of the parties;
(g) death or bankruptcy.

Chapter 6

Standard forms of contract

It is a widespread practice in the construction industry to use standard forms of contract. In the case of minor extensions and alterations to property, such a device is not normally necessary and a simple contract is entered into in the usual manner. Where the work is complex and expensive it is more convenient and safer to use a standard form. Such a form gives the professional and trade parties to the contract a degree of certainty as to the provisions of the contract while its constant use in practice means that the parties should be well versed in its application. A useful benefit is that it provides a means of settling disputes without having recourse to litigation.

Simply because a standard form is used does not mean that the ordinary rules of contract law can be avoided. The essential elements must be present and the vitiating factors will have the same effect. Moreover, it is open to the parties to agree amongst themselves to modify the forms where appropriate.

6.1 History

In 1931, the Joint Contracts Tribunal (JCT) was set up, consisting of representatives from the professions and the construction industry who were involved in major building works. The best known and most important publication produced by this body is the JCT Standard forms issued by other bodies include the Institution of This comes in the form of a private and local authority edition, with and without reference to quantities, and also for use with approximate quantities. The latest edition was produced in 1980. Standard forms issued by other bodies include the Institution of

Civil Engineers (ICE) conditions of contract, while government departments frequently use the form GC/Works/1.

Forms of sub-contract designed for use with the main forms are also available. Those issued by the JCT and the National Federation of Building Trades Employers (NFBTE) are the best known. The NFBTE is now the Building Employers' Confederation (BEC).

6.2 The standard form of building contract

It is the approved practice for a building contract to contain three sections. These are the articles of agreement, the contract conditions and the appendix.

6.3 Articles of Agreement

These are primarily concerned with definitions. Apart from setting out the names of the employer (the client) and the contractor (the builder), the articles deal with the contractor's obligations, the contract price and the identity of the architect. The quantity surveyor and the person acting as supervising officer are also named. Provision is made for replacement of these individuals where appropriate. There is also an arbitration clause (article 5) which specifies that in the event of a dispute the matter shall be referred to arbitration. If the choice of arbitrators is not agreed upon by the parties the appointment can be made by the Royal Institute of British Architects. Article 5 ends up by stating that the arbitrator's award shall be deemed to be binding and final on the parties concerned and that any dispute under the contract shall be dealt with in accordance with English law. Few building contracts are made under seal although local authorities still contract in this manner.

In the case of a speciality contract, a 50p stamp must be fixed to the document. Where a company is a party to the contract its seal will be affixed to the document to make it legally binding.

6.4 The contract conditions

Together with the contract bills and drawings, these form the substance of the contract. The conditions are divided into three parts. The first is of a general nature, the second part deals with nominated sub-contractors and suppliers and the third with fluctuations. As the name suggests, this last term is concerned with any changes which have come about in the amounts paid for labour and in the price of materials since the contract was entered into. Obviously, such deviations would affect the contractor's position.

Interpretation, definitions, etc. (clause 1)
Clause 1 is concerned with the method of reference to the appropriate clauses and it requires that the three parts of the contract be read as a whole. It also defines at length the terms used in the contract stating that they shall 'have the meanings given or ascribed in the article, clause or appendix item to which reference is made'.

Contractor's obligations (clause 2)
This important section requires the contractor to carry out and complete the work in accordance with the contract documents. In addition, it states that where appropriate, the quality of materials used and the standard of workmanship required shall be a matter for the opinion of the architect.

Clause 2.2 provides that the contract bills must be prepared in accordance with the Standard Method of Measurement of Building Works, 6th edition (SMM6), unless the contract states to the contrary in respect of a specific item or items. If in the ordinary course of events the SMM6 is not followed either by error or omission this is to be treated as a variation requiring the architect's instructions.

Clause 2.3 states that in the case of discrepancies or divergencies between documents the contractor must notify the architect in writing of the matter who will then issue appropriate instructions.

Contract sum additions or deductions, adjustment, interim certificates (clause 3)
This is concerned with the contract sum and adjustments to it by addition or deduction. Any alteration in this respect has to be taken into account when the architect issues the next interim certificate.

Certification is a method of confirming that the work complies with the contract. In a building contract, the certifier will normally be the architect. At stipulated periods (normally monthly) he will issue interim certificates showing the amount of work executed and the sums due to the contractor. When the architect considers that the works are virtually complete he will issue a certificate of practical completion. The architect must specify any defects and these must be remedied by the contractor at his own expense. A final certificate approves the completed works and states the sums due to the contractor for his services.

Architect's/supervising officer's instructions (clause 4)
This clause clarifies the architect's position. As a general rule, the contractor must comply with the instructions given to him by the architect acting properly in accordance with his powers under the contract. Any instruction issued by him must be in writing otherwise it is of no immediate effect. However, a verbal notice may be confirmed by the parties.

In the event of non-compliance by the contractor with the architect's instructions, the employer may seek a replacement to execute the appropriate works. Any sums due to this person may be deducted from the contractor's remuneration or can be recovered from him as a debt.

Contract documents, other documents, issue of certificates (clause 5)
These are crucial to the proper performance of the contract. The clause states that the original drawings and bills of quantities shall remain in the employer's custody but shall be available for inspection by the contractor at all reasonable times. Copies of these documents must be given to the contractor free of charge. In return, the contractor must provide the architect with copies of his master programme and any subsequent changes to it. On final payment under the contract the contractor can be required to return the contract drawings and documents to the architect. The appropriate documents may only be used for the purposes of the contract and the parties may not divulge the information contained therein.

Statutory obligations, notices, fees and charges (clause 6)
By clause 6, the contractor is given the task of ensuring that any fees or charges are complied with and that all appropriate notices are given. Unless originally provided for, any sums incurred will be added to the contract price.

Levels and setting out of the works (clause 7)
Responsibility for setting out the works rests with the contractor. The architect must supply the contractor with the appropriate information and drawings.

Material, goods and workmanship to conform to description, testing and inspection (clause 8)

This clause seeks to ensure that the materials used and the quality of workmanship adhere to the specifications given. Power is given to the architect to ensure these items are in accordance with the bills as far as this is possible. Provision is also made for the inspection of works and the testing of materials and goods.

Royalties and patent rights (clause 9)

Where patent rights are involved, royalties have to be paid. Taking out a patent gives an exclusive right to the holder to make use, sell or transfer the patent for a specific period of time (usually 20 years). Clause 9 provides that the contractor shall indemnify the employer against any claims brought against him in respect of patent rights being infringed. Where the contractor uses patented material in accordance with the architect's instructions the contractor shall not be liable for any breach and the royalties payable are added to the contract sum.

Person in charge (clause 10)

This clause requires the contractor to keep a 'competent person in charge' on site at all times that work is being carried out. Often it will be the site foreman. It is recognised that any instructions given to him by the architect or the clerk of works will be recognised as having the same effect as if they were given to the contractor personally.

Access for architect/supervising officer to the works (clause 11)

Under clause 11 the architect and his assistant are entitled to gain access to the works. This includes any place where work is undertaken for the contract. It will cover workshops used by sub-contractors.

Clerk of works (clause 12)

Where large building operations are concerned the employer may appoint a clerk of works to act as inspector. He operates subject to the architect's directions while the contractor must allow him reasonable facilities to carry out his duties.

Variation and provisional sums (clause 13)

During the execution of building works it frequently becomes necessary to vary the provisions of the original contract. Clause 13 covers this situation. To begin with it defines variations and states that the term covers the alteration or modification of the design, quality and quantity of the work as shown in the contract drawings and also the modification of obligations and restrictions imposed originally by the employer. The clause provides for the issuing of instructions by the architect requiring a variation and also for the payment of provisional sums under the contract in order that variations be carried out. Rules are laid down as to the method of payment for the variations.

Contract sum (clause 14)
This clause states that the quality of the work comprised in the contract sum is that to be found in the contract bills of quantities. Moreover, no adjustment or alteration shall be made to that sum except as stated in the conditions. The parties are deemed to have acquiesced in any error relating to the sum.

Value added tax, supplemental provisions (clause 15)
Value added tax (VAT) was introduced as a form of indirect tax by the Finance Act 1972. Clause 15 provides that the expression 'contract sum' is exclusive of VAT. The tax is to be recovered by the contractor from the employer. Sub-clause 15.3 allows the contractor to recover any benefit which he relinquishes by goods or services becoming exempt from VAT.

Materials and goods unfixed or off-site (clause 16)
This clarifies the position in respect of title to goods and materials waiting to be used under the contract. Where an interim certificate has been issued relating to specific items which have been paid for, ownership of the goods passes to the employer. Any goods not covered by such a certificate which are waiting to be used on site cannot be removed except with the architect's consent.

Practical completion and defects liability (clause 17)
The service of a certificate of practical completion by the architect is an indication that the works are nearing completion. The architect will signify the date of completion in the certificate and from that date liability for defects commences. The defects liability period will depend upon the size and the nature of the contract. Normally it will be set out in the appendix, but if no date is provided

for, the period will be six months. The contractor can be required to remedy any defect occurring within this period. Where defects have been made good to the architect's satisfaction he must issue a certificate of completion of making good defects. The contractor is not liable for damage by frost which appears after practical completion unless the architect certifies that the appropriate damage was in existence before that date.

Partial possession by employer (clause 18)
Provision is made for the employer to obtain possession of premises partially completed before practical completion of the works. The contractor is entitled to payment in full for the relevant part and the architect must issue a certificate estimating the approximate total value of the part. Where possession has been taken in these circumstances, the practical date of completion and the defects liability period operates from the date upon which occupation took place. Adjustments are allowed for in respect of the contractor's liability for insurance and the liquidated damages payable in the event of a breach.

Assignment and sub-contract (clause 19)
There is a fundamental distinction between the assignment of a right and a sub-letting. An assignment consists of a transfer whereas a sub-letting gives rights to others without diminishing those of the original parties. Neither of the two main parties can assign the contract without the other's consent. If the architect gives consent in writing, the contractor may sub-let. A person to whom the contractor sub-lets under this clause is known as a *domestic sub-contractor*. It is the practice for a number of sub-contractors to be mentioned in the bills of quantities so that the main contractor may make an appropriate selection.

Fair wages (clause 19A)
This is an administrative provision which attempts to ensure that the contractor provides reasonable conditions of service for his employees, gives adequate information as to their conditions of employment and keeps appropriate records. In particular it deals with wage rates, hours of work and conditions of labour. The contractor is required to recognise the right of the work force to belong to trade unions and he must make available information relating to any relevant agreement made between contractor and workforce

which may affect those working for him. There is a requirement for wage books and time sheets to be kept which may be inspected by the employer or his agent at any reasonable time. This clause, which only applies to local authority editions, was based on the Fair Wages Resolution of the House of Commons, passed in 1946. The present government has withdrawn this provision but no amendment has yet been made to the clause.

Injury to persons and property and employer's indemnity (clause 20)
This section deals with personal injury claims. In the event of such a claim, liability rests with the contractor and he must indemnify the employer. A similar provision applies in respect of damage to property.

Insurance against injury to persons and property (clause 21)
Clauses 21 and 22 are insurance provisions. Clause 21 relates to insurance cover against injury to persons and property. If called upon to indemnify the employer on the basis outlined in clause 20, the contractor must have sufficient financial backing. Therefore, he is required to take out insurance to guarantee the payment of his liabilities. Similar rules apply to sub-contractors. The appropriate policies and premium receipts must be produced if so required. In the event of default by the contractor, the employer may take out insurance making an appropriate deduction from any monies due to the contractor. For risks other than those arising out of or caused by the carrying out of the appropriate works, a provisional sum may be set aside in the joint names of the contractor and employer.

Insurance of the works against clause 22 perils (clause 22)
This is more specific. Those items to be covered by insurance are known as clause 22 perils. The clause provides that the contractor, in his own name and that of the employer, shall insure against loss or damage up to full reinstatement value. The insurers must be approved by the employer. Three alternative provisions are laid down relating to different types of works undertaken.

Date of possession, completion and postponement (clause 23)
On the date of possession, the contractor must commence work and proceed 'regularly and diligently' up to completion date. The power of the architect to postpone works where he thinks fit is also stated.

Damages for non-completion (clause 24)

If the contractor fails to complete the works by the completion date he is in breach of contract and the architect must issue a certificate to that effect. Consequently, liquidated damages become payable and the employer may deduct appropriate sums from the original contract completion date up to the date of practical completion. The rates will be set out in the appendix.

Extension of time (clause 25)

A common feature of construction works is delay. Where a contractor is unable to complete by the agreed date he will be in breach of contract and liable to pay liquidated damages. Where the delay is not the contractor's fault, he should protect his position by notifying the architect. If the delay is due to a specified cause such as bad weather, *force majeure*, failure to receive proper instructions or default on behalf of the suppliers, the architect will fix a new completion date.

Loss and expense caused by matters materially affecting regular progress of the works (clause 26)

This protects a contractor from losses through no fault of his own. Where the progress of work is impaired, the contractor must apply to the architect in writing stating the matter of which he complains. If the architect is satisfied with the application, he will assess the sum and add it to the contract sum. This only applies if the contractor is unable to obtain payment through any other provision in the contract. The list of matters which the contractor may rely upon are to be found in the clause. Nominated sub-contractors may also rely on this provision.

Determination by employer (clause 27)

Clause 27 states the grounds upon which the employer may determine the contract. Generally speaking, it depends upon default by the contractor and the grounds include suspension of works without reasonable cause, failure to proceed diligently and regularly, refusal to remedy defective works and materials, and assignment and subletting without consent. Insolvency and corruption by the contractor also terminates the contract. If the contractor continues in default for 14 days, the employer may exercise his right to terminate after due notice from the architect. The contractor remains liable to the employer for any loss due to the determination of the contract.

Determination by contractor (clause 28)
Where the employer is in default, the contractor is entitled to terminate the contract after due notice. The right automatically arises if the employer does not pay on a certificate or the works are suspended for specific reasons. These include instructions from the architect, *force majeure*, failure to receive proper information in time, and the opening of works for inspection. The condition states the respective rights of the parties in such circumstances. The contractor must remove any equipment and materials from the site and he must be paid for any work completed. He is entitled to be compensated for any loss or damage caused by the employer terminating the contract.

Works by employer or persons employed or engaged by employer (clause 29)
Where the employer wishes to execute certain works himself he must state this in the bill of quantities so that the contractor can distinguish this work from that which he must undertake himself. If the specification does not provide for this, the contractor's consent must first be obtained. Any person carrying out works on behalf of the employer under this clause is treated as the client's responsibility and not as a sub-contractor.

Certificates and payments (clause 30)
Reference has been made earlier to the system of certification which is a characteristic of building contracts. This system operates subject to the right of an employer to retain a sum of money as a guarantee that defects will be remedied and that all the work will be satisfactorily completed. This is known as a retention fund. The amounts which can be retained under this clause depend upon the value of the interim certificate. They are estimated on a percentage basis and are stated in the appendix. Complete performance is normally a condition precedent to payment of the retention monies. Appropriate adjustment must be made to the contract sum before the final certificate is issued.

Finance (No. 2) Act 1975: statutory tax deduction scheme (clause 31)
This act has attempted to fill a loophole whereby sub-contractors were avoiding payment of tax. The provision requires an employer to deduct income tax at the statutory deduction rate from any

sub-contractor unless the sub-contractor can produce an appropriate certificate that tax has been paid.

Outbreak of hostilities (clause 32)

This covers the position in the event of an outbreak of hostilities. Both parties may determine the contract in such circumstances while the contractor may claim payment for any work done.

War damage (clause 33)

This is an extension of the previous clause and relates to war damage. Where works are so affected, the architect must give instructions to the contractor as to the method of remedying damaged work. Compensation for war damage is also dealt with.

Antiquities (clause 34)

Where objects of interest and value are discovered on site as the work is in the process of execution, these items become the property of the employer and the contractor must deliver such items to the architect or the clerk of works. Any loss suffered by the contractor in such circumstances must be added to the contract sum.

Nominated sub-contractors (clause 35)

Part 2 of the Standard Form of Building Contract, 1980 is concerned with nominated sub-contractors and nominated suppliers. A characteristic of the construction industry in the United Kingdom is the right of the employer to choose specialist sub-contractors. Such persons are known as *nominated sub-contractors*. If instead, they supply goods, they are known as *nominated suppliers*. The main contractor has overall responsibility for efficiency and defects and is in full control of the work. Any defect by the sub-contractor is the responsibility of the main contractor. The main contractor has no cause of action against the employer in respect of the sub-contractor's defects.

Clause 35 deals with the appropriate aspects of the sub-contractor's appointment. Matters dealt with include procedure for nomination, methods of payment, extension of time limits and determination of employment. In particular it should be realised that in the ordinary course of events a nominated sub-contractor has no cause of action against the employer for the contract price. However, sub-contract form NSC/2 creates a direct relationship between the employer and the nominated sub-contractor on certain matters.

Nominated suppliers (clause 36)

Similar provisions apply to nominated suppliers. Safeguards are included to limit the liability of the main contractor if the nominated supplier is attempting to reduce his liability under the contract.

Fluctuations (clause 37)

Fluctuations are dealt with by clauses 38, 39 and 40 which form part 3 of the conditions. Frequently during the course of a building contract, changes will take place in the cost of items such as labour and materials. Normally the trend is upwards. Provision has to be made to ensure that the main contractor does not suffer loss by such changes. The parties have a choice of fluctuations provisions and the one chosen must be stated in the appendix. Specifically, clause 38 deals with contributions, levy and tax fluctuations, clause 39 with labour, materials cost and tax, while clause 40 is concerned with use of price adjustment formulae.

6.5 The appendix

The appendix completes the contract by filling in appropriate information and detail. In particular, it states the contract completion date and the date for possession. This is where the interim certificate period and the defects liability period are recorded.

6.6 Sub-contracts

Reference has been made already to the position of nominated and domestic sub-contractors together with their relationship to the main contract. Whether the sub-contractor is nominated or not, standard forms of sub-contract are available to cover the situation. Where there has been a nomination, JCT Form NSC/4 may be used. Domestic sub-contractors are now covered by a procedure laid down in clause 19 of JCT 80.

Form NSC/4 is available for sub-contractors who have tendered on the appropriate NSC/1 document and executed NSC/2 which creates a degree of contractual obligation between employer and sub-contractor. NSC/3 specifies the sub-contractor nominated for the particular works under the Standard Form of Building Contract 1980 (clause 35.10.2). Form NSC/4 is drafted on a similar basis to the main contract form. After setting out the articles, the sub-contract clauses relate to the documents, mention the sub-contract sum and then deal with the sub-contractor's position under the contract. Determination of employment under the sub-contract and the termination of the main contractor's employment under the main contract are dealt with. As in the main contract, there is a choice of fluctuations provisions.

6.7 National house-building agreements

Since 1936, the National House-Building Council (NHBC) (formerly the National Housebuilders Registration Council) has been in existence. This body was established by leading builders on a voluntary basis to encourage consistent high standards in house building. The system operates by the maintenance of a register of builders whose work adheres to the standards prescribed by the council. An insurance scheme operates to cover any defects which arise in dwellings constructed by members of the scheme. To apply, the defects must become apparent and be notified to the council within the first 10 years of construction. The standard notice of insurance cover brings the insurance policy into operation.

To regulate the system, the council employs officers to inspect the work completed. In the event of non-compliance, a builder may be removed from the register. The normal procedure is for registered builders to enter into a standard form agreement with the purchaser. The agreement is normally made on exchange of contracts. After stating that he is a party to the scheme, the builder warrants that the property has been built properly and that it will comply with the council's requirements. The initial guarantee period is normally two years from completion. Under the insurance scheme, the council undertakes to indemnify the purchaser on the builder's bankruptcy or insolvency. Moreover, the contract will specify the obligation of the council to satisfy any judgment obtained by the purchaser against the builder relating to defects in construction of a dwelling. The council will also agree to make good the cost of major defects within a 10-year period. Subsequent purchasers may also obtain the benefit of the agreement. A purchaser may have alternative remedies in contract, tort or under the Defective Premises Act 1972.

Chapter 7

The law of tort

7.1 The nature of a tort

A tort is often described as a civil wrong. Like contract, the law of tort is part of the civil law and developed from common law principles. Therefore, a plaintiff who commences an action based on tort will be looking for compensation as his principal remedy.

The law of tort has a number of particular characteristics. To begin with, there is an overlap between tortious liability and the criminal law. The same set of circumstances will frequently result in both civil and criminal proceedings. Examples include road accidents and certain accidents at work. However, each set of proceedings must be dealt with separately, one aiming to compensate the victim and the other to punish the wrongdoer. The same act may also be a tort and a breach of contract. A person who commits a tort is known as a tortfeasor.

Another characteristic of this area of the law is that liability is not dependent upon the contents of any agreement or other written document. Instead, obligations in tort are fixed by the law itself attempting to adjust losses and to keep a fair balance of interests. The law of tort recognises certain rights and if these are infringed an action may be brought by the plaintiff.

7.2 Liability in tort

This has traditionally depended upon fault, that is, the intentional or negligent causing of harm by one party to another. As an exception, certain torts do not require this element to be present and they are known as torts of strict or absolute liability. In such a case, liability arises whatever the state of mind or blameworthiness of the defendant. Examples include the rule in *Rylands* v. *Fletcher* (1876) (see 7.9), liability for dangerous animals and breaches of certain statutory duties such as the Factories Acts.

As a general rule the law of tort is not concerned with a person's motive. Consequently, a malicious motive will not make an otherwise lawful act unlawful, and conversely a good motive cannot legitimise an otherwise wrongful act. The classic illustration of this principle is *Bradford Corporation* v. *Pickles* (1895) where the defendant lawfully interrupted a supply of water to the corporation by sinking a shaft on his own land in order to influence the authority to buy the land from him at his asking price. The court decided that the act was lawful and the defendant's motive was irrelevant. A similar position was reached in *Chapman* v. *Hoenig* (1963) where a landlord maliciously served a valid notice to quit on his tenants but was deemed to have committed no tort.

7.3 Vicarious liability

At times, a person is deemed to be legally responsible for torts committed by others. This liability arises because of the relationship between the parties and it is known as vicarious liability. The most common example of this rule in operation is between employer and employee. The principle is that an employer is liable for torts committed by his servants in the course of their employment but he is not liable for the torts of an independent contractor. Difficulty sometimes arises in distinguishing between the two relationships and a number of tests have been devised for the purpose. It is sometimes said that a servant is an employee with a contract of service whereas an independent contractor has a contract for services.

SERVANTS
The traditional test for determining the existence of the master/servant relationship is the degree of control which the employer has over the employee. An employee can be told what to do and the manner in which he should do it. Sometimes this test is unsatisfactory and instead all the circumstances must be taken into account such as methods of payment and the employer's rights to dismiss the workforce.

The tort must be committed during the course of the servant's employment if the employer is to incur liability. In *Lloyd* v. *Grace, Smith & Co.* (1912) a firm of solicitors were vicariously liable for the acts of their conveyancing clerk, where, in the course of his employment, the clerk fraudulently conveyed property to himself, subsequently disposing of it and keeping the proceeds.

An act prohibited by the employer may well be performed in the course of employment. In *Limpus* v. *London General Omnibus Co.* (1900) the defendant's driver raced his bus against another belonging to a rival company. Despite the fact that drivers had been warned not to race, this action was held to be within the course of employment.

A servant is one who works as an integral part of a business. The question is whether the conduct prohibited formed part of what the servant was employed to do. In *Rose* v. *Plenty* (1976), contrary to instructions, a milk roundsman permitted a 13-year-old boy to help him with deliveries. When the boy was injured due to the negligent driving of the roundsman, the latter's employer was deemed to be vicariously liable. If the employee acts beyond the scope of his employment, the employer will not be liable as in *Beard* v. *London General Omnibus Co.* (1900) where the plaintiff was injured due to the negligent driving of a bus conductor.

Where an employee is lent out or hired by another employer, the original employer will generally be liable for any torts. In *Mersey Docks & Harbour Board* v. *Coggins & Griffiths Ltd* (1947) the Harbour Board lent out a mobile crane together with a driver to a firm of stevedores. The board continued to pay the driver and had power to dismiss him, although for the period of hire the employee was subject to the control of the stevedores. When the driver negligently injured another person the Harbour Board was held to be vicariously liable for his acts.

An employer will not be liable if the servant is engaged in a 'frolic of his own'. In other words if he commits a tort outside the course of his employment, the servant will personally be liable. In *Hilton* v. *Thomas Burton (Rhodes) Ltd* (1961) employers were not liable where four workmen on a demolition site knocked off to go to a café 7 miles from the site. Just before reaching the café they decided to turn back and one of their number was killed due to the negligence of the driver.

In situations where the employer is deemed to be vicariously liable for his servant's acts, the plaintiff may always sue the servant instead of the employer. However, a plaintiff should always choose his tortfeasor with care as an employer is normally more likely to be able to satisfy any judgment obtained against him.

INDEPENDENT CONTRACTORS

The general rule is that an employer is not liable for the torts of an independent contractor unless he has authorised them explicitly or implicitly. An independent contractor is one who is his own master, is engaged to do work but is free to select his method of doing it. Such a contractor is bound by contract but not by the employer's orders. The following are situations where an employer may be liable for the acts of an independent contractor.

Negligence in selecting the contractor

This issue arose in *Haseldine* v. *Daw & Sons Ltd* (1941) where the employer was considered to have satisfied his obligations in this respect when he employed 'a first-class firm of lift engineers' to inspect and report upon certain hydraulic lifts. Consequently, the employer was not liable.

Strict liability

An employer cannot normally delegate a duty which is imposed by statute or by the common law. Hence a master cannot avoid the obligations imposed by the Factories Act 1961 to fence dangerous machinery and to provide safe means of access. In *Darling* v. *Attorney-General* (1950) the Ministry of Works was liable for the negligence of an independent contractor who left a heap of timber on a field and thereby injured the plaintiff's horse. The ministry had statutory powers to do the work. A similar position arises at common law. Therefore, where the rule in *Rylands* v. *Fletcher* (1876) is applicable, or fire escapes from the employer's premises because of the actions of an independent contractor, a master is liable for the torts of his independent contract. Similar rules apply to dangerous animals.

Acts of an 'extra hazardous' nature

Where works are carried out which involve a special danger to others, public policy will not allow an employer to avoid liability by employing an independent contractor. The leading case is *Honeywill & Stein Ltd* v. *Larkin Bros Ltd* (1934) where the plaintiff employed the defendants as independent contractors to take photographs by flashlight in a cinema belonging to a third party. When the cinema caught fire the plaintiffs were held to be liable to the owners for the damage caused. A similar result was reached in *Matania* v. *National Provincial Bank* (1936) where a nuisance was caused by noise and dust emanating from large-scale building works.

A similar rule applies where an independent contractor is engaged to undertake extraordinary operations upon a highway. In *Hardaker* v. *Idle DC* (1896) a gas main was broken, thereby causing an explosion, because of the failure to pack soil around it while constructing a sewer. Likewise, in *Holliday* v. *National Telephone Co.* (1899) the negligent soldering of pipes caused an explosion for which the employer was liable. In *Tarry* v. *Ashton* (1876) the defendant employed an independent contractor to repair a lamp overhanging the highway. The plaintiff, who was injured when the lamp fell on him, succeeded in an action in tort and the employer was held liable for the acts of the independent contractor.

However, in *Salsbury* v. *Woodland* (1970) it was decided that an employer is not liable for the acts of an independent contractor carried out near to a highway which cause injury to persons on the highway. The Highways (Miscellaneous Provisions) Act 1961 imposed liability on the highway authority for accidents arising out of the failure of the authority to repair the highway. This is the case even though contractors are at fault, unless correct instructions were given to the contractor and carried out. If an employer subsequently confirms or ratifies the contractor's acts or previously authorises them he will be vicariously liable on ordinary common law principles.

Collateral negligence

Acts of collateral or casual negligence committed by the servants of an independent contractor, which are unconnected with the work they are engaged to do, will not render the employer of the contractor vicariously liable. If the employer is to be liable the danger must be an ingredient of the work. The major problem is to determine which negligence is collateral and which is not. The leading case is *Padbury* v. *Holliday & Greenwood Ltd* (1912) where one of the sub-contractor's workmen placed a tool on the sill of a window. The wind blew a casement open whereby the tool was knocked off the sill and fell on to a passer-by. The employer was found not liable because he could only incur blame for those risks caused by the works which the employer was having done.

7.4 General defences

Even where the plaintiff has established all the ingredients of a particular tort the defendant may prove a defence in order to escape liability. Some torts have special defences which are only of application in respect of that specific tort. These are described in later sections of this chapter. General defences are those which can be relied upon to answer the vast majority of claims in tort.

STATUTORY AUTHORITY

If a statute or secondary legislation authorises a particular act, no action will succeed in tort and the injured party has no remedy unless the statute provides for compensation. This defence is of importance in connection with nuisance and the rule in *Rylands* v. *Fletcher* (1876).

CONSENT (VOLENTI NON FIT INJURIA)

That to which a person consents cannot be considered an injury. Where a person consents to run the risk of damage he cannot later bring an action in tort if he has suffered loss. Knowledge of the risk on its own is not sufficient; consent to run the risk must be established. In *Smith* v. *Baker & Sons* (1891) the plaintiff was employed to drill holes in a rock cutting. While he was working, a crane continually passed overhead carrying crates of stones. When a stone fell out of a crate and injured him, he brought an action based on tort and succeeded. Although he knew of the danger, he could not be said to have consented to it. A similar result was achieved in *Bowater* v. *Rowley Regis Corporation* (1944) where the plaintiff was required as part of his employment, to take out a horse known by him and his employers to be unsafe. When he was injured by the horse it was determined that he had not consented to run the risk.

Behaviour which may give rise to the defence of *volenti* often amounts to contributory negligence (see under 7.5). The courts nowadays tend to prefer an apportionment under the Law Reform (Contributory Negligence) Act 1945 to the defence of consent.

Rescue cases

It is an established principle that the defence of *volenti* does not apply to rescue cases. That is where a person risks harm while in the process of rescuing another person or saving property from injury. As the plaintiff elects to run a risk after the defendant has acted he cannot be said to have consented to the defendant's tortious act.

In *Haynes* v. *Harwood* (1925) a policeman was injured while attempting to prevent a runaway horse from causing injury in a crowded street. As he was acting under a moral duty he succeeded in claiming damages as he himself had not consented to run the risk. A similar result was reached in *Baker* v. *T.E. Hopkins & Sons Ltd* (1959) where a doctor died after descending into a gas-filled well in order to rescue two workmen overcome by fumes.

The legal position seems to be different where there is no imminent danger to others. In *Cutler* v. *United Dairies Ltd* (1933) the defence of *volenti* succeeded where Cutler was injured while attempting to pacify a runaway horse on a country road.

INEVITABLE ACCIDENTS

If resultant damage was inevitable and could not have been avoided by any reasonable precaution, the defence of inevitable accident may be successfully pleaded. This defence has been accepted since *Stanley* v. *Powell* (1891) where the plaintiff, who was employed as a cartridge carrier for a shooting party, was injured when the defendant fired at a pheasant and the pellet ricocheted from a tree at an angle. Inevitable accident was held to be a good defence in *National Coal Board* v. *J.E. Evans Ltd* (1951) which concerned trespass to chattels in the form of electric cables of whose existence the defendants were not expected to be aware.

ACT OF GOD

There is authority, *Nichols* v. *Marsland* (1876), which suggests that where the commission of a tort is due to the operation of natural forces which no human foresight can envisage, the defence of act of God is available. In this case, heavy rainfall caused lakes to burst their banks causing flooding to the plaintiff's land.

REMOTENESS OF DAMAGE

Remoteness of loss is an important concept. It has already been discussed in connection with the law of contract under the guise of the rule in *Hadley* v. *Baxendale* (1854) (see under 5.16). In tort also a person will not be liable for consequences which are too remote. The test is now one of 'foreseeability'. Therefore, if a defendant cannot reasonably foresee the damage which ensues he will escape liability. To incur liability, the type or kind of damage which occurs must be foreseeable but not the exact manner in which it occurs or the degree to which the plaintiff is harmed. In *Overseas Tankship (UK) Ltd* v. *Morts Dock & Engineering Co. Ltd (The Wagon Mound)* (1961) oil spilt from a ship and spread to a wharf 200 yards away. Welding operations were in progress on the wharf. Sparks from these works set the oil alight, causing damage to the wharf and to slipways adjacent to it. The Judicial Committee of the Privy Council decided that the appellants could not have reasonably foreseen that the plaintiff's wharf would be damaged by fire.

The defendant must take the plaintiff as he finds him. If the danger is reasonably foreseeable, it is not relevant that the plaintiff suffers to a higher degree than the reasonable man because of personal characteristics. This 'egg shell' principle is well illustrated by *Smith* v. *Leech Brain* (1962) where the plaintiff suffered a burn on his lip owing to the negligence of the defendant. The burn activated a pre-malignant cancer from which the plaintiff died.

For any action to succeed, there must be a chain of causation which is left unbroken. Sometimes an intervening act or event will break the chain of consequences which can be reasonably foreseen. Where this *novus actus interveniens* occurs, the defendant will not usually be liable for the intervening act of the third party which breaks the chain of causation. If the third party act is itself reasonable or foreseeable, the defendant will be liable.

7.5 Negligence

Negligence has become the most important independent tort and nowadays it covers wide areas of activity. It is not actionable *per se*, and therefore loss must be proved by the plaintiff as a result of the commission of the tort. To succeed in an action based on negligence, the plaintiff must prove that:

(a) the defendant owed him a duty of care;
(b) the duty was broken by the defendant;
(c) the plaintiff suffered damage as a consequence.

Duty of care
This is a matter of law. Before 1932, there were situations where the courts recognised the existence of a legal duty of care and a plaintiff could recover damages in respect of a negligent act. However, there was no firm principle relating to the duty of care. In

Donoghue v. *Stevenson* (1932) Lord Atkin pronounced a more general test and stated that a person owes a duty of care to his neighbour. He then defined a neighbour as a person 'so closely and directly affected by my acts that I ought reasonably to have him in contemplation as being so affected when I am directing my mind to the acts or omissions which are called in question'. In this case, a man bought a bottle of ginger beer for his girl friend. The girl became ill because the bottle contained the decomposed remains of a snail. The design and materials from which the bottle was made prevented detection of the snail's presence until most of the liquid had been consumed. No claim in contract could be brought as the girl had not bought the drink. However, a claim succeeded in tort against the manufacturer.

The neighbour test has become the condition precedent to a successful claim in negligence and the situations in which such a duty arises are numerous. It is sufficient that a duty is owed to a particular class of person to which the plaintiff belongs. In *Haley* v. *London Electricity Board* (1965) the defendant's employees left a hole in the pavement unfenced during a work break. As a precaution, they placed a hammer in a railing which would have been observed by a normal-sighted person, but which was insufficient to prevent the plaintiff, who was blind, from falling into the hole and becoming deaf as a result of his injuries. Blind persons regularly used the area where the works were in the process of being undertaken and consequently the board owed a duty to the plaintiff and blind persons as a class.

In *Home Office* v. *Dorset Yacht Co. Ltd* (1970) the House of Lords considered that the *Donoghue* v. *Stevenson* test ought to apply generally unless excluded on grounds of public policy or remoteness. Because they owe their duty to the court and to the administration of justice generally, barristers are immune from liability in tort in respect of work done in the conduct of litigation and as regards the drawing of pleadings. As far as remoteness is concerned, in *King* v. *Phillips* (1963) it was decided that the plaintiff was outside the range of the defendant's duty of care where a mother saw a taxi reverse down a road onto the tricycle which her son was riding. She heard his scream and consequently suffered shock which caused depression. Recently in *McLoughlin* v. *O'Brien* (1982) the House of Lords decided that the test of liability for damages for nervous shock was reasonable forseeability of the plaintiff being injured by nervous shock as a result of the defendant's negligence.

Breach of the duty of care

Breach of the duty of care depends upon the standards of the 'reasonable man'. The existence of a breach is a matter of fact which is applied by an objective test. Many factors must be taken into account. Likelihood of harm is important. In *Bolton* v. *Stone* (1951) the plaintiff was struck by a cricket ball which had travelled some 100 yards and climbed a 17 feet fence. As it was improbable that the ball would be hit out of the ground or cause injury if it did, the defendant was not liable.

The seriousness of the injury risked is another consideration. In *Paris* v. *Stepney Borough Council* (9151) the plaintiff, who had only one good eye, was blinded in that eye during the course of his employment. He contended that his employers were negligent because they had not provided him with goggles. His argument was upheld. The House of Lords intimated that a higher degree of care is always required when dealing with persons suffering from a mental or physical disability. A similar higher standard is required in dealings with children and old people.

The utility of the defendant's act is also of importance. The risk must be balanced against the end to be achieved. In an emergency, a lesser degree of care may be acceptable. In *Watt* v. *Hertfordshire County Council* (1954) a fireman was injured in an emergency. A jack on the back of a lorry upon which he was travelling was incorrectly secured. The court decided that in the circumstances there was no failure to take reasonable care.

Another factor to be considered is whether or not adequate precautions have or ought to have been taken to minimise any risk. In *Latimer* v. *AEC* (1952) a factory was flooded because of an exceptionally heavy rainstorm. This resulted in the factory floor becoming grease covered. Although the employers did everything they could to get rid of the effects of the flood, the plaintiff slipped and injured himself. The plaintiff argued that the factory ought to have been closed because of the flood. The court decided that the company had not been negligent because the risk of injury on the slippy floor was not sufficient to justify the closure.

If a claim relates to a situation where some degree of professional knowledge or skill is required, the standard expected is the degree of competence of the ordinary competent practitioner. In *Wells* v. *Cooper* (1958) the owner of a house fitted a new door handle so loosely that when the plaintiff pulled at it he lost his balance and was injured. The same degree of skill required of a professional carpenter working for reward would not be required in these circumstances. It may be that a professional man who specialises in a particular field may be required to show a greater than normal expertise in that area of work.

Damage has been suffered

Loss is a prerequisite to a successful claim in negligence. The tort is not actionable *per se* and therefore some form of damage must be suffered which is not too remote. This may be damage to property or personal injuries. Although it is established law that there may be liability for financial loss arising from negligent misstatements (see later), in general, it was thought that liability in tort did not extend to economic loss on its own without any physical damage, see *Spantan Steel & Alloys* v. *Martins Construction* (1982). However, recently it has been decided that damages are recoverable for financial or economic loss arising from defective goods and materials.

In *Junior Books* v. *Veitchi* (1982) the plaintiffs instructed builders to install a floor in a factory. Specialist sub-contractors were instructed by the builders and these were the defendants to the action. On account of bad workmanship and materials, a crack appeared in the floor which had to be replaced. In addition to the cost of replacement, additional sums were claimed. These consisted of the cost of renovating machinery, loss of use of machinery together with interference with the business and loss of profits. The court decided that these sums were recoverable.

THE BURDEN OF PROOF

In civil cases, the burden rests upon the plaintiff to show that on the balance of probabilities the defendant was liable. Therefore in negligence cases, the burden of proving breach of duty of care and consequent damage falls upon the plaintiff. Sometimes it is difficult for the plaintiff to prove negligence because he is unable to show how it actually happened. To a considerable extent, the problem is overcome by the doctrine of *res ipsa loquitor* ('the facts speak for themselves'). This principle applies where the facts are so unusual that the defendant must have been negligent or the act would never have taken place. The circumstances are such that they raise the inference of the defendant's negligence so that a prima facie case exists. Negligence is assumed simply because the event has taken place.

The leading case is *Scott* v. *London & St Katharine Docks* (1865) where a successful claim was brought by a customs officer who was injured when bags of sugar fell on him from the upper floor of a warehouse. Where the doctrine is raised, the burden of proof is in practice reversed and the onus of disproving the negligence is put upon the defendant. If the defendant offers a reasonable explanation it is up to the plaintiff to prove the case in the normal way. The principle has been applied where a swab was left in a patient's body after an operation, see *Mahon* v. *Osborne* (1939); and where a household gas system disintegrated, see *Lloyds* v. *West Midlands Gas* (1971).

SPECIAL LIABILITIES

Premises

At common law an occupier of premises had a duty of care to those who visited him. Nowadays, this topic of liability for defective premises is governed by the Occupiers Liability Act 1957 as amended by the Defective Premises Act 1972. Both occupiers and lawful visitors are affected by the legislation. The Occupiers Liability Act provides that the occupier of premises or the landlord, if responsible for repairs, has a common duty of care to ensure that all lawful visitors will be reasonably safe when using the premises.

'Premises' includes any fixed or moveable structure and also covers vehicles, ships and aircraft.

Liability rests with the occupier and not beyond. An occupier is one who has control over the premises and it is a question of fact in each case as to who has occupation. Premises may have more than one occupier. Where large-scale building works are in progress, the site owner and the main contractor may be both in occupation, see *AMF International* v. *Magnet Bowling* (1968). Where a lease or tenancy agreement is executed, liability normally passes to the tenant.

An empty building may well be occupied. In *Harris* v. *Birkenhead Corporation* (1975) the local authority failed to block up a derelict house subject to a compulsory purchase order and they were held liable as occupiers. Again, in *Morrison Holdings Ltd* v. *Manders Properties Ltd* (1976) a tenant who had given up his tenancy but still retained the keys was held to be in occupation.

Lawful visitors: Occupiers owe a duty of care to lawful visitors. A lawful visitor is a person who expressly or by implication has been given the right to enter premises. This will include persons who have the right to enter premises under a contract after paying for entrance and those who have the right to enter premises in the exercise of a right authorised by law, such as officials of the gas and electricity boards and customs officers.

Normally an occupier may revoke the right of a lawful visitor to remain on premises at any time. Any person entering premises 'in the exercise of their calling' must not exceed the purpose for which they are present on the property or they become trespassers.

While on the premises, the occupier must take care to see that the visitor will be reasonably safe in using the premises for the purpose for which he is invited or permitted to be there. An occupier may satisfy the required duty of care by giving adequate warning of any danger. In this case, the normal rules relating to exemption clauses apply. Consequently, if the occupier takes all reasonable steps to bring the conditions to the visitor's notice, liability may well be avoided, see *Ashdown* v. *Samuel Williams* (1957).

Any limitation of liability must be read subject to the Unfair Contracts Terms Act 1977 (see under 5.15). An attempt to exclude liability for death or personal injury will not be upheld while, unless the restriction is reasonable, the occupier is unable to limit his liability for other damage caused by negligence.

The degree of care depends upon the type of visitor. A higher standard is owed to those under a disability. This is particularly the case with children. Dangers to which children may be specially attracted or allured must be particularly guarded against, while hidden dangers which children may not understand must be made known. However, an occupier can expect very young children to be accompanied by adults.

Where a person is injured because of the faulty work of an independent contractor, the occupier may avoid liability if he can show that he was careful in selecting the contractor and that where possible he supervised the work and subsequently checked it.

Trespassers: Trespassers are not covered by the Occupiers Liability Act. In general, an occupier of premises owes no duty of care to trespassers and they must take the consequences for their acts. An occupier may protect his property by barbed wire or insert spikes or broken glass on to the top of a boundary wall, but he must not intentionally harm a trespasser whom he knows to be present by shooting at him nor may he create hidden dangers such as traps and manholes. Until 1972, an occupier was only liable to a trespasser if he intentionally injured him or acted in reckless disregard of his presence on the land, see *Addie* v. *Dumbreck* (1929).

In 1972, the case of *Herrington* v. *British Railways Board* was decided. This concerned a 6-year-old boy who was electrocuted on a railway line after climbing through a fence which had not been properly maintained. Children regularly played near the railway line and the local station master had been informed that children had been seen on the line. Local inhabitants also crossed the line as a short cut. Although it was admitted that the boy was a trespasser, the House of Lords decided that the Railways Board owed a duty to the plaintiff and were consequently liable. The court stated that the duty of care owed to a trespasser is that of common humanity. The defendants were aware that children played upon the railway line, the presence of trespassers could easily be anticipated and there was a serious risk of danger. Simply warning children of dangers may not be a sufficient exercise of common humanity.

In *Pannet* v. *McGuinness & Co. Ltd* (1972) the plaintiff, aged five, trespassed on to land and fell into a fire used by the defendant company to burn rubbish. The plaintiff had been warned off the site on several previous occasions and the defendant's servants had been keeping a lookout for children who frequently trespassed on to the land. Even so, the defendants were liable because they realised the extreme likelihood of infant trespassers coming on to the land but had failed to take common-sense precautions to keep children off the site.

Non-occupiers liability: The law has been slow to recognise the liability of non-occupiers in negligence mainly because of the doctrine of *caveat emptor*. At common law, vendors and lessors of premises were immune from actions in tort even though they might incur contractual liability. In *Billings & Sons* v. *Riden* (1957) contractors who were removing a ramp from the front of a house were liable when the respondent, a 71-year-old woman, fell into a sunken recess. At common law, however, builder/vendors and builder/lessors were not liable in tort for negligence even though in contract they could be liable on the basis of breach of an implied warranty. Recent developments have modified the position.

The Defective Premises Act 1972: This act came into force on 1 January 1974. It provides that a builder of a dwelling house and those professional persons involved in its construction are under a duty of care to ensure that the work is executed in a professional and workmanlike manner, that proper materials will be used, and that it will be fit for habitation when completed. This applies to the initial erection of a dwelling or an alteration by enlargement or conversion. The duty is owed to any person who subsequently acquires an interest in the dwelling. In addition, the act imposes on a landlord a wider duty of care in respect of his obligations or right to repair the demised premises. Contracting out, or restricting the provisions of the act is not allowed.

The practical effect of the act is limited. If the dwelling is covered by a National House Building Council certificate the act does not apply. The vast majority of newly-built houses are covered by this scheme. In addition, these provisions only apply to dwelling houses and not to commercial properties. Finally, there is a strict limitation period of 6 years which runs from completion date of the dwelling whether damage has become apparent or not.

Case law: As a supplement to the changes in the law on a statutory basis, the courts have developed principles which have attempted to modify the *caveat emptor* rule. The duties of care imposed by the cases have turned out to be more far-reaching than the statutory duties. In *Dutton* v. *Bognor Regis UDC* (1972) the local authority was held liable for the acts of its servants who negligently inspected the foundations of a new house built on a tip and failed to notice that they were not satisfactory. The plaintiff, who was the second owner of the house, bought it two years after it was built. Because of the insecure foundations, serious defects appeared inside the house. The Court of Appeal decided that the plaintiff was within the principle of *Donoghue* v. *Stevenson* and that the plaintiff was entitled to damages for repair of the house and fall in market value. In *Dutton's* case, the claim against the builder was settled on the basis that a builder/owner was not liable in negligence. The Court of Appeal took the view that if the builder had been sued he would have been liable as well.

The law was developed further in *Anns* v. *London Borough of Merton* (1977). This was another case of failure to inspect foundations in a proper manner. The House of Lords stated that local authorities owe a duty to take reasonable care to ensure that building regulations are complied with, but to have the basis of a negligence claim a plaintiff must prove that the action taken was not within the limits of a discretion which was exercised bona fide. The duty was owed to owners and occupiers. All foreseeable damage arising from a breach of duty of care was recoverable. *Dutton's* case was approved by the House of Lords in *Anns*. The decision goes a long way to protect a subsequent purchaser of a dwelling house, as the ultimate owner is able to sue both the builder and the local authority.

Another issue which arose in *Anns* was that of limitation periods. The case appeared to accept a more flexible approach to limitation periods by accepting the decision in *Sparham-Souter* v. *Town & Country Developments (Essex) Ltd* (1976) that a plaintiff could commence his action at any time within six years of suffering damage. The case seemed to indicate that time did not run until the plaintiff with reasonable diligence could have discovered the defective state of his property. Recently, in *Pirelli G.C. Works Ltd* v. *Oscar Faber & Partners* (1982) the House of Lords stated that the 6 year limitation period in an action in tort alleging negligent design of a building ran from the date that the damage came into existence. The fact that the fault was discovered only later or could not have been discovered at all did not affect the period.

Negligent statements

An important development in the law of tort emerged with the decision in *Hedley Byrne* v. *Heller & Partners* (1966). Hedley Byrne were advertising agents about to contract with a customer. As a safeguard, they required a banker's reference as to the customer's creditworthiness. This was given by the defendants, a firm of merchant bankers. The bank reported that the customer was considered good for ordinary business arrangements. Relying on this report, the advertising agents gave the customer credit in the sum of £17,000. The customer proved to be far from sound and the plaintiffs lost the £17,000. Consequently, they sued the bankers for negligence in giving the report. Although the bank had been careless they had headed their report 'without responsibility', and on the strength of this disclaimer they were held to be not liable.

The House of Lords, in a series of *obiter dicta* considered the state of the law and took the view that there may be liability for fiduciary loss arising from negligent misstatements. In order for such liability to exist, there must be a special or fiduciary relationship between the parties, while the person giving the advice must have realised that the person making the inquiry intended to rely on the advice or information given. The use of a disclaimer may avoid liability. However, such a provision may be ineffective because it falls within the terms of the Unfair Contracts Terms Act 1977 which applies to disclaimers as well as exemption clauses. The plaintiff must show that the defendant had a particular skill or expertise. If the statement is made by someone without such knowledge on a purely casual basis liability will be avoided.

This decision had important implications for professional advisers. A valuer, for example, may incur liability for a negligent valuation to a party who suffers loss in consequence of placing reliance on it. Estate agents have also been held liable on this basis in a number of cases. Apart from any obligations in contract, a valuer of property owes a duty of care to a third party who suffers loss as a result of relying on a negligent valuation. This is the case if he realises that his negligent valuation will be passed on by his client to a third party and he understands that the third party will rely on the valuation. In *Singer & Friedlander Ltd* v. *John D. Wood & Co.* (1977) the defendant firm was commissioned by a developer to value a site which they owned and wished to develop. The valuer who visited the site was aware that the plaintiffs would rely on his company's valuation in deciding whether or not to lend to the developer. The defendants were considered to owe a duty to the plaintiffs under the rule in *Hedley Byrne* to take care when carrying out their valuation. Consequently, they were held liable when the plaintiffs suffered loss owing to their negligence.

The degree of skill and care expected of a valuer by the courts is the same as in the case of other professional persons. That is the standard of a reasonably skilled and competent valuer. If the defendant has acted in accordance with the general and approved practice of his profession he will probably avoid liability provided that he uses 'a well practised professional method of reaching a conclusion'. Therefore a skilled valuer is expected to have a sound knowledge and understanding of the legal principles relevant to the valuation process.

Ignorance, or failure to apply these may well amount to negligence. In *Weedon* v. *Hindwood Clarke & Esplin* (1975) a valuer, retained to negotiate compulsory purchase compensation with the district valuer, was liable when he failed to take into account in his negotiations a decision which altered the assessment of the compensation in his client's favour. Hence, a valuer who is commissioned to value residential property is taken to have a sound understanding of the law relating to landlord and tenant, and in particular the statutory provisions relating to security of tenure. Similar principles apply in connection with commercial and agricultural properties. Planning matters and the principles of the law of compulsory purchase should also be known. Legislation which could impose an obligation on a property owner to spend money on his property should be appreciated. In *Corisand Investments* v. *Druce & Co.* (1978) a valuer acting for a prospective mortgagee (lender of money) failed to appreciate that the hotel which he was estimating the value of required a fire certificate under the Fire Precautions Act 1971. Liability was incurred when he failed to deduct from his valuation a figure to take account of the cost of alterations to the hotel in order to obtain a certificate.

Location is important. A valuer is expected to know the state of the market and existing property values where he is undertaking valuations. In *Baxter* v. *F.W. Gapp & Co. Ltd* (1939) an estate agent retained to value a house in Berkshire was held liable on this basis. If a surveyor is making a valuation outside an area he knows he should enlist the help of local estate agents. Obviously, a site visit should be made when making a valuation. If acting for a prospective mortgagee, the valuer must attempt to estimate the value of the property on the market in the event of the mortgagee having to exercise his power of sale because of the borrower's default. Although he cannot foretell the future, the valuer ought to be able to estimate the state of the market in 6-12 months' time. In the *Corisand* case, a valuer was liable where he included in his figure a high 'speculative' content when that side of the market was coming to an end.

In *Perry* v. *Sidney Phillips & Sons* (1982) a surveyor was liable where he overestimated the value of a property because of his negligent failure to detect structural defects. The Court of Appeal stated that where a prospective buyer of a house is misled because of a negligent survey into paying more for a property than it is worth, the measure of damages payable is the difference between the price actually paid and the market value assessed as at the date of purchase together with interest until the payment of damages. It is not the notional difference in value as at the date of the hearing. The court considered that this was the case regardless of whether the plaintiff intended to remain in the property or whether he had cut his losses by resale. On the particular facts of this case, the plaintiff was also entitled to damages for inconvenience and discomfort.

The recent case of *Yianni* v. *Edwin Evans & Sons* (1981) has recognised that a valuer will be expected by a court to assume that a prospective buyer is unlikely to commission an independent survey as an added protection especially at the lower end of the market. Instead, the purchaser will place reliance on a building society survey, like 90 per cent of borrowers. In this case, the defendants undertook a building society survey and on the strength of a favourable report, the society made an offer of a loan. The defendants told the plaintiffs that if they required a report for their own information and protection they should consult an independent surveyor. The plaintiffs did not take this step. Instead, they accepted the offer of the society's loan. Some months after the purchase of the house they discovered that there were serious defects in the foundations of the house which would cost £18,000 to rectify. When the plaintiffs brought an action in negligence, the judge held that the defendants owed a duty of care under the *Hedley Byrne* principle and were completely liable. The defendants knew that the building society would rely on their valuation report in assessing the adequacy of the house as security for a loan and the actual amount of the loan. In addition, the defendants were aware that no independent survey would be relied upon.

A person who holds himself out as having professional skills or who undertakes work requiring such skills may incur liability under this principle. In *Freeman* v. *Marhall & Co.* (1966) an unqualified surveyor who had undertaken a structural survey could not plead ignorance where he failed to realise that a house was subject to rising damp.

Breach of statutory duty

Where a defendant is liable in tort, he is also frequently in breach of an act of parliament or regulations made under statute. The normal remedy for breach of a statutory provision is a fine, while in tort a plaintiff will be looking primarily for a sum of money by way of damages. One problem which arises is whether a breach of a statute can automatically give rise to a civil action in tort known as breach of statutory duty, as well as resulting in criminal liability.

A number of hurdles must be cleared before a plaintiff can succeed in such an action. The first consideration is whether the statute confers a private right of action. The plaintiff must prove that the statute was intended by parliament to confer a civil remedy for its breach and that the duty owed to the plaintiff was broken. The injury must be of a kind that the statute was intended to prevent. The breach of duty must be the cause of the damage which is not too remote. In *Ginty* v. *Belmont Building Supplies Ltd* (1959) statutory regulations required workers and employers in the roofing business to use crawling boards when working. The defendant contractors supplied the boards but the defendant, an experienced workman, failed to use them and fell through a roof. Although they were technically in breach of the statute, the defendants were acquitted because they had done everything that could be expected in the circumstances and the plaintiff's breach was the direct cause of the accident.

Many statutes fail to state whether or not damages are recoverable in the event of a breach. Most actions commenced in this area of the law are concerned with employer safety legislation. According to the Health and Safety at Work Act 1974, civil liability is imposed for breach of the building regulations. It was suggested in *Anns* v. *London Borough of Merton* (1977) that a householder can claim damages from a builder for breach of the building regulations. Consent and contributory negligence (see below) are the major defences to an action on this ground.

SPECIFIC DEFENCES

In addition to the general defences which may be raised in respect of a number of torts, there are also specific defences which have application in respect of an individual tort. In negligence actions, apart from showing that one of the essential elements is missing, the defendant may allege the plaintiff's consent to run the risk as a bar to an action. More frequently used is the defence of contributory negligence.

Contributory negligence
This defence is established where it is proved that an injured party failed to take reasonable care of himself and thus contributed to his own injury. Before 1945, a successful allegation of contributory negligence was a complete defence to the plaintiff's claim. Nowadays, the Law Reform (Contributory Negligence) Act 1945 regulates the position.

The effect of a successful claim of contributory negligence is to reduce the damages awarded to the plaintiff. In effect, the court makes an apportionment between the parties according to the degree of fault. Therefore a plaintiff's damages are reduced to the extent that the court considers him liable for the loss suffered. The defendant must show that the plaintiff failed to take reasonable care for his own safety and that his failure to do so would lead to harm to himself or his property. This defence may also be used to answer a claim for breach of statutory duty.

The principles laid down in *Herrington* v. *British Railways Board* have now been given statutory effect by the Occupier's Liability Act 1954, which is operative from May 1984.

7.6 Trespass

Although often associated with the criminal law, trespass is a long established tort. It occurs where there is direct interference with the person, goods or land of another. As it is actionable *per se*, there is no need to prove damage as a consequence of the tort.

TRESPASS TO THE PERSON

There are three types of trespass to the person.

Assault

This is a tort (and a crime) where one person causes another to fear the immediate application to himself of unlawful physical violence. Spoken words without bodily movement cannot constitute an assault. The term is often used to include battery.

Battery

This comprises the intentional application of unlawful force by one person upon another without his consent. It includes the slightest force and no actual harm need result. Consent, self-defence and the exercise of parental authority may be defences. It is also a criminal offence and conviction in a criminal court may be used as evidence in a civil action.

False imprisonment

This amounts to an unjustifiable act which totally deprives a person of his liberty. It must be intentional. There may be unlawful detention or a threat of force. It is unnecessary that there should be any actual use of force. Taking control of the person without consent is the governing factor. Imprisonment must be complete and definite. There must be no way out. If the plaintiff may proceed in another direction, although restrained from his original passage, there is no false imprisonment. Hence no action for false imprisonment was sustained where a person was prevented from passing along the highway and was compelled to return the same way, see *Bird* v. *Jones* (1843).

TRESPASS TO GOODS AND CHATTELS

This consists of direct physical interference with a chattel in the possession of another person without legal justification. Trespass to goods is actionable *per se* without any proof of actual damage. Any unauthorised touching or moving of a chattel is actionable although no damage results. Possession is the basis of the tort and only a person who possesses the goods at the time of the interference may actually sue. The interference may consist of actual damage or destruction of a chattel. Intermeddling with goods or dispossessing a person of them will also amount to a trespass.

Conversion

This is an act in relation to a person's goods which constitutes a serious and unjustifiable denial of that person's title to them. The usual remedies sought are damages and an injunction. This complex tort includes wrongfully taking goods, dealing with them, or destroying them. In *Oakley* v. *Lister* (1931) the plaintiff leased some land for the purpose of depositing hardcore belonging to him on it. The defendant acquired the freehold and wrote to the plaintiff informing him that he would not be allowed to remove the material claiming that it belonged to the defendant. In addition, the new freeholder used some of the material. The Court of Appeal held that the defendant had converted the material and interfered with the exercise of the plaintiff's rights.

Detinue

Detinue was an action in which the plaintiff sought the return of goods which had been wrongfully detained. The action was based on repossession. The claim was for the return of the chattels or their value together with damages for detention. To succeed to such a claim it was not necessary to show that a denial of the plaintiff's title had taken place. This tort was abolished by the Tort (Interference with Goods) Act 1977. This act was passed as a result of the Law Reform Committee's recommendation that the law relating to trespass to chattels be altered and replaced with a single tort of 'wrongful interference with goods'.

TRESPASS TO LAND

This consists of direct interference with the plaintiff's possession of land without any justification. The interference may be intentional at the outset, or alternatively it may arise when a person's lawful right to remain on land has been revoked. The interference may come about in a number of ways. Normally, it will be by entering on to the land. Instead, it can come about by throwing or placing something on the land. Flying over or tunnelling beneath land may amount to a trespass. The slightest entry on to land is sufficient to constitute this tort. The right of entry may also be abused. A person who enters land for a specific purpose, even under statutory powers, will commit a trespass if he exceeds the purpose for which he is there. Hence a person who uses the highway other than to pass and repass will become a trespasser, see *Harrison* v. *Duke of Rutland* (1893). Also, to refuse to leave the plaintiff's land is as much a trespass as to enter originally without right.

Rights in land are considered to extend upwards to infinity and downwards to the subsoil. Therefore an invasion of air space is a trespass. Overhead cables and sign boards come into this category. In *Woolerton & Wilson* v. *Costain Ltd* (1970) the swinging of a crane over other land was considered to be a trespass. Aircraft are normally protected from actions in this respect by the Civil Aviation Act 1948 as long as they fly at a reasonable height. This defence succeeded in *Bernstein* v. *Skyviews Ltd* (1978). If the act is broken or there is damage to property, liability will accrue. Interference with mineral rights may well amount to a trespass.

Again, trespass to land is a tort against possession rather than ownership. As a general rule, trespass is not a criminal offence and only gives rise to civil remedies. Certain statutory provisions prove to be exceptions to this rule and impose a fine for trespassing.

REMEDIES

Damages

The plaintiff's normal remedy will be damages. The tort is actionable *per se* and if no loss occurs, damages will be nominal in most circumstances.

Injunction

This equitable remedy may be available if the trespass is of a variety that is likely to recur. This may be combined with an action for damages.

Ejection

The occupier may use reasonable force to eject a trespasser. A trespasser who has entered without force must first be asked to leave and given reasonable time to do so.

Action for recovery and mesne profits

Where a person is dispossessed of his land and is prevented from returning he may bring an action against the wrongdoer. When he recovers possession, he may claim compensation for depreciation of the premises and use of the land. This would include lost rents and the costs of the action. Mesne is pronounced 'mean'.

Distress damage feasant

An occupier of land may take any chattels unlawfully upon his land and detain them until he is compensated for any damage they have caused. Therefore, an occupier is not obliged to return a ball which has broken a window pane. The most frequent application of the rule was in respect of animals which trespassed. Since 1971, distress damage feasant has not applied to animals. Instead, the occupier may exercise a power of sale.

DEFENCES

Apart from the normal general defences, the following may have application in respect of trespass to land:

(a) entry by authority of law;
(b) regaining possession of one's own property;
(c) necessity;
(d) entry by licence.

7.7. Nuisance

Nuisance comes in two main varieties: public and private. In addition, certain acts constitute a statutory nuisance (see later). Public health legislation, in particular, allows local authorities to proceed quickly where antisocial conduct amounting to a nuisance is taking place.

PUBLIC NUISANCE

This is essentially a criminal matter and the person responsible may be prosecuted. It has been defined as an act or omission which materially affects the reasonable comfort and convenience of life of a class of Her Majesty's subjects. Examples include obstructing the highway, making the highway dangerous for those who use it, polluting a public water supply and selling food unfit for human consumption. Public nuisance is not limited to interference with land. In *Dollman* v. *Hillman Ltd* (1941) a person recovered damages where he suffered injury because of fat left on the pavement outside a butcher's shop. However, in order to prevent a multiplicity of actions, a plaintiff may only sue for damages if he can show that he has suffered a particular form of damage over and above that suffered by the public at large. Such extra damage is known as special damage and frequently takes the form of personal injuries, see *Castle* v. *St Augustine's Links Ltd* (1922). It is not limited to this variety of harm and can be interference with property rights. Where the matter is one of public interest, a private person may ask the Attorney-General to bring an action on his behalf. Such an action is known as a *relator* action.

PRIVATE NUISANCE

This is a tort which protects a person from interference with the land he occupies. The plaintiff must have a proprietary in the land which is affected. Unlike trespass, private nuisance is a tort against enjoyment of land and the injury is indirect. It is normally not actionable *per se*. Therefore, actual damage must be proved.

ESSENTIAL ELEMENTS

Interference
This may take many forms. Dirt, smells and noise are traditional areas of litigation. Sewerage, tree roots and branches, fumes and vibrations from engines causing structural damage to houses have all constituted interference.

Damage
Although it is probably easier for a plaintiff to succeed in private nuisance if he can show actual damage, any substantial interference with the enjoyment of his land will suffice. If the plaintiff is relying on personal discomfort it must be material. Some state of affairs

over and above the everyday inconveniences which exist in a locality must be present. As an exception, if the interference is with an ease-ment (right of way) or similar property rights, it is not necessary to prove actual damage. A state of affairs which threatens discomfort or damage may constitute a nuisance.

Reasonableness
The essence of this tort is that it is a form of action against unreason-able behaviour. Therefore, if a person uses his land in a reasonable way so as to cause no undue inconvenience to others it is unlikely that he will have committed the tort. The court attempts to balance the interests of the occupier against those of the defendant. The longer the interference lasts and the greater its extent, the more likely it is that it will be a nuisance. It seems that where building operations of a temporary nature such as conversions or demolition are carried out with a reasonable degree of care so as not to cause undue inconvenience to neighbouring properties, no tort is com-mitted. This principle was applied in *Andrae* v. *Selfridge* (1938) where hotel proprietors complained of building works taking place nearby. When judging the standard of reasonableness, the following are of importance:

Sensitivity: The law of nuisance fails to assist those who require more protection than the community in general because of undue sensitivity. In *Bridlington Relay Ltd* v. *Yorkshire Electricity Board* (1965) the plaintiffs carried on a business of relaying sound and television broadcasts. The defendants' newly-erected power line interfered with their transmissions. Consequently the plaintiffs sought an injunction. The action failed. The plaintiff's use of their aerial for this particular purpose was of a special kind unusually vulnerable to interference. Other activities would not be affected by the powerline.

Locality: Where an occupier is complaining of interference with his enjoyment of land, an important factor is the nature of the locality. Different standards apply in different localities. Occupiers in urban and industrial areas may have to put up with more dis-comfort than those in more residential areas. In *Sturges* v. *Bridgman* (1879) a doctor claimed an injunction where noise from a neigh-bouring confectionery business interfered with the use of his con-sulting room at the back of his garden. The area was, in fact, one where doctors had their consulting rooms and the injunction was granted. If, however, the plaintiff has suffered material injury to his property, locality is irrelevant. In *St Helens Smelting Co.* v. *Tipping* (1865) vapours from the defendant's copper smelting works killed off the plaintiff's trees and crops. The plaintiff's action succeeded because location was no defence where actual damage occurred. In any case, whatever the utility of the alleged nuisance, the allegation that it is for the public benefit is no defence.

Malice: Malice (improper motive) is not an essential ingredient of private nuisance, but its existence may be evidence of unreasonable behaviour. In the well-known case of *Christie* v. *Davy* (1893) the plaintiff used her house for frequent musical evenings. The defendant, who lived in the adjoining semi-detached house, became so exasperated with the playing that he retaliated by knocking on the walls, beating trays and shrieking. The defendant's actions amounted to a nuisance as it was made for the sole purpose of annoyance. A similar result was reached in *Hollywood Silver Fox Farm Ltd* v. *Emmett* (1936) where, because of a dispute over a sign, the defendant sent his son to discharge a shotgun near to the plaintiff's land in order to interfere with the breeding of the plaintiff's foxes. This was an actionable nuisance and an injunction was granted to restrain him in the future. In general, the law of tort is not concerned with malice, see *Bradford Corporation* v. *Pickles* (1895) at 7.5.

Continuity

A nuisance must normally be of a continuing nature before it becomes actionable. There must be in existence some state of affairs which repeatedly affects the plaintiff's land. Despite this, isolated incidents of escapes of dangerous things have constituted nuisances. The question is whether the defendant has maintained on his land a state of affairs which may turn out to be a potential nuisance. In *Midwood Ltd* v. *Mayor of Manchester* (1905) the plaintiff recovered in nuisance for damage caused by a single escape of gas. Also, in *Spicer* v. *Smee* (1946) the plaintiff's bungalow was destroyed through fire caused by defective wiring in the defendant's adjoining bungalow. As there was a dangerous state of affairs at the defendant's dwelling he was held liable in nuisance.

THE PARTIES TO AN ACTION

The right to sue in private nuisance depends upon having an interest in the land. Therefore a plaintiff must be an occupier. This will cover an owner-occupier and where appropriate, any tenant in occupation. Where a permanent injury has been caused to the property, a landlord may sue despite the fact that he is not in possession. In *Masters* v. *Brent Borough Council* (1978) an occupier of a dwelling house successfully claimed damages for harm caused by the roots of a neighbouring lime tree. The damage had been caused before and after the plaintiff acquired the property. He was entitled to the full cost of repair.

The person primarily liable for the nuisance is he who creates it. This will often be the occupier of land. A person may also be liable in nuisance even though he has given up actual occupation of the land and therefore cannot enter the land to abate the nuisance. A person may incur liability simply because the nuisance exists on the land he occupies. If the occupier is not responsible for the nuisance, he must take reasonable steps to abate it, otherwise he may well be liable. In *Sedleigh-Denfield* v. *O'Callaghan* (1927) trespassers laid a pipe on land occupied by the defendant. Because the pipe became blocked, adjoining land was flooded. There was evidence that the defendants' employees had cleared out the ditch where the pipe was situated. The defendants were liable, because they ought to have known of the nuisance and taken appropriate steps to abate it. However, the defendant will not be liable if he takes reasonable steps.

Where premises are leased, the tenant will primarily be liable. Where the landlord creates the nuisance and then leases the property or authorises the tenant to commit or continue a nuisance, he may well incur liability. The authorisation may be express or implied. In *Harris* v. *James* (1876) the landlord as well as the tenant was liable as the former had authorised the commission of the nuisance.

REMEDIES

A plaintiff in an action based upon private nuisance will normally be looking for damages, together with an injunction. The latter is particularly important if there is a chance of the nuisance recurring and causing further damage to the plaintiff. As it is an equitable remedy, an injunction will not be granted if it would cause undue hardship to the defendant.

An alternative remedy is self-help or abatement. This is a process whereby the injured party may stop the nuisance by remedying the cause. The usual example given of this procedure is where roots and branches projecting on to another property are cut off by the affected occupier, see *Lennon* v. *Webb* (1895). Abatement is 'a remedy which the law does not favour'. Unless there is an emergency, the offending occupier should be informed and given a reasonable time to comply with the abatement of the offending matter. If an occupier exercises his rights and abates the nuisance he cannot subsequently bring an action for damages. If abatement is chosen, no unnecessary damage must be inflicted on the offending property.

DEFENCES

The following are of relevance in an action based on private nuisance:

(a) *volenti*;
(b) statutory authority;
(c) contributory negligence;
(d) prescription.

Certain private nuisances may become lawful if they have been exercised for 20 years or more.

7.8 Liability for animals

An owner of animals may incur liability in tort on account of his animal in the normal way. Therefore, he may be negligent, create a private nuisance or be liable in trespass. Since the enactment of the Animals Act 1971, the law has been updated to cater for modern conditions. At common law, injury caused by an animal attracted different treatment from harm inflicted by premises and dangerous chattels. The 1971 Act preserves the distinction between dangerous and non-dangerous species. The act imposes strict liability upon the keeper of an animal for any damage caused by an animal belonging to a dangerous species. The keeper of an animal belonging to a non-dangerous species is also strictly liable if the particular animal causes damage which flows from dangerous characteristics known to the person in control.

  If the injury is the fault of the plaintiff or if he validly accepted the risk, there will be no liability. If the plaintiff was a trespasser at the time of his injury he can only recover if he can show that the animal was an unreasonable guard of persons or property. In *Cummings* v. *Granger* (1974) the plaintiff's action failed where an untrained alsatian dog attacked a trespasser. The court said that it was not unreasonable for the defendant to keep a dog on the premises to protect him and the plaintiff ought to have known of the dog's existence for an appropriate notice was put up outside the premises.

Since the Guard Dogs Act 1976, adequate warning of a guard dog's presence on premises must be displayed. Unless the dog is chained up, a capable handler must be on the premises to keep the dog under control. Where a dog causes damage by killing or causing injury to livestock, the keeper is prima facie responsible for the damage. Section 9 of the 1971 Act entitles a farmer to shoot a dog which is worrying livestock where such an action is necessary for the protection of his animals. Another example of strict liability is where livestock straying on to someone else's land cause damage to that other person's property. In that case, the owner must pay for any damage or expenses incurred. Where animals stray on to the highway, it is no longer open to the defendant who is sued in negligence to plead that he was under no duty to fence or otherwise prevent his animals from straying. There are certain exceptions to this principle in the case of common land and other land not normally fenced.

7.9 The rule in Rylands v. Fletcher (1876)

In this case, the defendant, a mill owner, employed independent contractors to build a reservoir on his land. This was for the purpose of supplying water to run his mill. Unknown to the defendant and the contractors, an old mine shaft lay underneath the land. This led to the plaintiff's mine on neighbouring land. When the reservoir was filled, the water escaped through the shafts and flooded the plaintiff's mine. The plaintiff sued for damage incurred. Although it was established that the defendant had not been negligent and that the contractors were competent, the defendant was held to be liable. The reason for the decision is normally stated as follows:

A person who for his own purposes brings on his lands and collects and keeps there anything likely to do mischief if it escapes, must keep it at his peril, and if he does not do so, is prima facie answerable for all the damage which is the natural consequence of its escape.

ESSENTIALS

Control
The defendant must be an occupier of land or be the owner who is in control of things on the land.

Accumulation and non-natural use
The defendant must have brought on to his land some item which is likely to do mischief if it escapes. The item must not be 'naturally present on the land'. Therefore, the rule does not apply to the land itself, to rocks or to natural lakes. In addition, the actual use of the land by the defendant must be non-natural. This is a question of fact in each case. In order to satisfy this requirement, the use must in some way be uncommon.

Mischief
The item causing the mischief has included vibrations, oil, gas and electricity. Even a falling flagpole and a fairground chair have come within the definition.

Escape
There must be an escape from the place in occupation or control of the defendant to other land. In *Read* v. *Lyons* (1947) a Ministry of Supply inspector was injured by an explosive shell in a munitions factory. As she was unable to prove negligence, she relied upon *Rylands* v. *Fletcher*. The House of Lords decided that the rule had no application as there had been no escape from the factory premises.

Damage
The tort is not actionable *per se*. There must be proof of actual damage to the person or to property.

DEFENCES
Although liability is strict, certain defences are available.

Act of stranger
If the escape was caused by the act of a stranger over whom the defendant had no control he will not be liable. This means a person acting without the authority of the occupier and not a servant of the defendant. In *Rickards* v. *Lothian* (1913) the plaintiff's premises were flooded when an unidentified person left taps on

in premises of which the defendant was tenant.

Default by the plaintiff
Consent
Act of God
Statutory Authority
This will cover local authorities and statutory undertakers. In *Green v. Chelsea Waterworks Co* (1894) the defendants were liable, in the absence of negligence, where a water main burst and flooded the plaintiff's premises. The defendants were authorised by statute to lay the main.

7.10 Defamation

The essence of defamation is the publication of an untrue statement which tends to lower a person in the estimation of right-thinking members of society. It is a tort which is designed to protect reputation and the burden rests on the defendant to prove the truth of his statement. There are two forms of defamation: libel and slander.

LIBEL
This is defamation in a permanent form. Although it will normally consist of writing or printing, cases on paintings, statues and films have come into this category. Libel is actionable *per se*, and therefore the plaintiff has no need to prove financial loss after publication.

SLANDER
This is defamation in a transitory form. Normally it will take place by word of mouth or by gesture. In slander, the plaintiff must normally prove actual damage except where the following are imputed:

(a) that the plaintiff has committed a crime punishable by imprisonment;
(b) that the plaintiff has an infectious disease;
(c) unchastity in a woman;
(d) unfitness to carry out a particular trade or profession.

ESSENTIAL ELEMENTS OF THE TORT
The defamatory statement must be:

A reference to the plaintiff

It is up to the plaintiff to show that a third party would connect the defamatory statement with him. Therefore, a class of persons as such cannot be defamed. However, the plaintiff need not be the person to whom the defendant intended to refer.

Defamatory

Mere abuse does not amount to a defamatory statement. In order to be defamatory, the statement must discredit the plaintiff or make him repugnant to ordinary responsible people. Sometimes, a statement may appear quite harmless on the face of it but nevertheless in the circumstances it may have a secondary or hidden meaning. This is the innuendo. In *Monson* v. *Tussauds Ltd* (1894) an effigy of the plaintiff was placed next to those of convicted murderers. This was deemed to constitute libel.

Published

The statement must be communicated to a third party either in writing or by word of mouth. The requirement of publication may be satisfied not only where the defendant has purposely made the statement to another person, but also where he ought to have foreseen its publication. This is the reason why publication is presumed where postcards and telegrams are despatched. Before the defendant incurs liability, the third party must understand the defamatory nature of the statement and realise that it referred to the defendant. In *Sadgrove* v. *Hole* (1901) the plaintiff quantity surveyor brought an action for libel in respect of statements written on postcards relating to a bill of quantities which he had prepared. The defendant sent these cards to a third party. No reference appeared to the plaintiff's name on the cards and no other person would have understood that the statements referred to the surveyor. There was no publication. Every time that a defamatory statement is repeated it is actionable, although a person who merely supplies defamatory material such as a newsvendor will not incur liability unless the publication is intentional.

DEFENCES

Justification

If the defendant can prove that the statement was substantially true, this will be a complete defence.

Fair comment on a matter of public interest

The defendant must show that the words complained of were statements of opinion and not activated by malice. The statements must amount to honest comment on a matter of public interest. The defence will not apply to a misstatement of fact. Purely private matters are not relevant. Irrelevant comments will not be protected.

Privilege

Some statements are privileged. This means that in certain circumstances, no action will flow despite the defamatory nature of the comments made.

Absolute privilege: Statements made in parliamentary proceedings and in the law courts are privileged even if made maliciously. Such privilege attaches itself to a number of other situations where the law considers that a person should not have to consider the likelihood of proceedings in defamation because of the nature of the activity.

Qualified privilege: Sometimes, proceedings will be privileged unless the person who made the statement was prompted by malice. Examples include statements made because of some legal or moral duty and reports of parliamentary and judicial proceedings.

Offer of amends

Where innocently, a newspaper publishes a libel, the publishers may apologise, make an offer of amends and, where appropriate, print a correction. This will constitute a good defence. An apology will normally constitute a mitigating factor when assessing damages, whoever the defendant.

A prospective plaintiff in defamation proceedings should always remember a number of significant factors. Defamation is a very expensive form of litigation; no legal aid is available, while proceedings can only be brought and defended in the High Court. The County Court has no jurisdiction. Moreover, civil juries are still used in such proceedings.

Chapter 8

An introduction to land law

8.1 The meaning of property

In most legal systems, a distinction is made between land and other types of property. English law is no exception. Another distinction which is also made is between the ownership of property and possession of it. Possession is usually a matter of physical fact, implying the intention and power to control. Ownership, or title to property, is simply a right which the law recognises.

REAL AND PERSONAL PROPERTY

The primary distinction in English law is between real property or realty, which comprises freehold land, and personal property or personalty, which comprises all other forms of property. In theory, at least, all land in this country is owned by the Crown. For historical reasons, it is possible for a person to have rights over land. The greatest right which a person may have in land is an estate. Since 1925, the law only recognises the existence of two estates in land: the *freehold* and *leasehold*.

There are historical reasons for the leasehold estate being classified as an item of personal property. In the early development of land law, a real action protected a freehold estate in land. Therefore, if a freeholder had his land taken from him, he could bring a real action to recover the land itself from the person who had dispossessed him. Hence the term real property is applied to freehold land. Rights to other forms of property, including the leasehold, were limited to claiming compensation in respect of the property taken. Recovery of possession of the land itself could not be enforced therefore when a leaseholder was dispossessed of his land. Consequently only a personal action could be brought in

146

respect of personal property.

Personal property is sometimes known as chattels. 'Personalty' is divided into *chattels real* and *chattels personal*. It is only for historical reasons, already stated, that the leasehold estate is classified as an item of personal property. In fact, it is inseparably related to real property. The leasehold is known as chattels real.

Chattels personal comprises every other type of property and is divided into *choses in possession* and *choses in action*. The former are rights over tangible moveables and such rights may be enjoyed simply by physical possession. The latter are rights such as debts and copyrights which may be enjoyed or protected only by legal action. Since 1925, the distinction between real and personal property is not of great importance. It would be of more value today if English law adopted the classification of immoveable property (land) and moveable property (personal chattels) as in most other legal systems.

8.2 The historical background of English land law

The development of English land law is often said to begin with the Norman conquest of 1066. At this date, all land became vested in King William I. Soon after coming to power, the King began to grant rights in land to his most senior followers and also to certain of the English barons who submitted to his control. These senior followers became known as tenants-in-chief or holders of the land. These tenants-in-chief were themselves able to grant rights to others in respect of the whole or part of land they had received. Likewise, the recipients of land from the tenants-in-chief were able to make sub-grants to others. This system of granting rights over land characterised by service to a sovereign or chief was known as the process of *subinfeudation*. To a large extent, this feudal system depended on the concept of tenure or the holding of land.

TENURE

In order to hold freehold land, particular services were rendered by a tenant to his superior. The terms upon which the tenant held were of various kinds and the expression *tenure* related to the conditions under which the land was held. The expression tenant is derived from tenure, meaning in general any holder of land. There developed in this context two particular types of tenure:

(a) free tenure;

(b) unfree tenure.

Free tenures

These were for fixed services. Once the specified services were performed by the tenant his time was his own and he was free to use the land as he desired. Examples include the following:

Knight service: This required the tenant to supply horsemen to his lord for 40 days in every year.

Sergeanty: This required personal services to one's lord.

Free socage: This required services of a non-military kind, normally agricultural, such as the provision of crops or livestock to a lord. Sometimes a small payment would be made instead.

Spiritual tenure: This consisted of saying masses for the superior lord or the giving of alms.

Unfree tenures

These consisted of rendering services of a servile nature. Medieval serfs held their land on this basis. Because of the nature of the tenure, they were not entitled to leave their holding of land. The varieties of unfree tenure varied from manor to manor. Because a record was kept by the manorial court, these tenures were known as *copyhold*.

Other obligations

Certain obligations were sometimes owed by the tenant to his lord and these were known as incidents. *Escheat* is a good example of this. In certain circumstances, land was forfeited to a superior tenant on death. In addition, certain types of tenure developed on a customary basis. By passage of time, the free and unfree tenures became freeholds. Today, little remains of the former varieties of tenure and at the present time only two forms of tenure remain; namely the freehold and the leasehold.

ESTATES

The expression estate in land applies to the length of time for which a tenant was traditionally entitled to hold land. Therefore it classified rights in land according to their duration. Since the sixteenth century, two estates have been recognised by the law:

(a) freehold estates, where duration is not known;
(b) leasehold estates, whereby one or more persons have the exclusive right to occupy land for a fixed period of time.

Freeholds

Since 1925, the only freehold estate of any importance is the *fee simple absolute in possession* which is the largest estate known to English land law. Another type of freehold estate was the fee tail where the land could only be inherited by specific descendants of the original person to whom the land was granted. In addition, it was possible to have a life estate of a freehold whereby a person would hold land for the duration of his life or the life of some other person (the estate pur autre vie). Nowadays, the only estate of freehold recognised and capable of existing at law is the fee simple.

Leaseholds

The essence of the leasehold estate is the creation of an estate in land for a fixed period of time whereby one person pays rent to another in return for occupation or use of the land. Its technical name is *the term of years absolute*. For most practical purposes the leasehold estate includes what is known as a tenancy agreement.

FUTURE RIGHTS IN LAND

Future rights in land are those which will come into existence at some future time.

Reversions

If A has an estate in fee simple and he grants to B an estate or interest of shorter duration than his own such as a lease, A is said to have his fee simple in reversion as the land will revert to him when B's rights terminate. In such a case, B is said to be a *reversioner.*

Remainders

If A grants his entire right in land by means of two successive transactions, e.g. to B for life and then to C in fee simple, the right to possession of the land is said to 'remain' away from A. Therefore C's interest is consequently known as a remainder and C is a *remainderman.*

Seisin

Where a person is said to be 'seised' of land, it meant in traditional land law that he had possession of it. As such, there is no practical significance in using the term but the expression is still to be found in old title deeds.

THE IMPORTANCE OF EQUITY IN ENGLISH LAND LAW

Equity developed because of the deficiencies of the common law. These included the formalised writ system, procedural complexities and inadequate remedies. The practice grew up whereby persons seeking a remedy would petition the King for assistance. These petitions would be passed on to the Lord Chancellor. As the number of these petitions increased the chancellor's jurisdiction developed into a court of law staffed by judges dealing with chancery or equity matters. As a consequence of this, a set of separate and rival courts grew up alongside the common law courts, but granting different remedies such as injunctions and specific performance.

The nature of equitable remedies

The courts of equity adopted a different attitude to cases from the common law courts. If a plaintiff proved his case in the common law courts, he was automatically entitled to damages. Equity was more flexible and originally would grant any remedy which it thought appropriate. Over a period of time the courts of equity became more formalised and the remedies available were classified. Equitable remedies are still discretionary and they will not be granted where the common law remedy of damages is adequate. In addition, a set of rules known as the *maxims of equity* governed the functioning of equitable remedies. For example:

(a) Equity looks to the intent rather than to the form. This means that as long as the parties intend to enter into a particular agreement, the lack of compliance with formalities will not make the transaction ineffective.
(b) Delay defeats the equities. Failure to commence proceedings within a reasonable time will mean that the jurisdiction of the courts of equity cannot be relied upon.
(c) He who comes to equity must come with clean hand. This means that any person who seeks the aid of equity must act honestly and in good faith.

8.3 Estates and interests

In English land law, the largest right which a person may have over land is an estate. Two estates became established as the most important rights which a person could have over land, namely the freehold and the leasehold. Any other right which a person possesses over land is an *interest*. A *legal interest* in land is a right which before the Judicature Acts (1873-75) was only recognised by the common law courts. An *equitable interest*, on the other hand, was an interest in land which was only recognised by the courts of equity before the Judicature Acts.

The concept of the trust is a good example of the distinction. This is a device, which has been used to give a person a future interest in land or personalty. If A transfers land to B in trust for the benefit of C, A is the *settlor* or *grantor*, B is the *trustee* and C is known as the *beneficiary*. The common law courts would only recognise the trustee's rights and not those of the beneficiary, while the courts of equity would recognise the beneficiary's interest under the trust.

THE 1925 PROPERTY LEGISLATION

By the end of the nineteenth century, it had become apparent that English law was still based on the feudal system and not appropriate to the needs of an expanding industrial society. Many ancient doctrines still survived, especially as to tenure, while different rules were in existence relating to real and personal property. The biggest problems concerned the transfer or conveyancing of land which was complicated and cumbersome. Because of these difficulties, a series of acts was passed in 1925 bringing about important changes in English land law. The underlying purpose was to simplify the conveyancing of land. The principal act was the Law of Property Act (LPA) while the Settled Land Act, Trustee Act, Land Registration and Land Charges Acts were also of great importance.

THE CONCEPT OF ESTATES AND INTERESTS AFTER 1925

Section 1 of the Law of Property Act 1925 states that only two legal estates are capable of recognition at law after 1925. These are the *fee simple absolute in possession* and *the term of years absolute*. As stated before, a person may have a right in land which does not amount to an estate and this is known as an interest. Interests in land may be of a legal or equitable nature. Section 1 goes on to say that only five legal interests are capable of existing. Of these five, only two, the easement or similar right over land and the charge by way of legal mortgage, are of importance nowadays. The act goes on to state that any other interest is of an equitable nature. Consequently, if an interest in land is not within those stated in section 1 of the Law of Property Act, it is automatically an equitable interest.

LEGAL AND EQUITABLE INTERESTS

Despite the attempt in 1875 to combine the administration of the common law and equity, differences do still exist. A legal right or interest is said to be a *right in rem*. This means that an action can be brought against the property. An equitable interest is said to be a *right in personam*, giving the plaintiff a right to sue the person responsible.

A legal right is said to be enforceable against the world at large so that whoever acquires the estate in land is bound by that legal interest whether he knew of it or not. Any person having the benefit of a legal right of way or similar benefit may enforce it against the purchaser of a legal estate whether the latter knew of its existence or not.

An equitable interest is a personal right which, although generally may be enforced against the community at large, is subject to one major exception. This is the so-called bona fide purchaser for value of the legal estate who has taken without notice of the existence of the equitable interest, and a person who claims through him. This doctrine of the bona fide purchaser or 'equity's darling' contains a number of expressions which are explained as follows.

Bona fide

This simply means that the purchaser must act in good faith. Any fraud or underhand practice will forfeit the privilege of the doctrine.

Purchaser

The word is used in its technical sense to indicate a person who takes property.

Value

Consideration must have been given for money or monies' worth.

Legal estate

The purchaser must obtain a legal estate.

Notice
There are a number of different types of notice: actual, constructive, imputed and statutory.

Actual notice: A person has actual notice or knowledge where, from any circumstances, he has acquired knowledge of the existence of the right.

Constructive notice: A person has this type of notice where it is presumed that if he had made proper inquiry the existence of this interest would have been revealed. Such notice is deemed to exist where a person deliberately refrains from making proper inquiries in an attempt to avoid having notice or where a person is too careless to make proper inquiry.

Imputed notice: Where a person employs a solicitor or other agent to act on his behalf, any notice received by the agent, acting in his capacity as agent, will be imputed to the purchaser.

Statutory notice: Since 1925, registration of an interest in land has constituted statutory notice of the existence of that interest to any intending purchaser. Registration takes place in the Lands Charges Register and by section 198 of the Law of Property Act 1925; this is considered to be equivalent to actual notice. The system of registration has done much to minimise the importance of the doctrine of notice in recent years. Failure to register the interest renders it void against a purchaser. Some equitable interests are not registrable. In that case, the other types of notice must be relied upon.

Certain equitable interests are overreached on a sale of land. This means that a purchaser of a legal estate may disregard them even if he has actual notice of their existence. The person entitled to the benefit of the interest is recompensed by a monetary payment.

8.4 The freehold estate

Since 1925, the only freehold estate recognised at law is the fee simple absolute in possession. This is the greatest estate known to English law. Although in theory all land is vested in the Crown, for all practical purposes this estate gives rights in perpetuity over land and gives to its holder extensive powers over the land. Those other categories of freeholds which were recognised before 1925 now only exist as equitable interests. By its definition, the holder of the fee simple may normally transfer the estate to any person he so wishes. At one time, complicated rules applied in respect of the language which had to be used to transfer a fee simple. These were known as words of purchase and words of limitation. Nowadays, it is sufficient to indicate in the conveyance or other document that the property has passed from one person to another.

THE RIGHTS OF THE FREEHOLDER

The holder of the largest estate known to English law has traditionally enjoyed wide powers of control, disposal and use of land. As a characteristic of his ownership, a freeholder enjoys certain natural rights which arise from his possession of the fee simple.

Right of support

This means that a landowner is entitled to such support from his neighbour's land as is necessary to keep the landowner's soil at its natural level. In *Redland Bricks Ltd* v. *Morris* (1970) excavations by the brick company resulted in the plaintiff's market garden slipping on to the defendant's land due to lack of support. The right of support does not apply in the case of support for buildings, which normally operates as an easement.

Right of air

A landowner has the right to receive air in an unpolluted state where it flows on to his premises.

Right of alienation

Generally speaking, a freeholder may dispose of his property to any person he wishes. In addition, he may transfer part of the land if he so desires. Alienation may be by will or by deed.

Enjoyment

A freeholder has extensive rights of enjoyment including the right to enjoy everything on, above and beneath the land. In addition, he may 'waste' (alter the nature of) the land if he so wishes.

RESTRICTIONS ON A FREEHOLDER'S RIGHTS

Rights of others
A freeholder will take his estate subject to any rights of way over his land and rights of tenants under leases. The holder of the fee simple may also be bound by a restrictive covenant.

Liability under the general law
Liability may arise particularly in tort. The freeholder may be liable for any nuisances he causes. He may also incur liability under the rule in *Rylands* v. *Fletcher* (1876). Liability in negligence is another important factor. If a landowner fails to exercise his duty of care in respect of those persons who have rights over his land, liability may well be incurred.

Minerals
The rule is *cujus est solum*. That is, the freeholder owns his land to the depths of the earth. There are restrictions on a freeholder's rights to claim minerals beneath his land. It may also be the case that the vendor of the land has reserved them out of the sale on the previous conveyance of the land. In such circumstances, the purchaser will take free from them. Major exceptions to the *cujus est solum* rule are gold and silver, which normally belong to the Crown. Interests in coal are vested in the National Coal Board. Where treasure trove is found (gold and silver objects deliberately hidden of which the true owner cannot be found), this belongs to the Crown.

Air space
Any interference with the air space of a freeholder will normally amount to a trespass. The Civil Aviation Act 1949 prevents a freeholder from bringing an action in respect of interference with air space by a civil aircraft, provided that the aircraft is flying at a reasonable height, see *Bernstein* v. *Skyviews Ltd* (1978). Intrusion of air space by telephone wires and overhanging branches is probably both a nuisance and a trespass.

Wild animals and fishing rights
Although a freeholder has no absolute rights over wild animals on his land, he does have qualified rights to catch and appropriate such animals on his land. As soon as animals are killed, they fall into the ownership of the landowner even if killed by trespassers.

The right to fish in a non-tidal river is deemed to belong to the river owner or any person to whom he has granted such a right. In a tidal river, the public usually has a right to fish up to the point of ebb and flow of the tide. Separate riparian owners of the two river banks possess the right to fish up to the centre line.

Water rights

At common law, a landowner had the right to draw percolating water from his land. Since the Water Resources Act 1963, water can only be taken for domestic purposes if a licence is granted by the water authority. A person who owns land adjoining a stream (a riparian owner) has certain rights relating to the watercourse.

Entry by right conferred by law

This is normally governed by statute. If the individual in question exceeds his rights he will be a trespasser.

Limitations on the right to alienate

Normally, the owner of the fee simple may dispose of his property to whom he so wishes. Where property is left in a will, the testator must ensure that he is making reasonable provision for his spouse and children if they have been living together at the date of death. This is governed by the Inheritance (Provision for Family and Dependants) Act 1975.

Statutory social control

These provisions are probably the most important restrictions on the right of the freeholder to deal with his land as he pleases. Examples include planning legislation, the law relating to compulsory purchase, public health and housing law. Tenants of certain types of property are protected by statutory provisions, and in other cases they are given the right to purchase the freehold.

FIXTURES

A fixture is an object which changes its nature from a chattel and becomes part of the land upon which it is found. The fixture may be changed back to a chattel by separating it from the land. The basic rule is that fixtures pass with the land but chattels do not. Therefore, on a transfer of land, chattels may be removed, but not fixtures which have become a constituent part of the land. In order to distinguish between chattels and fixtures, two tests are applied.

These are particularly important in deciding whether or not a garage or a greenhouse can be removed on the sale of property or the termination of a lease.

Test one: the degree of annexation

This is the primary test. Such a test is applied to show how permanently the object has been attached to the land. Therefore, if an object is attached or annexed in any way to land by nailing, screwing or being set in concrete, it is a fixture. Fireplaces and panelling are good examples. If the article rests on the ground by its own weight, there is a presumption that the item is a chattel. In *Holland* v. *Hodgson* (1872) Blackburn J illustrated this principle where he stated that a pile of stones stacked together in a yard would be considered as chattels, but the same set of stones forming a wall would be part of the land.

It is possible to challenge this presumption. In *Leigh* v. *Taylor* (1902) tapestries which were fixed to battens which were screwed to the walls of a house were deemed to be chattels because the degree of annexation was slight and the purpose of fixing the tapestries was to enjoy them in their own right. However, a chattel which is attached to land, albeit slightly, is deemed to be a fixture.

Test two: the purpose of the annexation

This test is used if the first is difficult to apply. The test here is to ascertain the object of the annexation and whether or not the item has been fixed with the purpose of permanently improving the land. Where an item is placed on land or fitted in a way that shows an intention to improve the use of the land, it is deemed to be a fixture. Each situation depends upon its own set of facts. In *Vaudeville Electric Cinema Ltd* v. *Muriset* (1923) and *Lyon & Co.* v. *London City and Midland Bank* (1903) different results were reached on similar facts relating to seats in a cinema. If there is a conflict between the tests, the 'purpose' test will take priority.

Removal of fixtures

The fundamental rule is that fixtures pass with the land whereas chattels do not. Consequently, on a sale of land, fixtures must be left for the new fee simple owner. In certain cases special rules apply. One major example concerns the 'tenant's fixtures', which may be removed from a holding by a tenant at the end of his lease. This may have important consequences. In *New Zealand Govern-*

Property Corporation v. *VHM & S Ltd* (1982) the revised rent of the Haymarket Theatre was based upon the assumption that the tenant had the right to remove 'trade fixtures'.

8.5 Interests in land

EASEMENTS

Interests in land may be of a legal or an equitable nature. One of the most common forms of legal interest is the easement. These are private rights enjoyed by successive landowners over the land of another. Examples are rights of way and rights of light. The right of support for buildings may also exist as an easement. It must be remembered that an easement is a private right and not one which may be exercised by any member of the public at large. Occasionally it is possible for an easement to exist as an equitable interest and in that case it should be registered in the normal way to bind a bona fide purchaser for value. Traditionally there are four essential aspects of a valid easement.

There must be a dominant and a servient tenement
This means simply that there must be a piece of land which benefits from the easement (the dominant tenement) and another parcel of land which has the burden of the interest over it (the servient tenement). In the normal course of events, the easement will pass with the land on any transfer of the dominant tenement.

The easement must accommodate the dominant tenement
The right must be to the advantage of the dominant tenement, thereby improving the utility of the land, or enhance some aspect of it. A personal right which does not benefit the land or a mere licence to use land will not constitute an easement. In *Hill* v. *Tupper* (1863) the right to let out boats on a canal for fishing purposes was deemed simply to be a personal right and was not beneficial to the land as such. Although the two properties must be near to each other, they need not necessarily be adjacent to each other.

The dominant and servient tenements must be owned by separate parties
The essence of an easement is that it operates as a right against the land of another. A person cannot have rights against himself. Where

a person habitually exercises rights over part of his own land, which if that part were occupied by another would be an easement, that is said to be a quasi-easement.

The easement must lie in grant

This combines a number of different factors. The parties to the easement must be capable of definition and have capacity while the right itself must be the subject of an actual grant. If the right is too vague, it will not constitute an easement.

Although rights of way, light and support are probably the most common forms of easements, all sorts of rights have been recognised as easements from time to time. The use of a letter box, the right to enjoy a park, an airfield, and to store casks on land have all been established as easements.

Method of acquisition

Apart from creation by statute, an easement must normally be acquired by *grant*. This may be done *expressly* by deed or, where the owner of two adjoining properties desires, he may reserve to himself an easement over the land sold. Sometimes a grant may be *implied*. Where a landowner sells part of his holding in land, the court will sometimes imply the grant of an easement or its reservation. This may come about under the rule in *Wheeldon* v. *Burrows* (1879) whereby any easements which are continuous, apparent and reasonably necessary for the enjoyment of the land will automatically pass to the purchaser. Such an easement will also be implied if it appears that the parties must clearly have intended from the circumstances of the case to create an easement.

Related to the intended easement is the easement of necessity. This is based on the concept of public policy that property should not be rendered unusable. The normal necessity will be a right of way to land but other examples include *Wong* v. *Beaumont Property Trust Ltd* (1965) where a ventilation duct for a Chinese restaurant was classified as an easement of necessity. Section 62 of the Law of Property Act 1925 is important in this context. By this section, all easements, rights and privileges automatically pass to a purchaser on the sale of land. This section is wider in scope than the rule in *Wheeldon* v. *Burrows*, and is not dependent upon the easement being continuous and apparent. Sometimes the easement is implied in favour of the grantor instead of the grantee.

Another method of creation of an easement is by *presumed grant* or *prescription*. The idea behind the concept is that where an interest is enjoyed over the servient land by long user and it is exercised as of right and not by permission from the servient owner, an easement may well come about. A presumed grant may come about on a common law basis if user can be shown since time immemorial. User since 1189 may be presumed if use of the property within living memory can be proved. This may be challenged if the use could not have possibly existed at some time since 1189.

Sometimes the courts will operate a legal fiction known as the *lost modern grant*. This presumes from use of at least 20 years that a grant has been made some time in the past but that it has been lost. This legal fiction revives the grant of the right by deed or charter.

More important in practice is acquisition under the Prescription Act 1832. By this act, 20 years' uninterrupted user as of right will create a valid easement unless it can be shown that the right was enjoyed by oral permission. After 40 years of uninterrupted use, the claim can only be defeated by showing that written permission was given. For both periods, the user must be *nec vi, nec clam, nec precario* and it must be 'next before' the claim. This means that the qualifying periods must run up to the time that the action is brought. Interruptions for less than one year are ignored.

Unless the easement is one of light, an easement can only be acquired by prescription by one fee simple owner against another freeholder. Easements of light have traditionally been subject to different rules. Here, there is only one period — 20 years' uninterrupted user. User need not be of right and oral consent or payment of money to exercise the right will not defeat the claim.

PROFITS A PRENDRE

This is an interest in land which gives a person the right to take some item from the land of another. Once it is taken, the item becomes a chattel. A right to cut and take timber or fish or fowl comes into this category. The right to take water from the land of another is not a profit although it may exist as an easement. Most of the rules relating to easements also apply to profits, but a dominant tenement is not essential to the existence of a profit while the profit need not be for the benefit of other land.

A profit *in gross* is one which exists even though it is unattached to any ownership of land, while a profit *appurtenant* is one which is attached to a dominant tenement. Another distinction is sometimes made between a *several* profit which is a right enjoyed by one person only to the exclusion of all others, and a profit *in common* which is one enjoyed by many people.

A profit, like an easement, may exist as a legal or equitable interest. The rules as to acquisition by prescription are similar but the time periods are different. Instead of the two periods of 20 and 40 years, the periods are 30 and 60 years. Profits and easements may be extinguished by release, statute or unity of seisin. The last occurs where both tenements pass into ownership of the same person. Sometimes the alteration of the dominant tenement will have the same effect.

RESTRICTIVE COVENANTS

A covenant is an agreement which may be positive or negative in nature. For example, the covenant may be to pay rent or not to allow premises to fall into disrepair. A restrictive covenant arises from an agreement by one person to restrict the use of his land in order to benefit other land. It is an equitable interest and cannot exist at common law. To bind a purchaser of land it should be registered as a land charge unless it is contained in a lease, in which case it is not capable of registration.

Examples of restrictive covenants are frequently to be found in conveyances of freeholds and in leases. Covenants to prevent a dwelling house being used for business purposes or the carrying out of an offensive trade are usual examples of this interest. A distinction has to be made between the covenantor who is agreeing not to use his land in a particular manner and the covenantee for whose benefit the covenant is entered into.

The extent to which a restrictive covenant is binding upon successors in title
The major problem with restrictive covenants is the extent to which they can be enforced by persons who were not original parties to the agreement. As essentially, a covenant is a contractual obligation, it is only enforceable at common law against the individual persons who agreed to be bound by it. To determine whether or not such a covenant can be enforced by a subsequent party, a distinction has to be made between the benefit and the burden of a covenant.

The burden
This means the obligation of having to adhere to the restrictive covenant. The rule here is that at common law, the burden of having

to adhere to the covenant cannot pass from the original covenantor. In equity, the burden of a covenant may 'run' or pass automatically with the ownership of the land provided that:

(a) it is negative in substance;
(b) it 'touches and concerns' the land;
(c) successors in title have notice of the covenant;
(d) the covenant benefits the land of the convenantee.

These rules are developed from the case of *Tulk* v. *Moxhay* (1848). In each case, it is the substance and not the form of the contract which must be regarded. In addition, the covenant must be intended to bind successors in title of the covenantor and it is commonplace when actually drafting covenants to state this intention. If there is evidence that the covenant is simply a personal one and does not benefit the dominant land, successors in title may well not be bound. To protect a restrictive covenant which affects freehold land it should be registered as a land charge to constitute statutory notice to any intending purchaser.

The benefit
Although the common law rule is that the benefit of a covenant can be assigned subject to normal contractual principles, the right to sue a successor in title of the original covenantor can only be passed on with the aid of equity. This normally may come about in one of three ways.

(a) annexation;
(b) assigning the benefit;
(c) building schemes.

Annexation depends upon the intention of the parties inferred from the language which is used in the deed creating the covenant. It is therefore a drafting matter and the intention to annex is expressly stated in the document. In the absence of annexation, an assignee of the covenantee's land may be able to bring an action for breach of covenant if he can show that he is an express assignee of the covenant itself. The assignee must obtain the benefit of the covenant at the same time as the land is conveyed to him. Recently, in *Federated Homes Ltd* v. *Mill Lodge Properties Ltd* (1980), annexation was deemed to have been effected under section 78 of the Law of

Property Act 1925 without the need for appropriate language in the conveyance of the covenantee's land. If this decision is correct, express assignment will not normally be necessary in the future to pass on the benefit of the covenant.

Where there is a building scheme, restrictive covenants may be enforced by one purchaser or his successors in title, against other purchasers or their successors in title. Such a scheme normally arises where a housing estate is sold in freehold plots to various purchasers. Each purchaser enters into similar covenants relating to the use of the land. Each covenant becomes mutually enforceable between the various purchasers and their successors in title so that each purchaser and his assignees can sue or be sued by every other purchaser and his assignees for a breach of restrictive covenant. The leading case on the topic is *Elliston* v. *Reacher* (1908) where the following rules were formulated as the conditions which must exist before the scheme becomes operative insofar as the benefit and burden of restrictive covenants can pass to successors in title:

(a) Both plaintiff and defendant must derive title from a common vendor.
(b) The estate must be laid out in a defined area.
(c) The restrictions must be intended by the vendor to be for the benefit of all the lots sold and the purchasers bought the plots on that basis.

Modification and discharge of restrictive covenants
Apart from being expressly released by the person entitled to the benefit of the covenant or unity of ownership of the two parcels of land, a person interested in the land may apply to the Lands Tribunal under section 84 of the Law of Property Act 1925 for total or partial discharge or removal of the covenant. The covenant must be attached to freehold land or to a lease originally granted for at least 40 years with 25 or more years unexpired. Application is made to the Lands Tribunal who have a discretion where appropriate. They may order compensation to be paid to any person entitled to the benefit of the covenant. There are four grounds upon which application may be made:

(a) A change has occurred in the character of the property or neighbourhood.
(b) The continuous existence of the restriction would impede some

reasonable use of the land.
(c) The parties involved have agreed expressly or impliedly to the removal.
(d) The proposed discharge or modification will not injure the persons entitled to the benefit of the restriction.

Current planning policies of the local authority should be taken into account.

MORTGAGES

Definition
A mortgage is traditionally defined as a transfer of an estate or interest in land in order to secure the payment of a debt. The borrower gives rights in property to the lender as security for a loan. The borrower is known as the mortgagor and the lender the mortgagee.

Legal and equitable mortgages
A legal mortgage is the transfer of a legal estate, or occasionally an interest, to act as security for the repayment of a loan.

An equitable mortgage arises where the borrower has no legal estate or interest but wishes to raise a loan. Such a mortgage simply creates an equitable interest.

Where a person is buying a freehold or leasehold estate with the aid of a mortgage given by a bank or building society, this will be a legal mortgage. In the case of default by the borrower, the lender will be able to enforce his security by entry on to the land which is mortgaged. Where a person simply requires a loan unconnected with the purchase of an interest in land he will normally have an equitable mortgage. In this case, the lender will only be able to sue for the money owed. He rarely has any rights against the land.

A legal mortgage is normally effected by means of a mortgage deed in which the mortgagor agrees to pay interest on the loan at a given rate and covenants with the mortgagee as to such matters as repair and insurance of the property. Nowadays, it is commonplace for mortgages to deal with periodic payments of capital as well as interest. The date specified in the mortgage deed on which the principal and interest will be repaid by the borrower is known as the legal or contractual date of redemption. This gives the borrower the right to redeem at law on the contractual date and a right in equity to redeem after that date has passed.

Creation of a legal mortgage

A mortgage of an estate in fee simple can be created by:

(a) a demise for a term of years absolute subject to a provision for cesser on redemption; or
(b) a charge expressed to be made by way of legal mortgage under section 85 of the Law of Property Act 1925.

The essence of the demise is that it operates as a transfer of the estate in land to the mortgagee until the borrower pays off the loan. It is now the normal practice to use a legal charge to effect a legal mortgage. The actual form of legal mortgage is short and simple, while it brings into existence a legal mortgage without the need for any transfer of the estate in land to the mortgagee. However, the legal mortgagee has similar rights and remedies to those he would possess if the legal estate had been transferred to him. Similar rules apply if the mortgage is of a leasehold although in the case of a demise a sub-lease must be granted for a period shorter than the lease.

Equitable mortgages

If the mortgagor has no legal estate or interest to mortgage, any mortgage which he effects must necessarily be equitable. Equitable mortgages sometimes come about where the lender is given the title deeds of the mortgagor's property to act as security for the repayment of the loan. Sometimes an equitable interest, such as a life interest, may be mortgaged. To be effective, such a mortgage must be in writing and signed by the borrower to comply with section 53 of the Law of Property Act 1925.

An equitable charge will also operate as an equitable mortgage. This is where the parties to a loan agree informally that property shall stand as security for a debt, but there is no transfer of ownership or possession. Where there is a written agreement which acknowledges a loan together with a promise to enter into a legal mortgage, an equitable mortgage is immediately created. When the appropriate deed is executed the agreement is converted into a legal mortgage. Unless the equitable mortgage is protected by a deposit of title deeds with the mortgagee any equitable mortgage ought to be registered as a land charge to bind a purchaser for value of the legal estate.

The equity of redemption
This is a proprietary interest in land and the parties to a mortgage cannot agree to prevent its exercise. Any agreement which 'clogs' the equity or makes it more difficult to redeem the mortgage will not be recognised by the courts if it is unreasonable. The mortgage deed will state the date of redemption. In practice, this will normally arise six months from the date of the loan so that the mortgagee's powers arise virtually immediately. The mortgagor has no right in law to redeem at any other time and therefore he will be relying upon his rights in equity. The right to redeem has certain characteristics attached to it by law.

State of property: The borrower must receive the property at the termination of the mortgage in the same state as he mortgaged it.

Redemption: A mortgage cannot be made totally irredeemable.

Postponement of the right to redeem: If not oppressive, an agreement to postpone the contractual date of redemption may be enforceable. The court will consider all factors including the relative bargaining powers of the parties, their legal status and the amount of loan involved. In *Knightsbridge Estates* v. *Bryne* (1939) a 40-year postponement of the right to redeem was valid where the mortgagor sought redemption because cheaper interest rates could be found elsewhere.

Collateral advantages: In some cases, the mortgagee may in addition to requiring repayment of the loan together with interest, contract in the mortgage for an additional benefit. Any agreement to confer this advantage will be upheld unless it is oppressive or violates the right to redeem.

Powers of the mortgagor and mortgagee
Both mortgagor and mortgagee have rights which arise automatically from the mortgage apart from those outlined in the mortgage deed. The borrower has an automatic right to enjoyment of the property, while, subject to any contrary provision in the mortgage where the loan has been made by deed, the mortgagor may grant agricultural or occupation leases not exceeding 50 years and building leases for not more than 999 years. Certain conditions must be met and any lease which does not fulfil these requirements will bind the mort-

gagor but not the mortgagee — that is, unless the lender is estopped from denying the existence of the lease by demanding rent to be paid to him or something similar. As the mortgagor is given powers to lease, he may also accept surrenders of leases unless there is shown to be contrary intention. A similar restriction may appear in a mortgage deed which prevents the mortgagor from compelling the mortgagee to allow the transfer of the mortgage to a third party. The mortgagor may inspect the title deeds to the property and make copies from them, while, if in possession or entitled to the receipts and profits from the property, he may bring actions on his own behalf.

A legal mortgagee of land has extensive rights. Apart from having the right to sue on the personal covenant for principal and interest owing, he has extensive rights against the land. The right to sell is important. The power itself arises when the contractual date of redemption has passed but it may only be exercised if interest and/or principal are in default or there has been a breach of some other covenant. Before the sale takes place, the mortgagee must obtain vacant possession while the sale may be by private treaty or by auction. There is a statutory obligation upon a building society mortgagee to obtain the best price reasonably obtainable while other lenders should also attempt to obtain the best market price. This may mean selling when the market is buoyant.

A more drastic measure is foreclosure. In that case, an account is directed to be taken of the monies due under the mortgage and a time is fixed for payment of the sum involved. If the money is not forthcoming at the date fixed the mortgagor will lose his equitable right to redeem. Where it appears to the mortgagee that in the long term the borrower will be viable enough to pay the loan but at the moment the mortgagor is in difficulties, the power to appoint a receiver may be exercised as long as the mortgagee is entitled to exercise his power of sale. This device is particularly useful in the case of a company borrower. The receiver may collect rents and exercise other management powers while there is an established order in which money which comes into the receiver's hands must be applied. Once a mortgage is entered into, the mortgagee has an immediate right to enter into possession. The main reason why a lender will not do this is that he must account for money which he has received on a strict basis. In any case, the County Court has wide powers to postpone an order for possession of a dwelling house where a defaulting borrower under an instalment mortgage is in arrears of payment and there is a reasonable chance of it being paid.

Further mortgages

It is possible to have more than one mortgage on a specific property. Subsequent mortgages can be of a legal variety or they may be equitable. There are a number of reasons why such a mortgage may be unsatisfactory. Normally, the first mortgagee will have the title deeds to the property, while the risks of tacking and consolidation are present.

Tacking arises where a subsequent mortgagee may insist on repayment of his loan before payment of a prior mortgage. Consolidation occurs where a mortgagee has more than one mortgage on different properties which are created by the same mortgagor. In such circumstances the lender may refuse to permit the redemption of one without the other if certain conditions are satisfied. If the first mortgagee forecloses, subsequent lenders are placed in a difficult position. The greatest problem for the later mortgagee however is that his only remedy in practice will be to sue for the money lent.

LAND CHARGES

This is governed by the Land Charges Act 1972. Because of the doctrine of the bona fide purchaser, the person entitled to the benefit of an equitable interest in land and any potential purchaser of land must respectively be able to protect and learn of the existence of any equitable interests affecting the legal estate. The object of this system is to provide a register of equitable interests together with certain legal interests so that interested parties can discover with relative ease the existence of an encumbrance. Registration under this system is the equivalent of actual notice. If proper registration takes place, any purchaser of the land will be bound by it. If the interest is not registered, it will fail to bind a purchaser for value of the land, even if the purchaser actually knew of its existence.

The register

The Land Charges Register is one of five registers of incumbrances kept by the Land Registry at Plymouth. There are also five classes of land charge which an intending purchaser should investigate. Of these, Classes C, D and F are of importance. These refer to such items as equitable charges and restrictive covenants. Class F was created by the Matrimonial Homes Act 1967 and it gives a spouse the right to occupy the matrimonial home where the other spouse is entitled to the complete beneficial interest in the property.

The practical effect of these rules is that an interested party must make a search in the Land Charges Register. This is a form of inquiry which is sent off to Plymouth. Alternatively, the applicant may visit the registry in person or inquire on the telephone. Preferably, an official certificate of search should be obtained as this is conclusive evidence. The search must be made against the name of the person who created the charge. If the interests are unregistrable, a purchaser has to rely on his own inquiries (or those of his legal advisers) by inspecting the vendor's legal title and the land itself.

Local authorities also keep registers dealing with matters such as planning restrictions and compulsory purchase orders. Such charges are registered against the land and nowadays failure to register a local land charge does not affect its enforceability.

LICENCES

A licence is a mere equity which confers no interest in land. It is simply a permission given by an occupier of land allowing the licensee to do some act which would otherwise constitute a trespass. Such a licence may be granted by word of mouth or in writing. In recent years, it has become increasingly important to determine whether a lease or a licence has been granted because the former will often give statutory protection as to security of tenure while the latter will not. As a licence is simply a personal agreement it can be revoked at any time and it cannot bind a third party. This is particularly the case as far as a bare licence is concerned. This is where no consideration has been given. Sometimes, a licence is coupled with an interest such as a profit. The right to fish and take away those caught would be an example. In this case, while the interest to which it is coupled continues, the licence will be irrevocable while a third party who was aware of its existence will be bound by it.

The principles of estoppel apply to licences. Therefore, where a party only has a licence to occupy, but the landowner has permitted or acquiesced in that person's use of the land, the licence may well become a proprietary interest which cannot be revoked by the licensor. It will also bind a third party. The ordinary contractual licence which exists where consideration has been given creates problems. At common law such a licence was revocable but in equity, it cannot be revoked for the time during which the parties intend it to exist. There are varying authorities as to whether such a licence will bind a third party.

8.6 The leasehold estate

This is the second legal estate capable of existing at law since 1925. Its technical name is the term of years absolute which implies that it is granted for a fixed period of time and that it will not cease to exist on the occurrence of some uncertain event which is not within the control of the parties. For a valid leasehold estate to exist, there must usually be:

(a) compliance with the required formalities;
(b) creation of the estate for a fixed period of time;
(c) the right to exclusive possession of the property let.

FORMALITIES

A lease must normally be created by deed (section 52 of the Law of Property Act 1925). As an exception, a lease for a term of three years or less, at the best rent reasonably obtainable without taking a fine, may be made orally or informally in writing. The rule only applies to the creation of a lease and not to an assignment of an existing term of years. A lease for more than three years which is not made by deed will pass only an equitable interest.

A long lease is often preceded by an agreement to create the lease. If this agreement contains sufficient evidence of the intention of the parties to create a lease, effect will be given to the agreement despite the absence of a deed. Even if there is a complete absence of a written agreement, the existence of a lease may be recognised if the court is certain that the parties desired to enter such an agreement. If possible the parties should enter into a formal deed as an agreement for a lease is only an equitable interest and not an estate in land.

FIXED PERIOD

At common law a lease must commence on a fixed date and terminate on a fixed date. This is not the only type of agreement which comes within the scope of a term of years absolute. Often, instead of having a fixed term of years there will be in existence a tenancy agreement. Such a periodic tenancy is described by reference to the period when rent is payable such as a weekly or monthly tenancy. The fixed term here is the period when rent is payable. The lease as such automatically repeats itself when the specified period runs out unless either party gives notice to quit to the other. If either landlord or tenant wishes to determine the tenancy by notice, at least one period of notice must be given. In the case of a yearly tenancy at least six months' notice must be given. Sometimes statute requires longer periods to be given. A weekly tenant of a dwelling house must be given at least 4 weeks' notice while in the case of a tenanted farm the period is 12 months. The periodic tenancy may arise expressly or by implication.

EXCLUSIVE POSSESSION
Although exclusive possession does not necessarily indicate the existence of a lease, the right of possession to the exclusion of the lessor is an essential element of a lease. This exclusive use is not lost because the landlord retains some right to visit the premises for rent or to view the state of repair. The test is one of intention as to whether the premises are being transferred for a period of time to the tenant or simply a personal right of occupation has been given.

COVENANTS IN LEASES
Modern day leases and tenancy agreements contain many covenants of positive and negative nature setting out with care the obligations of the relative parties. This is particularly the case if the landlord is a major institution such as a large property development company. It is still the case that many periodic tenancies, especially those of short duration are entered into on a less formal basis with little reference to the obligations of the parties other than to rent and description.

OBLIGATIONS IN THE ABSENCE OF EXPRESS COVENANTS
Where the agreement is silent except as to essential information such as length, parties, premises and rent, certain obligations are inferred into the lease. The landlord impliedly covenants that he will give the following.

Quiet enjoyment
The tenant is entitled to peaceful enjoyment of the premises without any interruption from the landlord or a person acting on his behalf.

Examples of breach of the covenant have included threats to the tenant and cutting off gas and electricity supplies. The tenant may recover damages if his quiet enjoyment is disturbed in a substantial way while the landlord may well be guilty of a criminal offence under the Protection from Eviction Act 1977.

Non-derogation from grant
This is related to quiet enjoyment. It arises when the landlord substantially interferes with the use of the demised premises in respect of the purpose for which they were let. Where a block of flats were obviously to be used for residential purposes there could be breach of this covenant if the greater part is subsequently let for business purposes.

Fitness
The common law position is that there is no implied covenant on the part of the landlord that the premises are fit for habitation or will be in the future. Certain exceptions to the rule arise, mainly by statute.

In the case of a furnished letting, there is an implied condition that the dwelling house will be reasonably fit for habitation at the commencement of the letting. Therefore if the drainage is defective or the house is infested with bugs as in *Smith* v. *Marrable* (1843) the tenant may repudiate the contract and recover damages. The Housing Acts of 1957 and 1961 also give some protection. The 1957 Act applies to houses at a low rent. In that case, there is an implied condition that the house is fit for human habitation at the commencement of the letting and that it will be kept so by the landlord during the tenancy.

The 1961 Act is more useful. This applies to leases of seven years or less. It implies a covenant by the landlord that he will keep the structure and exterior in good repair and that he will also have responsibility for other installations such as gas, electricity and sanitation matters. Regards must be had to the age and character of the dwelling and to the locality. Contracting out is not allowed.

The Defective Premises Act 1972
This has been mentioned before in connection with non-occupiers' liability (see under 7.5). It imposes an obligation upon those involved in the construction of a dwelling whether by initial erection or

conversion whereby they owe a duty of care to see that the work is carried out properly and that the property will be fit for habitation when completed. For the defects relating to this statute see Chapter 7.

Obligations of the tenant

As far as the tenant is concerned, he covenants that he will:

(a) pay rent;
(b) pay rates and taxes;
(c) not be liable for waste.

This means that the tenant must not alter the character of the land so as to diminish the landlord's reversion.

A tenant for a fixed term is liable for voluntary waste such as pulling down buildings or removing fixtures. Apart from these acts of a destructive nature, the fixed-term tenant may also be liable for permissive waste which arises from an act of omission such as failure to repair a building. A periodic tenant is liable for voluntary waste but the main obligation of weekly and yearly tenants is to keep the premises in a 'tenant-like' manner. This seems to indicate that the tenant must simply do such work as is necessary for his own reasonable enjoyment of the premises. Any tenant who commits wanton acts of destruction, known as equitable waste, will be restrained by injunction.

The 'usual covenant'

If a lease or tenancy agreement is said to be subject to the 'usual covenants', it is a question of fact which is dependent upon the circumstances of each case. It has been long established that certain covenants are always usual and these are similar to the implied covenants together with a covenant by the tenant to deliver up the premises in repair and to allow the lessor to enter and view the state of repair. Other considerations must also be taken into account such as trade usage, the character of the property and the practice in a particular neighbourhood. In *Chester* v. *Buckingham Travel Ltd* (1981) a right of re-entry for breach of any covenant was deemed to be usual in respect of a lease of a garage workshop in Chelsea.

EXPRESS COVENANTS

The vast majority of leases and tenancy agreements will be formally drafted. The type of agreement, i.e. business, residential or agricultural, will determine the variety of covenants entered into. In particular, the parties will agree the rent payable, how often and where it is to be paid, date of commencement of the term and its duration. Nowadays most agreements will also contain machinery for review of the rent at periodic intervals. The various liabilities which arise in connection with ownership such as rates, repairs, insurance and similar regulatory matters tend to be dealt with by express provision.

Covenant to pay rent

The rule is that rent is payable in arrears unless the agreement expressly refers to payment in advance, as it frequently does. Unless the agreement provides otherwise, payment of rent continues even in the event of destruction by fire or some similar calamity. In the event of default, the landlord has the option of bringing an action for arrears in which case up to six years' arrears are recoverable or, in the case of a tenanted farm, one year's.

Where this is inappropriate the landlord may levy distress through the County Court. This is the right to take property from the tenant's possession in order to satisfy any debt owing to the lessor. The court bailiff will seize chattels found on the premises to satisfy the sum owing. The goods are sold by auction while the tenant is given the option of paying off the arrears.

If the agreement gives the landlord the right to re-enter the land on non-payment or rent, the lease may be forfeited. Unless equity grants relief, the tenant will lose his rights under the lease.

Covenant to repair

Either of the parties to the agreement may be liable for repair of the demised premises. Alternatively, there may be an apportionment between them of obligations. It is sometimes said that after making allowances for the age, character and locality of the premises, the covenantor must maintain the premises as they would be kept by a reasonably-minded owner taking all these matters into account.

Repair does not mean improvement or reconstruction. The tenant is under an obligation to deliver up the premises to the landlord in substantially the same condition as they were let. Hence the lessee is under no obligation to install new foundations in an old house, although recently it has been decided that the underpinning of foundations of a newly-built restaurant in a hotel complex were deemed to be repair work.

The covenant to repair is often qualified by the words 'fair (or reasonable) wear and tear excepted'. The rule is that a tenant is not liable for damage resulting from reasonable use of the property. The landlord may commence proceedings for damages or where appropriate for forfeiture. There is a rule which says that the amount of damages payable must not exceed the sum by which the value of the reversion has diminished.

Covenant against assignment and sub-letting

Unless there is a prohibition in the lease, a tenant may assign or sub-let as he so wishes without obtaining the landlord's consent. Therefore it is commonplace in a lease for a landlord to include provisions limiting the right of the tenant to part with the estate or to sub-let. Such covenants are normally in absolute or qualified form. An absolute prohibition prevents any assignment in express terms. If the covenant is a qualified one which prevents assignment without written permission, certain provisions are implied by statute. The consent to the assignment must 'not be unreasonably withheld' while no fine or similar sum of money shall be payable for the giving of the consent unless there is an express provision in the lease to that effect. If an assignment takes place in breach, the transfer will be valid but it will normally give rise to a claim for damages or forfeiture against the assignor.

SECURITY OF TENURE

At common law, a lease starts on a fixed day and terminates on a fixed date, while a periodic tenancy will repeat itself until either party to the agreement gives due notice to the other. Sometimes these provisions are purely academic because a number of statutory provisions assist tenants of agricultural, business and residential properties by giving them the right to remain in possession of the demised premises after the original agreement has ended. Many of these provisions are of necessity complicated and are outside the scope of this book.

The usual condition precedent for protection is to be a tenant. Apart from licensees who work on a farm and live in accommodation tied to the farm, this requirement must be satisfied. Tenant farmers, at the moment, have the right to transfer their holding to an 'eligible person' on death, while in those cases where the tenant quits his farm after notice to treat by the landlord he may claim compensation for disturbance. Tenants of business and professional premises are entitled to apply to the court for a new tenancy when their original agreements come to an end. As long as the appropriate time limits are adhered to and certain grounds of opposition are not satisfied, the court may grant a new lease of up to 14 years' duration.

Both public and private sector residential tenants may be entitled to a varying degree of protection relating to security of tenure and rent payable. The Housing Act 1980 gives public sector tenants the right to buy their houses, while the Leasehold Reform Act 1967 allows certain tenants holding under long leases at low rents and occupying their houses as residences, either to purchase the freehold or extend their leases for a further period up to 50 years.

8.7 Agreements for the sale of land and the granting of leases

Before a freehold can be conveyed or a lease granted, a formal deed must be made (section 52.3 of the Law of Property Act 1925). Sometimes a prior agreement or a contract to sell the land is made. Occasionally the courts are prepared to grant specific performance to a plaintiff should he seek performance of the contract. This can only be done if section 40 of the Law of Property Act 1925 is complied with. This states that 'a contract for the sale or other disposition of land or any interest in land is unenforceable unless in writing or evidenced by a written note or memorandum signed by the party to be charged or by his duly authorised agent'.

THE MEMORANDUM
The following must be satisfied before there can be compliance with section 40. The agreement must contain:

(a) the names of the parties or their description;
(b) description of the property;
(c) price or rent;
(d) the terms of the sale;
(e) the signature of the party to be charged or his agent. This could mean the vendor or the purchaser. Alternatively it could be his solicitor or estate agent.

Therefore, the memorandum must evidence the agreement and set out its terms. It may consist of several documents. If the section is not complied with, the contract is unenforceable, but it is not void.

Part performance
Where there is non-compliance with section 40 but an act of part performance has followed an oral agreement, equity will not allow 'a statute to be used as a cloak to a fraud'. Therefore, an action for specific performance of the agreement may be brought. The act of part performance must satisfy three conditions:

It must be exclusively referable to a contract such as that alleged: In *Rawlinson* v. *Ames* (1925), parties entered into an oral contract to grant a lease subject to certain alterations being made. After these works were executed, the tenant refused to take up the agreement. The court decided that a valid contract was in existence and ordered specific performance. At one time, payment of money on its own would not amount to part performance but this proposition has now been rejected by the House of Lords.

The act must not be simply introductory: Therefore, the act must be in furtherance of the alleged agreement not simply an administrative act or one which is ancillary to the contract. Making a valuation or measuring land would be introductory. Taking possession of the land would be consistent with the alleged agreement.

Fraud: It must be such that it would render it a fraud to rely upon the statute.

CONVEYANCING
This is the process of transferring land from one person to another. Freeholds are conveyed while leaseholds are assigned. At this moment in time there are two methods of conveyancing:

(a) The traditional method where the title to the land is unregistered.
(b) Registered title conveyancing where the state guarantees proof of ownership of the land in question.

Some 70 per cent of the population of England and Wales is now covered by the system of registration of title. Once an area becomes one of 'compulsory registration', application for first registration must be made after the first conveyance or grant of an appropriate lease takes place in respect of a property in that area. The other 30 per cent of the country, mainly in rural areas, is subject to the older procedures of having to investigate the title to the land. If a person wishes to find out whether or not the title to an individual property has been registered, he can make application to the Land Registry at Plymouth for a search in the parcels index. This will provide the appropriate information.

CO-OWNERSHIP

Where one beneficial owner of land transfers his estate to another, no problem of joint ownership arises. More commonly, land is shared by a number of persons. Two types of joint ownership are recognised by the law:

(a) the joint tenancy;
(b) the tenancy in common.

The essence of a joint tenancy is that each co-owner owns all the estate of the land in question. They are considered by the law to be one person although the joint tenants amongst themselves have separate rights. The predominant characteristic of the joint tenancy is the right of survivorship. This means that on death the property will automatically pass to the surviving joint tenant. In addition, the joint tenants have the same interest and title to land at the same time. Possession of the land is vested in all the joint tenants.

The tenancy in common can only be an equitable interest in land. In this case, the shares in the land are not necessarily equal and there is no right of survivorship. Each tenant in common is entitled to a share of the whole and the tenant can leave his share by will when he dies. There is no right of survivorship.

UNREGISTERED TITLE CONVEYANCING

Pre-contract

Once there is an agreed transaction, the appropriate procedural steps have to be carried out on behalf of vendor and purchaser. It is the job of the vendor to prepare a contract from the information contained in the title deeds to the property and also from the conditions of the proposed sale. While this is being done, the purchaser must make various investigations and enquiries relating to the property. These include the following:

(a) local lands charges search;
(b) local authority enquiries;
(c) enquiries before contract;
(d) mining search;
(e) Commons Registration Act search.

Contract

The normal practice is for the vendor (or more likely his solicitor) to prepare the contract in duplicate. It must be remembered that it is not necessary to have a formal contract to have an enforceable agreement for the sale of land. As long as there is compliance with section 40 of the Law of Property Act or a sufficient act of part performance, there may well be a valid contract. Because of this state of affairs, it is common practice to head all correspondence 'subject to contract'. This prevents any binding contract coming into existence until there is a formal exchange.

For the purchaser it is necessary to ensure that the vendor has the right to sell the land which he is purporting to sell. Hence the need for the purchaser to investigate the vendor's title to the land. There is a binding contract from the date when the vendor sends his part contract duly signed to the purchaser.

The conveyance

As soon as an enforceable contract is made, the beneficial ownership in the property passes to the purchaser. Before the formal conveyance is handed over to the purchaser with the other title deeds, the purchaser will raise requisitions on title which are inquiries to the vendor relating to the property and in particular the appropriate completion date. An official land charges search should be made before completion to check the existence of any encumbrances.

REGISTERED TITLE CONVEYANCING

The object of registering the title to the land is to simplify the method of conveyancing. The Land Registration Act 1925 introduced a system whereby gradually a detailed record would exist of every dealing with land in England and Wales. In such a case there is no need to investigate the title as the state guarantees that it is correct. One document known as the Land Certificate takes the place of the title deeds. Instead of a formal conveyance a short form of transfer will suffice.

Chapter 9

Industrial and business law

9.1 Sale of goods

In addition to considering the methods by which land may be transferred, it is also necessary to look at similar rules in respect of personal property. The law relating to the sale of goods is essentially contractual in nature. Therefore, all the essentials of a valid contract such as consideration and the intention to create legal relations must be present. Also, the vitiating factors such as mistake and misrepresentation may well affect the validity of the contract. In assessing damages for breach of a contract for the sale of goods the usual rules as to remoteness and the classification of damages will apply. The Sale of Goods Act 1893 codified the common law. The act does not make a contract, but instead defines the obligations of the parties.

The current act is the Sale of Goods Act 1979. The law was developed in the nineteenth century, firmly based on the concept of *caveat emptor* ('let the buyer beware') and equality of bargaining power between the parties. These presumptions are unrealistic in contemporary society, especially with the growth of the use of standard forms of contract. To a certain extent, recent legislation restricting the use of exclusion clauses and implying terms automatically into 'consumer' contracts has made the legal position of the parties more equitable.

TERMINOLOGY

A contract for the sale of goods is one whereby the seller transfers or agrees to transfer the property in goods to the buyer for a money consideration called the price. 'Goods' includes all personal chattels other than money and choses in action (see Real and personal property, Chapter 8.1). The definition has been held to include a ship and a coin sold as a curio.

A distinction is made between specific goods, which are those identified and agreed upon at the time the contract is made, and unascertained goods which are defined only by a description applicable to all goods of that type.

Another major distinction is between a sale of goods and an agreement to sell goods. Where the property passes immediately under the contract, it is a sale of goods. Where it passes at some future date or when some condition is fulfilled, the transaction is known as an agreement to sell.

For there to be a contract for the sale of goods the price must be in money. This may be fixed in the contract, left to be fixed in the manner agreed therein, or determined by the course of dealing between the parties.

IMPLIED TERMS

The Sales of Goods Act 1979 implies terms into contracts for the sale of goods.

Title (section 12)

In every contract for the sale of goods there is an implied condition on the part of the seller that he has a right to sell the goods or that he will have the right at the time when the property is to pass. If this condition is broken, the buyer may treat the contract as at an end, even though he has done some act which would otherwise have amounted to acceptance.

Description (section 13)

Where there is a contract for the sale of goods by description, there is an implied condition that the goods shall correspond with the description. The vast majority of sales will be by description. It will cover every situation where the buyer has not seen the goods but is relying on the description alone. It will also cover specific goods which the buyer has seen if they correspond to a description. If the goods are exposed for sale and selected by a buyer, this will be a sale by description. The section also extends to matters such as measurements, quantity and methods of packing.

Merchantable quality (section 14)

This section only applies where goods are sold in the course of business. In such a case, there is an implied condition of merchantable quality except as regards defects specifically drawn to the buyer's attention before the contract is made, or where the buyer examines the goods before the contract, as regards defects which the examination ought to reveal. 'Merchantable quality' means that the goods are fit for the purpose for which goods of that type are normally bought as is reasonable to expect having regard to description, price and other relevant circumstances. The goods must remain merchantable for a reasonable time.

The condition of fitness (section 14)

There is an implied condition where the seller sells goods in the course of a business, that the goods are reasonably fit for any purpose which the buyer makes known to the seller. This purpose will usually be implied, especially where goods have only one purpose and that is the reason the particular item is required. If goods have a number of purposes the buyer must indicate the one for which he requires them. If it appears from the contract that the buyer does not rely upon the seller's skill or judgement or it is unreasonable for him to do so, the section will not apply.

Many contracts in the building industry are for work done and materials supplied instead of being purely for the sale of goods. It has been decided on a number of occasions that a person contracting to do work and to supply materials warrants that the materials will be of good quality and reasonably fit for the purpose for which they are to be used, unless the circumstances of the contract are such as to exclude any such warranty. In *Young & Marten Ltd* v. *McManus Childs Ltd* (1968) the problem arose as to whether under a contract to supply and fix roofing tiles described under a brand name (Somerset 13) the suppliers were liable for damages in respect of latent defects which, in effect, made the tiles useless. These tiles were obtainable from one manufacturer only. It was decided that the suppliers were liable in damages on the basis of an implied warranty of quality of the tiles and the fact that the tiles were only obtainable from one manufacturer was not sufficient to exclude the implied term.

However, in *Gloucestershire County Council* v. *Richardson* (1968) any warranty by the contractor relating to quality or fitness was excluded where design, materials, quality and price of prestressed concrete columns were fixed by the employer and nominated suppliers without reference to the contractor. Similar principles were applied in *Test Valley Borough Council* v. *Greater London Council* (1979), where substantial defects appeared in overspill dwellings forming part of a town development scheme, and in *IBA* v. *EMI & BICC* (1980), where a television mast collapsed.

Sale by sample
Certain items such as carpets and wallpaper, are often bought on the basis of a sample inspected before the sale takes place. A contract is made by sample where there is an express or implied term to that effect. In such a case, the following conditions are implied:

(a) that the bulk will correspond with the sample in quality;
(b) that the buyer shall have a reasonable opportunity of comparing the bulk with the sample;
(c) that the goods shall be free from any defect, rendering them unmerchantable, which would not be apparent on reasonable examination of the sample.

Stipulations as to time are dealt with by section 10 of the 1979 Act. This enacts that, unless a different intention appears from the terms of the contract, time of payment is not of the essence in a contract for the sale of goods. Stipulations as to time of delivery are normally of the essence in commercial transactions.

EXCLUSION OF THE IMPLIED TERMS
The extent to which sections 12-15 of the Sale of Goods Act 1979 can be excluded depends upon the Unfair Contract Terms Act 1977 (UCTA). Any of the terms implied by the act may be excluded or varied by the contract subject to UCTA. The act states that any clause purporting to exclude section 12 (title) is void. In a consumer sale any term excluding sections 13, 14 or 15 (description, quality, fitness and sample) shall also be void. A consumer sale arises where:

(a) the seller is making a sale in the course of business;
(b) the goods are of a type ordinarily bought for private use or consumption;
(c) the buyer does not purchase the goods in the course of a business.

In a non-consumer sale, made in the course of business, a seller may exclude his liability under sections 13-15 if he can show that it is fair and reasonable for him to do so. The majority of sales in the construction industry will be non-consumer sales. The act gives guidelines as to factors to be taken into account when applying this reasonableness test. They are as follows:

(a) the relative strength of the bargaining position of the parties taking into account the availability of suitable alternative products and sources of supply;
(b) whether the buyer received an inducement to agree to the term;
(c) whether the buyer knew or ought reasonably to have known of the existence and extent of the term;
(d) the extent to which the goods were manufactured, processed or adapted to the special order of the buyer.

An auction sale or a sale by tender is not a consumer sale, so if a private buyer buys at an auction, an exclusion clause may be valid subject to the reasonableness test. It is presumed that a sale is a consumer sale, but once the seller has proved it is a non-consumer sale, it seems that it is for the buyer to show that it would not be fair and reasonable to rely on the term.

REMEDIES

The seller
A seller of goods may have personal rights against the buyer or if he is unpaid he may also have rights against the goods. If the goods have been delivered to the buyer and he refuses to pay, the seller may bring an action for the price of the goods. Where the buyer wrongfully refuses or neglects to pay for the goods, the seller may maintain an action for damages for non-acceptance. A seller also has rights over the goods where he remains unpaid. If the goods are still in the seller's possession he may exercise a lien over the goods. This means that he has a right to withhold delivery until he is paid. Such a right depends upon having possession of the goods and will not apply if the buyer has been given credit unless the credit term has expired. Those actually in possession of building materials may have a lien over them until duly paid, just as an architect has a lien over plans and documents which he has prepared until he receives his fees. The unpaid seller's lien is a lien for the price only and where the price has been paid it does not enable him to retain possession of the goods for any other purpose.

Also, the act provides a means whereby possession once lost may be regained. After the seller has parted with possession of the goods to a carrier for transmission to the buyer he can stop the goods in transit and retake possession. This power exists even though any credit given has not expired. The right which is known as *stoppage in transit* only applies if the buyer has become insolvent. Stoppage does not rescind the contract of sale, but merely restores possession of the goods to the seller. The seller has no rights to resell the goods except where:

(a) the goods are of a perishable nature;
(b) the seller gives notice to the buyer of his intention to resell and the buyer does not pay or tender the price within a reasonable time;
(c) the right of resale is expressly reserved.

The buyer
Where appropriate, the buyer may bring an action for damages for non-delivery. This will arise where the seller wrongfully neglects or refuses to deliver the goods. If the buyer suffers no loss or harm, damages will be nominal. Sub-contracts are generally disregarded unless the court considers that when the contract was made, both parties considered the possibility of sub-sales. This is frequently the case in the construction industry. Where appropriate, the buyer may bring an action for breach of warranty. Exceptionally, if the object is unique, specific performance of the contract may be ordered. Special damages (the second limb of *Hadley* v. *Baxendale* (1854)) may also be claimed.

9.2 Contracts for the supply of services

A contract for the sale of goods must be distinguished from a contract for services. The distinction is important because a sale of goods is governed by the Sale of Goods Act 1979, while contracts for services are not. The distinction has led to much litigation in the past because situations may arise where it is difficult to ascertain whether the essence of the contract is the passing of the goods or the actual supply of services. Contracts involving the installation of new appliances or of building materials seem likely to come into the second category. Recently the Supply of Goods and Services Act 1982 was enacted which codified all the previous common law obligations and implied terms into contracts for services in a similar manner to those implied into contracts for the sale of goods.

CARE AND SKILL

The provider of the services must carry them out with reasonable skill and care. As usual, what is reasonable will depend upon the circumstances of the case. As in the case of the provisions relating to quality and fitness in contracts for the sale of goods, the term will only apply where the supplier of the services is acting in the course of a business.

TIME FOR PERFORMANCE

One complaint frequently made against those who supply services is the delay in performance of such contracts. Where no completion date is fixed, the implied term requires the works to be carried out within a reasonable time. Again, what is reasonable will depend upon the circumstances of each case and primarily it will be a question of fact.

CONSIDERATION

In an attempt to discourage extortionate bills, the act provides that where no price has been fixed for the services, the customer shall pay a reasonable price. The section only applies where no price has been fixed at the outset.

If the contract is essentially for the supply of services but also includes the supply of materials, implied terms similar to those in sections 12-15 of the Sale of Goods Act are to be implied into the contract.

The act does not indicate whether the terms implied by the 1982 Act are conditions or warranties. That would seem to be a matter of degree depending upon the circumstances.

9.3 Debts

Where a person fails to pay a sum of money which he owes to another, he has incurred a debt. Often the debt will have arisen through a breach of contract or the claim may represent damages awarded to a successful plaintiff which have been left unpaid. Where a debtor refuses to pay, the creditor may commence proceedings in the appropriate court. This ought to be preceded by a pre-action letter threatening action in the event of default as many individuals and businesses with the ability to pay often wait until litigation is imminent or even later before responding to pressure to pay. If a debtor fails to respond to a request for payment, the creditor may start proceedings in the appropriate court.

The vast majority of actions are commenced in the County Court by filing the particulars of the claim and the events giving rise to the action. Claims involving less than £5,000 will be heard in this court. If the sum owed exceeds £5,000 or the matter involves a difficult point of law, the case will be heard in the High Court in which case proceedings are commenced by the issue of a formal writ telling the defendant that a claim has been made against him. If the court is satisfied that the plaintiff's claim has been substantiated it will enter a *judgment* against the defendant. This means that the court has formally decided and pronounced that the debt is owing.

ENFORCING THE JUDGMENT

Writ of execution
The idea behind this procedure is to authorise a bailiff attached to the court to enter the debtor's premises to seize goods of sufficient value to satisfy the judgment debt. This procedure is applicable in both the High Court and the County Court. Threat of such action will frequently result in payment. The writ is issued for the sum owing together with the bailiff's charges and the costs which arise from the sale of the goods. Certain items such as clothing, bedding and the tools of any trade are excluded from the items which may be taken.

Garnishee proceedings
These are proceedings which enable a judgment creditor to have assigned to him the benefit of any debt owed by a garnishee to the debtor under a judgment. The third party (known as the garnishee) who owes money to the debtor must pay that debt to the judgment creditor. Banks are regular targets for this procedure but Post Office savings and building society accounts are exempt. An order nisi is made and unless the debt is successfully disputed the order is made absolute. Garnishee proceedings is one of several methods of enforcing a money judgment via the courts and it is the method most likely to be met with upon the insolvency of a building contractor.

If creditors of an insolvent contractor attempt to recoup their potential losses by means of a garnishee order, the matter should be placed in the hands of the appropriate legal advisers.

Attachment of earnings

Of major importance, providing the defendant is employed, is the method of attaching earnings. Although the order is made only by the County Court, it can be applied to High Court judgments. The plaintiff must apply to the County Court in the area where the defendant lives for the appropriate order. The court inquires into the defendant's income and commitments and contacts his employers to verify the information. At the hearing, the registrar will make an appropriate order after taking the information he has into account. The order will require the employers to deduct a certain sum from the defendant's earnings each week until the debt is satisfied. The order must state a 'protected earnings level' under which the defendant's income must not be allowed to fall.

Judgment summons

This is a method of inquiry into the defendant's means. It arises where there has been non-compliance with a court judgment and the creditor wishes to obtain a full examination into the means of the debtor. If it considers it appropriate, the court will order payments to be made at stated intervals. There is power to commit a judgment debtor to prison but it is used in very limited circumstances.

Insolvency

In the last few years, insolvency has become a frequent occurrence in the building industry. Insolvency is considered to arise where an individual or a company is unable to meet its liabilities as and when they become due. In the case of individuals or partnerships this may involve the legal concept of bankruptcy in which case the procedures involved under the Bankruptcy Act 1914 will apply. In the context of companies the matter is dealt with by the Companies Acts 1948-81. However, the term does not mean necessarily that the debtor has virtually no assets, nor that the creditors will not receive payment in full. Fluctuations in the demand for building works may create a 'cash flow' problem while the structure of the building industry, including as it does so many small and medium-size firms, is an important factor to take into account. Even nowadays a relatively small amount of capital is needed to set up a company without any limitations on trading while high interest rates and restrictions on credit may dry up demand and leave large sums outstanding on credit.

Insolvency and the law

There are usually indications of financial and liquidity problems before the state of insolvency is reached. A slow-down in the progress of building works, decrease in the labour force and reduction in the amount of materials on site are all significant factors. An even clearer indication is that nominated sub-contractors are not being paid the sums due to them. Most building contracts are concerned with companies and there are relatively few insolvencies of main contractors to which the bankruptcy acts will apply. However, where appropriate the procedure is as follows.

Bankruptcy

The purpose of bankruptcy law is to free an unfortunate debtor from his financial position, impose sanctions upon a dishonest debtor and as far as possible to secure a fair distribution of property amongst creditors.

Acts of bankruptcy

These are the grounds upon which the creditors, or even the debtor himself, may present a petition for the making of a receiving order against him. The 10 available acts of bankruptcy are all indications of the debtor's weak financial position.

Stages in the bankruptcy process

The petition: The creditor has three months after the commission of an act of bankruptcy to present a petition before the court inviting it to make a receiving order against the debtor. At least £200 must be owing. Credit must be given for the value of any security which is held. A copy of the petition will be served upon the debtor and a date fixed for the hearing of the petition. If satisfied that an act of bankruptcy has taken place the court will make a receiving order.

The receiving order: This prevents any action being taken against the estate without leave of the court. The order makes the official receiver custodian of the debtor's property. The order prevents the debtor from disposing of his possessions.

Statement of affairs: The debtor must provide the official receiver with this information within seven days of the receiving order.

Meeting of creditors: At the first meeting, the creditors will normally appoint a trustee in bankruptcy who is given responsibility for the payment of debts and the overall management of the bankruptcy. At such a meeting, the creditors may agree to ask the court to adjudicate the debtor bankrupt.

The public examination: This is a personal investigation, held in court, into the debtor's financial affairs which is taken on oath. The main purpose of the examination is to enquire into the cause of the debtor's financial failure.

The adjudication order: This is the order which actually makes the debtor bankrupt. Subject to certain exceptions, any property of the debtor becomes vested in the trustee in bankruptcy and the bankrupt's property can be dealt with for the benefit of the creditors. The debtor is now recognised as an undischarged bankrupt, in which case he cannot act as a company director and he commits an offence if he obtains credit without disclosing his bankruptcy. The undischarged bankrupt may at any time apply to the court for a discharge and if successful the bankrupt will be restored to his former status.

Liquidation (For Companies see Types of business associations, 9.5: If insolvency results in liquidation, the Companies Acts 1948-81 will apply. Liquidation is a process whereby the life of a company is ended and its property is administered for the benefit of its creditors and members. There are two main types of liquidation, compulsory, under an order of the court or voluntary, under a resolution of the company. Normally, the former occurs where the directors and those in control do not want the company to be liquidated whereas the latter occurs when they do. A liquidator may be appointed either by the court or by the company. His main task is to take control of the company, collect its assets, pay its debts and finally to distribute any surplus which remains amongst the members in accordance with their rights. If the liquidation is a compulsory winding up, the official receiver becomes provisional liquidator until the creditors' meeting when either the appointment will be confirmed or another person appointed. Clause 27.2 of JCT 80 provides that the employment of the contractor shall be automatically determined in the event of the contractor becoming bankrupt or on the making of a winding up order. The contractor's employment may be reinstated by agreement between the employer, the contractor and his liquidator.

Receivership: The fact that a company is having difficulty meeting its financial commitments does not necessarily mean that it will be wound up. Apart from issuing shares, a company may raise finance by borrowing. This is frequently done by the company giving its creditors debentures to show that they have lent money to the concern. A debenture is a type of document which acknowledges the indebtedness on the part of the company to the debenture holders. Normally, the debenture is secured by a charge over the property. This charge is fixed if it relates to a particular asset. If the assets which are charged are varied from time to time the charge is said to be floating. If the debenture holders consider that the security against their debentures is in jeopardy they may appoint a receiver through provisions in the document or through the courts. His function is simply to get in the assets charged, to collect the rents and profits, exercise powers of realisation and pay the net proceeds to the holders of the debentures. As such, the receiver has no powers to administer the affairs of the business. Consequently, he is invariably appointed manager as well as receiver by the terms of the document. This is the person with whom the quantity surveyor will deal if a building contractor becomes insolvent. For all practical purposes, he will replace the board of directors as on a winding up but he is not liable for those contracts entered into by the company even if he oversees their performance. If he enters new contracts for the purpose of the receivership he and the company will be personally liable thereon unless the contract provides otherwise. He has a right to be indemnified out of the assets.

A major problem which arises on insolvency in the construction industry is completion of the works outstanding. Reinstatement is one such method. In this case, there may be an assignment to another company of the use of the insolvent company's employees. An assignment is a method of transferring rights under a contract to a third party. The receiver/manager or liquidator must obtain the consent of the employer before the assignment. A novation is usually preferred to an assignment. The idea is that the rights and liabilities of the original contractor are transferred to a successor contractor under a deed of novation which the employer must sign. A novation brings into existence a new contract. The insolvent contractor releases his liabilities under the agreement while the new contractor becomes liable to complete the works outstanding for the appropriate part of the contract price which remains unpaid.

Companies
One relative luxury, which is rarely granted to professional men and women, is the right to form a company with limited liability. A registered company is a corporation: that is, a separate legal person distinct from its members. Consequently, the debts and contracts of a company are those of the company and not of its members. The vast majority of companies are limited in liability whereby members restrict the amount which they will have to contribute in the event of the company ceasing to trade. Occasionally an unlimited company is registered, in which case there is no limitation on the members' liability for the debts of the company. Such companies are not common and the major reason for such a course of action is that the unlimited company need not forward its reports and accounts to the registrar of companies. It may well be of interest to civil engineers and architects that companies for whom they are executing works are not subject to limited liability.

Although the formalities involved in the registration of a company are far more extensive than in the case of other forms of business association, the costs of formation only become excessive if a private company becomes a public company and invites members of the public to take shares in the company. One advantage which attaches to companies is that of perpetual succession. When a shareholder dies or retires, the company is not dissolved and no drain is made on its resources or the resources of other members. The property of the company belongs to it as such, so there is no need for any formal transfer of company property.

Traditionally, there have been severe limitations on the rights of professional persons to form limited liability companies. This has been the case particularly in those professions which handle large sums of money. Architects and chartered surveyors may now obtain dispensation from their professional bodies to form limited companies if certain conditions are complied with. These relate to a minimum paid-up share capital and professional indemnity insurance.

Directors are appointed by members to manage the affairs of the company on their behalf. Unlike a partnership, which usually conducts its affairs through its partners, members of a registered company are not agents of the company and have no powers to manage its affairs. This remains in the hands of the directors. However, shares in a company can easily be transferred or mortgaged by a member while in the case of a partnership there are severe restrictions upon a partner transferring his equity in the firm. Incorporation is becoming an attractive proposition to those in the professions who will be seeking to take advantage of this status where possible.

9.4 Insurance

Insurance is a familiar characteristic of contemporary life. Policies taken out cover a wide variety of risks. Apart from the well-known compulsory motor insurance scheme, and life and endowment policies, contracts of insurance covering damage and contents to property are a necessary precaution for the private individual. The business and professional world also has to consider liability insurance. This may be a professional negligence policy or an employer's policy covering his vicarious liability to a third party and his personal liability to his employees.

A contract of insurance is one whereby a person or company (the insurer) agrees in return for a premium to pay a sum of money to another person or company (the insured) on the happening of a certain event, or to indemnify the insured against any loss caused by the risk insured against.

A contract of insurance is one of the *utmost good faith* (*uberrimae fidei*). Consequently there is a duty upon the insured to disclose all material facts known to him when applying for renewal of the contract. In the event of non-disclosure, the insurer may avoid liability.

Unlike a wager, an insurance contract is made to guard against the consequences of a loss. Therefore, there must be an insurable interest protected by the policy. All this means is that the insured must have some interest to be protected at the time of the loss. If there is no such interest there is nothing to indemnify.

9.5 Types of business associations

There are a number of types of business organisations in this country whereby a professional person or tradesman may carry out his work. An individual frequently starts his business life by working for others. If he has some success he may be faced with the problem of deciding whether to become a sole practitioner, form a partnership with others or create a limited liability company. Much depends upon the type of profession or business, the degree of specialisation required, professional rules and regulations and the availability of or access to finance.

THE SOLE TRADER/PRACTITIONER
Such a person is liable for all his own actions. He makes the decisions and is fully responsible for any losses which he may incur. In the event of bankruptcy all the trader's property including his dwelling house may be included in the proceedings. On the other hand, any profits which are made belong entirely to the sole agent subject to taxation. No problems arise as to the use of capital and distribution of income.

Formalities are straightforward. In most cases they are virtually non-existent but certain professional bodies do not allow sole practitioners to operate completely freely. Certain professions regulate to an extent the geographical location of their members, while others only allow their members to operate as sole practitioners. The Bar is the paramount example of this. Sometimes a person may only practise on his own account if he has been admitted to his profession for a number of years.

Unless a practitioner is fortunate enough to fill a particular niche he may find it difficult to specialise in a particular area of work. Another problem which arises is future planning of the business. This may be difficult to organise because of a lack of perpetual succession. Finance is another consideration. Often the only method of raising money is by taking out further mortgages on domestic property. Insurance cover is also relevant. Premiums are often weighed heavily against the sole practitioner as the professional bodies concerned consider that lack of supervision can lead to mistakes being made and an easier misappropriation of clients' money.

PARTNERSHIPS
A partnership or firm is an unincorporated body with a common

objective. At the moment this is the way most construction and surveying professionals practise. It is defined as the relationship which subsists between persons carrying on a business in common with a view to profit. There are few formalities to be observed where a firm commences in business. Although there is no requirement to have a partnership agreement, for practical reasons it is better to have one. The agreement may be entered into for a fixed period of time or indefinitely. In the latter case, it is known as a partnership at will. Partners may normally choose any name for their firm as long as they are not attempting to pass themselves off as other traders. The Registration of Business Names register which required partnerships to give information about themselves has now been abolished by the Companies Act 1981.

Running a partnership

Agency law applies so far as partnerships are concerned and any partner can bind the firm by transactions entered into by him as long as they are within the ordinary course of business. It follows from this that as each partner is the agent of the others, all the partners are liable for any torts or breaches of contract committed by any of the other partners in the course of the firm's business. Each partner is liable with the others for all the firm's debts and obligations incurred while he is a partner. A firm does not have perpetual succession, so it is immediately affected by death, bankruptcy, mental disorder or retirement of any of its members. In these cases, subject to any agreement between the partners, the firm is dissolved and has to be reconstituted. Partnership property in England and Wales belongs to the individual partners. Consequently changes occur in the ownership of and title to the firm's property. No new partner may be introduced into the firm without the consent of the existing members.

The number of partners in any particular firm is limited to 20. Certain professions, including surveyors and estate agents are no longer subject to this restriction and may have as many members as they wish. One result of the limit is that partnerships find it difficult to raise large sums of capital while firms do not have much facility for borrowing. On the other hand, the cost of running a partnership is frequently less onerous. There is less publicity and exposure. Returns do not have to be made to the Registrar of Companies and partnership accounts are not open to public inspection. The *ultra vires* rule (acting beyond powers given) does not apply to partnerships; they can do anything lawful which the partners agree to do. In addition, a firm is not subject to the rules in connection with raising and maintenance of share capital.

COMPANIES

A registered company is a corporation, that is, a separate legal person distinct from its members. Consequently, the debts and contracts of a company are those of the company and not of its members. The great attraction of incorporation is limited liability. The vast majority of companies are limited in liability, in which case members restrict the amount which they will have to contribute in the event of the company ceasing to trade. This sum is equal to any amount outstanding on payment of shares.

Nowadays, the formalities involved in the registration of a company are extensive, and if a private company becomes a public company and invites members of the public to take shares in the company, the costs involved are excessive.

A company has perpetual succession and therefore it is not affected by death or retirement. When a shareholder dies or retires, the company is not dissolved and no drain is made on its resources or the resources of other members. The property of the company belongs to it as such, so there is no need for any formal transfer of company property if there is a change in share ownership.

Directors are appointed by members to manage the affairs of the company on their behalf. Unlike a partnership, members of a company do not have full powers to take part in the affairs of the company. The members of a registered company as such are not its agents and have no powers to manage its affairs. The members of a private company must not exceed 50 but in the case of a public company there is no maximum. Shares in a company can be transferred or mortgaged by a member easily, while in the case of a partnership there are restrictions relating to a partner transferring his equity in the firm. Companies may raise money by borrowing on the strength of their assets or by issuing shares.

9.6 Employment law

THE EMPLOYMENT RELATIONSHIP

Until relatively recently, employment law was embodied in case law. The most which a wrongfully dismissed employee could normally recover would be the wages due to him under a valid period of notice. The last 20 years have seen the emergence of new employment rights established by statute, aimed at preventing an employee from being unfairly dismissed and giving him the right to compensation if he is dismissed by reason of redundancy.

Common law rules are still important especially when determining whether a person is an employee or is self-employed. The relationship of employer and employee is essentially contractual in nature. An employee is a person who works for another (the employer) under a contract of service. This relationship is distinguished from a contract for services under which a self-employed person is to perform some task. It is a question of law which determines the category of the relationship and a number of tests have been devised. The traditional test for determining whether the contract is one of service is the amount of control exercised by the employer. Another test which has been used is the integration test which purports to solve the problem if the independent contractor can be shown not to be integrated into the business. Probably the most satisfactory test is the multiple test which asks a number of pertinent questions to determine the relationship. All the circumstances are to be considered when deciding whether or not a person is an employee. The name which the parties give to the relationship is a relevant factor but it is not conclusive.

THE CONTRACT OF EMPLOYMENT

Sometimes a senior employee of a company will have a written contract of employment which comprehensively deals with all the terms of his employment. More frequently an employee is sent his conditions of service or he is referred to the works rules. These may well incorporate any collective agreement which has come about as a result of negotiations between the employers and trade unions active in a particular industry. Express terms will take precedence over other stipulations, but certain terms are implied whether they have been negotiated upon or not.

Employers' duties

To pay wages: A right to remuneration is implied where a person does work where he would normally expect to be paid. Normally there will be a specific clause in the contract as to payment of wages.

To provide work: There is no general implied duty on the employer to provide work even where it is available. In a few special cases such as contracts involving commission or piece-workers the rule may be modified. Also in situations where part of the consideration involved is for the employee to enhance his reputation. The effect of this lack of an implied duty is that an employer may pay wages in lieu of notice instead of having to provide work.

Health and safety: At common law, the employer is under a common law duty to take care of his employees' safety imposed under the ordinary law of tort in accordance with normal negligence rules. This includes providing adequate plant, premises and machinery together with a competent staff and a safe system of work. The common law position is, of course, much supplemented by the appropriate health and safety legislation and regulations made under the Factories Act 1961 (see 9.7).

Indemnity: Employees are entitled to be indemnified by the employer in respect of expenses incurred by them in the correct performance of their duties.

Employees' duties

To act reasonably: An employee must exercise reasonable care in the performance of his services. Likewise, he must use any skill which he professes to have in a reasonable manner.

Good faith: The employee owes this duty and must not do any act which might prejudice or injure his employer's business. Consequently, where he is in a position of trust he must not allow his personal interests and his duties to conflict. In particular, he must not allow information which he has gained through his employment to be used for his personal benefit. In *Cranleigh Precision Engineering* v. *Bryant* (1964) the defendant, who had formerly been Managing Director of the plaintiff company invented a swimming pool which was marketed by the company. Mr Bryant decided to set up business on his own account, using the information which he had acquired while running the plaintiff company. An injunction was granted which prevented Bryant from competing with Cranleigh in the manufacture of swimming pools.

The employee must render faithful service. Where a person's employment has ceased he may well find that his business activities are restricted by a specific covenant in his contract known as a restraint of trade clause. Such a clause will only be upheld if it can be shown that it is reasonable and not contrary to public policy. Consequently, few of these clauses succeed.

Duty to obey lawful orders: Lawful orders only need be obeyed and not those which are unreasonable.

Statutory statement of terms of the contract

By section 1 of the Employment Protection (Consolidation) Act 1978 (EP(C)A) not later than 13 weeks after the commencement of an employee's period of employment he must receive a written statement of the main terms of the contract of employment containing the following particulars:

(a) identity of the parties to the contract stating when the employment began;
(b) hours of work and overtime arrangements;
(c) rates of pay and the intervals when paid;
(d) entitlement to holidays and holiday pay;
(e) effect of sickness or injury including any provisions for sick pay;
(f) pension schemes;
(g) period of notice required to terminate the contract;
(h) title of the job;
(i) rules relating to discipline and procedures for stating grievances;
(j) if a fixed-term contract, the date of expiration.

Although the statement of terms of the contract must be given to the employee, it may refer him instead to some other readily accessible document which contains full details of the necessary particulars. If there is a written contract of employment which contains details of the matters required to be included in the statement, there is no need for the particulars to be given — that is, as long as the employee has been given a copy of the contract or he has ready access to it. Any change in the terms must be notified in writing within one month. Where the employer fails to give a written statement as required, the matter may be referred to an industrial tribunal. Certain classes of workers, in particular registered dock workers and part-time employees are not eligible to receive a statement.

RECENT EMPLOYMENT LEGISLATION

Legislation introduced in the last 20 years has significantly improved the position of employees. The Redundancy Payments Act 1965 enabled an employee who is dismissed by reason of redundancy to obtain a lump sum from his employer based on age, length of service and wages, and the Employment Protection (Consolidation) Act 1978 (EP(C)A) allows an employee who is unfairly dismissed to obtain an order for reinstatement or re-engagement and/or a payment from his employer to compensate him for his loss.

Other legislation prevents discrimination as regards terms and conditions of employment between the sexes and renders unlawful certain acts of discrimination on the grounds of a person's sex or by reason of the fact that a person is married. Other provisions allow an employee absent from work on account of pregnancy to obtain maternity pay and the right to return to work as long as she informs her employer that she will be absent from work and certain time limits are satisfied. Full-time employees who are officials of recognised and independent trade unions have the right to take time off work with pay in order to carry out their duties in connection with industrial relations with the employer. Likewise, those employees who are members of recognised unions have the right to time off during working hours for taking part in union activities. Full-time employees who are holders of certain public offices have the right to a reasonable amount of time off during working hours for performing those duties. Examples include members of local authorities and justices of the peace.

TERMINATION OF THE CONTRACT OF EMPLOYMENT

A contract for a fixed term ends automatically at the end of that term and no provision for earlier termination by notice is implied. Where the contract is for an indefinite term (the majority of cases) the common law rule is that it can be determined at any time by reasonable notice by either party. This must be considered subject to the EP(C)A which imposes certain minimum periods of notice for long-service employees. One week's notice is required to be given by the employer for each year of continuous employment by his employees. This is subject to a maximum of 12 weeks' notice. An employee who has been employed for at least 4 weeks continuously must give at least one month's notice to terminate the contract. Either party may waive his right to notice or accept a payment in lieu. Instant dismissal without notice will only be justified if the employee has acted in a manner which is incompatible with his obligations to his employer.

UNFAIR DISMISSAL

This is governed by the EP(C)A 1978 as amended by the Employment Act 1980. An employee to whom the act applies has a right not to be unfairly dismissed. Certain employees are excluded from the scope of the legislation including:

(a) those with less than 52 weeks' continuous service with their employers (104 weeks in the case of small companies with less than 20 employees);
(b) part-time employees (less than 16 hours per week; 8 hours after 5 years' employment);
(c) employees older than the normal retirement age at the undertaking where they are employed;
(d) a person employed by his or her spouse;
(e) registered dock workers.

An employee is dismissed if his contract is terminated by his employer with or without notice or where the employee terminates the contract in circumstances where his employer's conduct entitles him to do so. This is known as *constructive dismissal*. It also occurs, less frequently, where a fixed-term contract expires and is not renewed under that contract.

The employer, when dismissing a member of his workforce must prove that the principal reason for the dismissal falls within section 57 of the EP(C)A or there was some other substantial reason justifying the dismissal. The reasons are as follows:

(a) the capability or qualifications of the employee;
(b) the conduct of the employee;
(c) the fact that he was redundant;
(d) the fact that the employee could not continue to work in the position where he was employed without contravening a statutory provision.

If the principal reason for the employee's dismissal is an inadmissible one, the dismissal will be unfair. This covers situations where:

(a) the employee was, or proposed to become, a member of an

independent trade union; or

(b) he had taken part in the activities of an independent trade union.

If an employee is dismissed for an inadmissible reason it does not matter that he is above the statutory age limit or has been employed for less than 52 weeks.

Remedies for unfair dismissal

Within three months from the effective date of dismissal a complaint must be presented to the tribunal. At this stage a copy of the complaint must be sent by the tribunal to a conciliation officer of the Advisory, Conciliation and Arbitration Service (ACAS) who must endeavour to promote a settlement. If the tribunal finds that the dismissal was unfair it must explain its powers to the claimant and ask him whether or not he wishes those powers to be exercised. If he does, the tribunal must consider whether or not to order *reinstatement* by restoring the employee's job and treating the employee as though he had never been dismissed. If the tribunal does not order reinstatement, it must consider whether or not to make an order for *re-engagement* whereby some other suitable employment with the employer or his successor would be ordered.

If the order for *reinstatement* or *re-engagement* is not complied with by the employer, the tribunal must make a *compensation order* and, unless the employer satisfies the tribunal that it was not practicable to comply with the order, additional compensation will be awarded to the employee.

Where the tribunal does not consider reinstatement or re-engagement to be appropriate, as is frequently the case, it may make a compensation order to compensate the employee for his loss which flows from the unfair dismissal. Such an award consists of:

(a) a *basic* award;
(b) a *compensatory* award.

The basic award is calculated in the same way as a redundancy payment (see below). This is estimated according to age, wages and length of service. The compensatory award is such sum as the tribunal considers just and equitable having regard to any loss sustained by the claimant. This may take into account lost benefits and expenses. The normal obligation to mitigate losses applies, and the compensation may be reduced by the claimant's own contributory fault. Appeal from the decision of an industrial tribunal lies to the Employment Appeal Tribunal on a point of law.

REDUNDANCY PAYMENTS

Where a person is dismissed from his employment by reason of redundancy he will be entitled to a redundancy payment. The statutory system was inaugurated by the Redundancy Payments Act 1965 which is now incorporated into the EP(C)A 1978. In order to qualify, the claimant must be:

(a) under retirement age at the time of his dismissal;
(b) continuously employed for a period of two years prior to the application;
(c) dismissed by reason of redundancy.

Dismissal must be treated as being by reason of redundancy if attributable to the fact that:

(a) the employer has ceased or intends to cease to carry on the business for the purposes for which the employee was employed; or
(b) the employer has ceased or intends to cease to carry on the business in the place where the employee was employed; or
(c) requirements for employees to carry out work of a particular kind or to do so in the place where the employee was employed have ceased or diminished.

Where an employer dismisses an employee and arranges for his work to be done by an independent contractor this will amount to a dismissal by reason of redundancy. Also, if the employer makes far-reaching changes so that the work has become fundamentally different from that which the employee originally carried out, there could be a redundancy situation. If the employee was dismissed for misconduct and the employer can prove it, the employee will not be entitled to a redundancy payment.

Calculation of a redundancy payment
As in the case of unfair dismissal, the sum depends upon the three factors of age, pay and service. The payment is not dependent upon the claimant's actual loss. Instead, the statutory formula

divides the claimant's working life with his employer into three periods. The calculation starts at the termination of employment while no account is taken of employment before the age of 18. For each year of continuous employment over the age of 41, one and a half weeks' pay is awarded. One week's pay is given for each year between the ages of 22 and 40, while half a week's pay is given for each such year between 18 and 21. A maximum of 20 years of service is taken into account. A week's pay is subject to an upper limit which is raised from time to time.

If the employer is unable to make the redundancy payment, the employee may recover it directly from the Department of Employment. When he makes the payment an employer can claim a rebate approximately equal to 40 per cent of the payment from the redundancy fund operated by the department. In the case of large-scale redundancies, an employer must consult with a recognised trade union. If he fails to do this, a tribunal can make a 'protective award' in favour of the employees affected.

9.7 Health and safety

The construction industry is one of the most dangerous in which to work. Accidents average some 40,000 per year. A fatality rate of 70 deaths in the first six months of 1983 was a significant increase in such incidents. This is despite the fact that the United Kingdom has one of the most far-reaching and sophisticated systems of health and safety legislation in Western Europe.

Prior to 1974, such legislation as there was existed on a fragmented basis, each industry having its own set of rules. In the construction industry, regulations were derived from the Factories Act 1961. The Health and Safety at Work Act 1974 (HSWA) implemented the main recommendations of the report of the Robens Committee. This committee was critical of the overall structure of safety legislation and, in particular, the fact that millions of people were not covered by any appropriate legislation at all. The new act applied to virtually every employer and employee, and now serves as the principal authority on this area of the law. Eventually the other acts and sets of regulations will be repealed and secondary legislation will be derived from the 1974 Act.

The act sought to lay down general policy rules covering employee safety at work; the requirements of the act are enforced by the

Health and Safety Executive who employ inspectors for the purposes of the act. The objects are stated in section 1 of the 1974 Act as follows:

(a) securing the health, safety and welfare of persons at work;
(b) to protect persons from risks arising from work premises or activities;
(c) to control the storage and use of dangerous substances;
(d) to control certain emissions into the air from premises.

Section 2 of the act requires every employer to ensure so far as it is reasonably practicable the health, safety and welfare of his employees while they are at work. This includes the provision of safe systems of work, appropriate information for employees, training and supervision and an adequate working environment. The employer is also required to provide a written statement relating to health and safety policy which sets out his arrangements and intentions. No standard form is prescribed for this statement but failure to draw up such a statement renders the employer liable to prosecution. The organisation used to carry out the named policy must be defined and the arrangements for making the policy effective must also be identified. Care must be taken by the employer in its preparation because the contents will be binding upon him, and an inspector will almost certainly use the statement of policy as a starting point in any systematic investigation. Consequently, the policy statement should be checked by a firm of professional advisers and revised and monitored as often as thought appropriate.

Employers also have a duty to consult safety representatives with a view to making arrangements which will enable them and their employees to co-operate effectively in developing and promoting measures which ensure the health and safety of the work-force. The effectiveness of such measures must also be checked. Apart from attending meetings of safety committees, each representative must investigate potential hazards and examine the cause of accidents. He should carry out inspections of the work place periodically and investigate any complaints relating to the employees' health, safety or welfare at work. Representations with management and with inspectors of the Health and Safety Executive are also his responsibility.

The Code of Practice which deals with safety representatives and committees also deals with training of such personnel. It suggests that this should be done as soon as possible after appointment and that recognised trade unions whose members are employed at the particular work place have the responsibility of nominating both the course and the representatives who are to take the course. A safety committee must be established when a request has been received by an employer from at least two safety representatives. Such persons are entitled to time off with pay to perform their functions and undergo training.

Liability for defects in any equipment supplied to the employees for their use at work rests with the employer, as does the correct installation of such equipment. Self-employed persons are covered by the legislation and there is an obligation upon them to conduct their work in such a way as to ensure that other persons are not exposed to risks to their health and safety. Employees are also affected by the legislation. Each individual employee must take reasonable care for his own health and safety and for the safety of others affected by his acts or omissions. Where necessary, the work-force must co-operate with the employer and observe the rules and instructions issued by him. They must not interfere with any installation which is provided for these purposes otherwise they may be liable to a fine.

Manufacturers and suppliers are under similar obligations. They must ensure, so far as is reasonably practicable, that:

(a) any article or substance is safe and without risk to health when properly used;
(b) any necessary research or testing is undertaken;
(c) the ultimate user of the article or the substance has sufficient information concerning the product.

These rules apply to any person who designs, imports, erects or installs any article or substance.

Enforcement of the act is in the hands of the Health and Safety Executive. A health and safety inspector has powers to make investigations, enter premises and take samples where necessary. If he thinks it appropriate, he may question persons who may be able to provide information relating to investigations, and he may inspect records, books and certificates.

The main task of the inspectorate is to advise industry but if an employer is found to be infringing the act (including the old Factories Acts and the regulations), he may well be served with an improvement notice setting out the alleged breach and indicating the time limit within which matters must be put right. Any appeal against the notice will suspend its operation while the matter is pronounced upon by an industrial tribunal. In serious cases where substantial personal injury may arise, a prohibition notice may be served. The effect of this is that the activities complained of must cease until they have been remedied. The notice has immediate effect. Notice of appeal does not suspend the prohibition notice.

The penalties which attach to the HSWA are essentially criminal in nature, providing for a fine and, in respect of certain offences, imprisonment for up to two years. This act does not prevent an employee who is injured at work from bringing a personal injuries claim in negligence against his employer.

CONSTRUCTION REGULATIONS

Although it is envisaged that eventually such regulations will be made under the 'umbrella' of the HSWA, at the moment specific regulations covering the construction industry emanate from the Factories Act 1961. These regulations 'fill out' the principal legislation by dealing with situations peculiar to the construction industry and covering day-to-day hazards. A person bringing a claim based on a breach of the regulations is concerned with civil liability and will be bringing an action for damages. Any claim based on breach of the regulations may also involve a breach of obligations under the HSWA or the Factories Act 1961. Therefore criminal liability may be incurred.

The Construction (General Provisions) Regulations 1961

These regulations apply 'to building operations and to works of engineering construction'. The main characteristic of the regulations is the requirement that a contractor and employer who carries out works to which the regulations apply must appoint safety supervisors to oversee any works which are carried out where more than 20 persons are normally employed. The supervisor is responsible for compliance with the safety legislation and must promote safe working practices. Other aspects dealt with include excavations, timbering, explosives and unhealthy working conditions.

The Construction (Lifting Operations) Regulations 1961

As implied, these are concerned with the construction, maintenance and inspection of lifting appliances. After dealing with the exemptions, the regulations refer to such matters as support, fixing and erection of lifting appliances. Rules are also made as to provision of platforms and cabins for crane drivers. The regulations deal with chains, ropes and lifting gear in detail and there are special provisions as to hoists. To prevent personal injuries, standards are laid down as to carriage of persons by means of lifting appliances and the secureness of leads. Appropriate reports and certificates are required to be kept.

The Construction (Health and Welfare) Regulations 1966
These relate to the provision of facilities for employees in the construction industry. In particular:

(a) first aid equipment;
(b) a first aid room: if more than 250 persons are employed upon the site, a contractor with more than 40 employees must provide such facilities;
(c) washing facilities
(d) sanitary conveniences;
(e) protective clothing;
(f) shelters and appropriate accommodation for meals and clothing storage.

The Construction (Working Place) Regulations 1966
These concern themselves with work place safety and satisfactory means of access and egress. In particular, the regulations deal in detail with scaffolding. Strengths, maintenance and erection are considered in detail, and sizes of gangways, guard rails and toe boards are specified.

Despite the existence of the HSWA and the construction regulations made under earlier legislation there is ample evidence that many, particularly smaller firms, are not adhering to the standards imposed. Reluctance by employees to wear safety equipment, especially helmets and safety harnesses, is still the cause of a large number of accidents, while reduction in the overall amount of work available in the last few years has led to competitive tendering which sometimes results in safety aspects being disregarded.

Another problem is effective supervision, especially where a contractor may have a number of sites in operation at the same time. Although the HSWA has been a significant development in this area of the law, we are still a long way from the stage where every employer realises that he is responsible for creating a safe system of work.

Chapter 10

Public law

This chapter is concerned with certain aspects of public law which are essential to the needs of trainee surveyors and those working in the construction industry generally. Public law is concerned with the State, and with rights and duties between individuals and the state. One significant aspect is administrative law, which is concerned with regulating and controlling the government agencies which adminster the legislative process. Those areas of law to be considered in this chapter are essentially statute based and to a degree they are all concerned with obligations between individual and State which help to maintain reasonable environmental standards and improve the quality of life generally. Some are products of the nineteenth century, while others are more sophisticated in nature and are geared to the problems which beset a highly industrialised nation with space at a premium.

10.1 Highway law

The principal act on highway law is the Highways Act 1980 which consolidated the previous Highways Acts and the Highways (Miscellaneous Provisions) Act 1961. The 1980 Act also contains certain recommendations of the Law Commission. At central government level, the Secretary of State for Transport is the Highway Authority. On a local government basis, the county councils and their metropolitan equivalents have major responsibility for the highway network although the other authorities have certain obligations. In the Greater London area the GLC is the principal highway authority. One particular feature of highway law is the use of agency agreements whereby other authorities carry out work on an agency basis in return for appropriate payment. This occurs frequently in connection with trunk roads where the Secretary of State for Transport delegates to the highway authorities the task of upkeep and repair of the way.

CREATION OF HIGHWAYS

A highway is usually described as a way over which the public at large have the right to pass and repass. Such a way may be created at common law by the dedication of a right of passage across land for use by the public or it may be created by statute.

Common law

Creation of a highway at common law requires three essential elements. The landowner must intend to make over a right of passage across his land for the benefit of the public at large. This intention may be express, in which case there may be a deed embodying an agreement entered into by the owner with the highway authority, or it may be implied if there is sufficient evidence of such an intention.

The position is now simplified by the Highways Act 1980. If a way has been enjoyed by the public as of right and without interruption for a full period of 20 years, it is deemed to have been dedicated as a highway. This presumption may be challenged if there is evidence to the contrary such as the display of an appropriate notice denying an intention to dedicate ('private road') or if the way is shut off at periodic intervals. The person who dedicates the way must be the fee simple owner because there can be no effective dedication unless the grantor is capable of giving a right over his land for all time. Although there may be restrictions as to the mode of user over the way, the right of passage must be capable of being exercised by the public at large and not limited to particular groups or classes of people.

Statute

A highway may be created by statute either by general or local act of parliament. The 1980 Act contains a number of provisions regulating the statutory methods by which a highway may be created. Section 24 of the 1980 Act gives major powers to the minister and to local highway authorities to construct new highways. The National Parks and Access to the Countryside Act 1949 governs ways which are mainly used by non-vehicular traffic.

RESPONSIBILITY FOR HIGHWAYS

At common law, responsibility for the repair of all highways fell to the inhabitants of the parish. Today there are four categories of repair responsibility to consider.

Highways which are 'maintainable at public expense'
This denotes that the highway is the responsibility of the appropriate highway authority. If the highway was in existence before 1835, it automatically comes into this category. If the highway has been taken over since that date by the highway authority under a statutory provision it will be formally adopted. Section 37 of the Highways Act 1980 allows for this. Section 38 is concerned with adoption by agreement.

Trunk roads
These are the principal roads which constitute the national system of routes for through traffic. Motorways do not come into this category. The Minister of Transport has liability but in practice the county councils undertake works of repair and upkeep.

Private road
The number of ways which are maintained by persons other than the highway authority are small in number. Where a body or individual persons have carried out repairs over a long period of time liability may arise by prescription. Liability to maintain may also pass with the land.

Private streets
There are certain ways for which nobody is responsible for repair. Ordinary repairs to these streets are the responsibility of no specific person although the highway authority may require frontagers (persons who own property which abuts onto the highway) to carry out emergency repairs. If the frontagers default, the authority may do the works and recover the cost from the owners concerned.

The adoption of private streets
A highway authority may decide that a private street ought to be adopted. In such a case, a procedural code based upon the Private Street Works Act 1892 will be put into effect. By this the highway authority:

(a) resolves to make up the way;
(b) prepares plans and specifications;
(c) estimates the costs involved and makes a provisional apportionment of costs among frontagers;
(d) gives notice of final apportionment.

Contribution by individual frontagers is estimated in accordance with frontage of their premises onto the street. Quite frequently, the authority will contribute either part or the whole of the expenses involved in the making up of a private street. Owners have extensive rights of objection, while an appeal to the Secretary of State for Transport is available when a frontager receives a demand for payment.

The Advance Payment Code is a method whereby the payment of sums involved in respect of the street works can be secured. By these provisions, no building can take place in a private street until the owner of the land where the works are to take place has paid or given security. Once development has reached a certain stage, frontagers are then able to require that street works be carried out.

STANDARD OF REPAIR

At common law a highway authority owes a duty of care to prevent injury to those persons likely to use the way. In *Haley* v. *London Electricity Board* (1965) the plaintiff, who was blind, became deaf as a result of injuries received when he fell into a trench which was the responsibility of the defendant's servants. This common law duty is reinforced by similar statutory obligations in the Highways Act 1980.

Another aspect of the highway authorities' liability is where they fail to repair the way or repair it negligently. At one time, an authority only incurred liability by misfeasance, i.e. carrying out repairs negligently or wrongfully. If the authority simply failed to carry out its obligations there was no remedy available. This defence of nonfeasance was effectively abolished in 1964; but if the highway authority can show that in the circumstances they have done everything possible to make the way as safe as possible, having regard to the character of the road and the traffic expected to use it, they will have a defence.

RIGHTS OF THE PUBLIC OVER THE HIGHWAY

The rights of the public in connection with the highway are limited to passing and repassing over the way. If this right is exceeded, a person may find that he has become a trespasser. In such circumstances, a person exceeding his rights may be restrained by the owner of adjoining land or in some cases by other users of the highway. Therefore, technically, a person who is picketing on the highway, other than in contemplation of a trade dispute, or an onlooker estimating the form of horses before a race from the road, may be exceeding his rights to pass and repass.

The law requires that these rules be construed in a reasonable manner as in *Rodgers* v. *Ministry of Transport* (1952) where lorry drivers were entitled to park their vehicles on a grass verge which formed part of the highway while having a meal as long as no obstruction was caused. The highway authority has a discretion whether to issue proceedings or not. The discretion must be exercised properly in accordance with the objects of highway law.

INTERFERENCE WITH THE HIGHWAY

Both the criminal law and the civil law protect the rights of the public to pass and repass over the highway without hindrance. The Highways Act 1980, Part 1, also contains many regulatory offences relating to such matters as builders' skips, scaffolding and the mixing of cement on highways.

In addition to the statutory offences created by the act, it is also an offence to obstruct the way at common law. Civil liability creates more problems. A plaintiff in this respect will often be looking for damages and an injunction to prevent the continuation of the hindrance affecting the way. Not every physical obstruction of the way will constitute a nuisance in law, but the plaintiff's claim will normally be in nuisance or in negligence. In *Chesterfield Corporation* v. *Arthur Robinson* (1955) the plaintiffs were awarded damages when they had to divert their bus service because a large load in the process of delivery by the defendants had been negligently transported.

One significant problem is that civil proceedings can only be taken by an individual in his own name if he can show that some private right of his has been interfered with as well as a public right, or if he can prove that he has suffered special damage over and above that suffered by the public at large. The action for the injunction will be brought by the highway authority in its own name or by the Attorney-General on behalf of some other person. In the latter case it is known as a *relator* action.

10.2 Environmental health law

The framework of public health law was laid in the nineteenth century as a result of the Industrial Revolution. The famous Public Health Act of 1875 provided the basis for subsequent general public health legislation passed in the twentieth century. The Public Health Acts of 1936 and 1961 contain the bulk of the general law relating to the environment, while many specific acts regulate the law on these matters. Examples include the Water Act 1973, the Clean Air Acts, legislation governing noise, and the Control of Pollution Act 1974. At local level, district councils have responsibility for the majority of everyday environmental health aspects although, where appropriate, certain specialist bodies such as the water authorities and port health authorities may be liable. Sometimes district councils may act together for administrative reasons and form a joint board.

SANITATION
Since the setting up of the regional water authorities under the Water Act 1973, these bodies have taken over the duties previously entrusted to the district councils in sanitation matters. To a certain extent, the water authorities and the district councils work together.

Definitions
By Section 343 of the Public Health Act 1936:

'*Drains*' are pipes which are used for the drainage of one building or of buildings or yards *within* the same curtilage;

'*Sewers*' are pipes used for the drainage of buildings or yards *not* within the same curtilage.

It is important to distinguish between the two because drains are always the responsibility of a private individual while sewers may be the responsibility of a private individual or of the water authority.

Public sewers
These are defined by section 20 of the 1936 Act as substituted by the Water Act 1973. Sewers coming within the definition are:

(a) those vested in the local authority in 1936;

(b) those constructed by the authority at any time and not simply for their own use;
(c) sewers constructed by the authority in pursuance of some statutory provision such as where a local authority adopts a private street;
(d) any other sewer vested in the authority for some purpose other than simply draining property belonging to the authority.

Private sewers
These are not defined in the act and are a private responsibility. They comprise sewers which do not come within the definition of public sewers and therefore include those constructed by private individuals, built for a profit, as a land drain, or by the authority simply for the drainage of its own property.

Duties of the water authorities relating to public sewers
There is an obligation on the water authorities to provide such public sewers as may be necessary for the proper draining of its area. In the event of no provision, the only remedy open to an aggrieved person is a complaint to the Secretary of State. In the event of a person suffering loss because of non-compliance with this obligation, damages may be obtained. It is also the duty of the water authority to maintain, cleanse and empty all public sewers vested in the authority. Sometimes the water authority may recover its expenses in respect of the maintenance of sewers.

While carrying out their functions, the authorities must act in such a manner so as 'not to create a nuisance'. In *Smeaton* v. *Ilford Corporation* (1954) this was taken to exclude liability for escapes of sewerage in the absence of negligence. In *Pride of Derby Angling Association Ltd* v. *British Celanese* (1953) a successful claim was brought against three defendants including Derby Corporation who were carrying out their obligations in such a way so as to cause pollution of the River Derwent.

The Public Health Acts and the Water Act 1973 allow owners and occupiers to have their drains or sewers drained into public sewers unless the discharge contains trade effluent. If the authority elects to make the connection itself, the cost will still have to be borne by the owner concerned.

STATUTORY NUISANCES
A nuisance is frequently defined as an indirect interference with a

person's use or enjoyment of land. The tort is known as private nuisance while nuisance may also be public in which case it is also a crime. Because of the difficulties involved in bringing these proceedings, such as cost, the problem of relator proceedings, and the effects of the industrial society and urbanisation, it has been essential to utilise a cheaper and speedier process. The remedy has been to define certain actions as statutory nuisances and to prescribe a procedure for dealing with them. The remedies are available to both local authorities (acting through their environmental health officers) and to private individuals. The advantage of dealing with nuisances in the Magistrates' Court rather than in the High Court is obvious.

Obligations and definitions

By section 91 of the Public Health Act 1936, district councils have an obligation to inspect their districts from time to time for the existence of statutory nuisances and to take steps to abate them.

Section 92 of the 1936 Act defines statutory nuisances as follows:

(a) premises which are prejudicial to health or a nuisance;
(b) an animal kept in such a place or manner as to be prejudicial to health or a nuisance;
(c) an accumulation or deposit which is prejudicial to health or a nuisance;
(d) dust or effluvia caused by a trade business or process prejudicial to health or a nuisance to the inhabitants of a neighbourhood;
(e) any work place with insufficient ventilation or so overcrowded as to be prejudicial to the health of the employees;
(f) contaminated water storage containers for domestic purposes which are prejudicial to health or a nuisance;
(g) a foul or choked watercourse which is prejudicial to health or a nuisance;
(h) any tent, shed or van which is used for habitation and which is so overcrowded or deficient in sanitary accommodation as to be prejudicial to health or a nuisance.

To satisfy the 'prejudicial to health or a nuisance' test, different standards have been applied over the years. At one time, it was decided that any state of affairs which might cause discomfort to occupants could amount to a statutory nuisance. Recent cases have resulted in a more legalistic approach being taken by the courts. To be prejudicial to health the state of the premises must be insanitary or fundamentally defective in which case it will constitute a statutory nuisance. If this condition is not satisfied, it is not sufficient for the nuisance to simply cause discomfort to the occupiers of the premises in question. In addition, it must affect neighbouring property.

Abatement of nuisances

Once the authority is satisfied that the statutory nuisance exists it may serve an abatement notice on the person responsible stating the alleged nuisance and the procedure to be followed to put it right. If the nuisance is likely to recur, a prohibition notice may be served stating the procedures required to prevent the continuance of the problem. Not only the authority, but also a private individual who is aggrieved by the existence of a statutory nuisance may initiate these proceedings. A private individual should make a complaint to a justice of the peace. If the complaint is substantiated, the proceedings will continue as if the local authority had commenced proceedings.

In the event of non-compliance with the notice, the authority may apply to the Magistrates' Court for a nuisance order. Failure to comply with this order may lead to a fine, and a daily penalty for as long as the nuisance continues. Where appropriate, the authority may do the work and charge the cost to the person responsible. An emergency procedure is available to the authority in which case nine days after serving the initial notice the authority may proceed.

10.3 Building regulations

Regulations relating to the imposition of minimum standards in connection with the construction of new buildings date back to 1875. The Public Health Act of that year gave authorities powers to regulate the construction of buildings in the form of building by-laws. These by-laws were superseded in 1936 by a further set of by-laws which dealt with such matters as materials used and methods of ventilation. These rules were primarily intended to relate to new buildings but some of the controls concern existing buildings. In 1961, the Public Health Act replaced the old building by-laws with a uniform set of regulations which applied throughout the country as a whole. In the old London County Council area the London Building Acts apply. The first set of building regulations appeared in 1965. Those in force at the moment were introduced in 1976 and have since been amended. The Health and Safety at Work Act 1974 extended the scope of the regulations significantly.

PLANS

The nature of building regulations approval is well illustrated by the rules relating to the submission of plans. Persons undertaking works which come within the scope of the regulations have a duty to submit plans together with specifications and other particulars. Where plans are submitted and the regulations are complied with, the authority has no alternative but to pass the plans. In other words the process is a regulatory one and there is no discretionary element, unlike the position where a planning authority considers an application. Statute provides for a number of situations where the plans must automatically be rejected by the authority. These include situations where there is unsatisfactory provision for drainage, proposed building over a sewer, or on ground filled with offensive materials. In two situations, where there is insufficient food storage accommodation and where there is a lack of adequate bathroom provision, the authority may reject the plans.

THE DECISION AND ENFORCEMENT

Notice of its decision must be given by the authority to the applicant. Sometimes, works may be approved in stages and in such circumstances conditions will frequently be attached requiring the deposit of further plans. Notice of the decision of the authority must normally be given within 5 weeks or such extended period not exceeding 8 weeks as may be agreed in writing between the parties. For planning applications the period is 8 weeks, and if the parties so desire, this time limit may be extended as long as they so wish. Where works are carried out in breach of the regulations the authority may require that the works be altered, or where appropriate, that the works be pulled down. If the person responsible ignores the notice, the authority itself may alter or pull down the works and charge the cost of the operation to the person on whom the notice was served.

The authority must act with diligence because the notice must be served within 12 months of the completion of the works or the unauthorised works become legitimate. The authority is mainly concerned with a fundamental breach of the regulations as opposed to technical slips. Sometimes it is appropriate for the authority to apply for an injunction for the removal or alteration of the contravening works. Relaxation of the regulations is possible, but regulations must be acted upon within three years otherwise the consent will run out of time.

10.4 Planning law

The first comprehensive planning act in this country dates from 1947. This was followed by consolidating legislation and in 1971 the present principal act on town and country planning law appeared on the statute book. Since then, many admendments have taken place but the Town and Country Planning Act, 1971, remains the major enactment. Unlike the law relating to housing or public health legislation which tends to relate solely to an individual property, planning law is concerned with the community at large. It places on the landowner an obligation to obtain permission before he may change or alter the use of his land thereby putting first the interests of society generally.

Planning law is statutory in nature and the courts play a relatively minor role. Day-to-day responsibility for planning matters is entrusted to local authorities while the role of central government is to supervise and determine overall policy. District councils have the responsibility for the majority of applications and enforcement of the legislation. The county councils are responsible for strategy and policy matters, only involving themselves in planning consents where the matter is out of the ordinary.

DEVELOPMENT PLANS

Since 1948 local planning authorities have been required to prepare and maintain development plans for their areas. Once prepared, such a plan forms the basis of planning control for the area. Until 1968, a single development plan was prepared by the counties consisting of a series of maps supported by a written statement indicating the method and stages by which the plan would be carried out. The plan had to be approved by the Secretary of State and provision was made for objections to the plan, all of which had to be considered. At least every 5 years the old style plan had to be reviewed.

For a number of reasons, in particular the cumbersome nature of the plan and the lengthy process for hearing objections, the system was replaced by the so-called 'new style' plan consisting of a structure plan and a local plan. Structure plans, which are prepared by the county highway authorities, are intended to form the overall framework for development. These plans, which are produced as a result of a survey instituted by the authority, will deal with all relevant aspects relating to the land together with population matters. Each structure plan must be approved by the Secretary of State at the Department of the Environment and any person wishing to make representations or objections to the plan may be dealt with by an 'examination in public'.

The local plans represent a detailed translation of the policy set out in the structure plan. These are the responsibility of district councils. The plans may take a number of forms, dealing with a particular area or subject such as transport policies or the green belt. Areas selected for early development are dealt with in action area plans. A plan consists of a map and a written statement and it will comprise such descriptive matter and illustrations as appropriate. Its purpose is to guide the authority and any intending developer in respect of possible development of the land covered by the plan. The local plan need not be confirmed. It is normally sent to the Secretary of State for information only, but in the case of conflict between structure and local plans the latter will take priority.

THE DEVELOPMENT AND CONTROL SYSTEM

The key word in planning law is development. If a particular activity concerning land amounts to development, planning permission will be required, but if the activity does not, no planning consent is required. Development means the carrying out of building, engineering, mining or other operations in, on, over or under land, or the making of any material change in the use of any buildings or other land. This is a two-fold definition comprising operations development and material change of use.

Certain operations and uses are declared by the 1971 Act not to be development. Alterations which do not materially affect the appearance of a building will come into this category, as will the use of a building within the boundary of a dwelling house which is incidental to the enjoyment of the property. Whether a particular activity amounts to development can be tested by applying to the local planning authority for a determination as to whether or not planning permission is required.

To constitute operations development, there must be a change in the physical character of the land. Material change of use is not defined by the act. It is essentially a matter of fact and degree which depends upon the circumstances and the character of the use. A change of use must be a material one while the relevant consideration is the nature of the user and not the identity or purpose of the individual occupier. Whether an activity amounts to a material change of use is a matter for the local planning authority. The choice of planning unit is important, and an intensification of user may amount to a change of user. A change of use within a 'use class' does not amount to development. A change from a jeweller's shop to a book shop will not amount to development but the change to a garage or to an estate agent's office will require permission.

PERMITTED DEVELOPMENT

Planning law recognises that not every activity which amounts to development should require consent. Therefore, from time to time, General Development Orders (GDOs) are enacted which automatically grant permission for various minor acts of development. The current GDO was amended in 1981 and it grants planning permission automatically to 23 classes of development.

In particular, the amended order substantially increased the limits on the permitted enlargement of a dwelling house. The limit is now 70 cubic metres or 15 per cent, whichever is the greater (50 cubic metres or 10 per cent in the case of a terraced house), subject to a maximum of 115 cubic metres. These limits are subject to limitations as to the amount of curtilage which may be covered by buildings and as to height and distance from the boundary. The limits for the permitted extensions of industrial buildings have also been increased.

APPLICATIONS FOR PLANNING PERMISSION

Application is made to the district planning authority. The form should be accompanied by plans and drawings indicating the location and the form of development. A certificate stating the applicant's legal interest in the land and, where appropriate, that notice has been given to the owner should also be submitted. The prescribed fee must also accompany the application.

In the case of operations development, an intending developer may wish to test the principle of whether or not the authority will allow him a consent. In that case, an outline application may be made indicating the proposed development. In such circumstances only a site plan need be filed.

The local planning authority may refuse the application, grant it, or give consent subject to conditions. Unless the parties agree to an extension, the planning authority has 8 weeks to come to a decision. If permission is granted, the development which it authorises must be begun within 5 years of obtaining consent. If the consent is given subject to conditions, these must be certain and reasonably relate to the proposed development.

APPEALS AND ENFORCEMENT

Where a planning authority refuses an application or imposes conditions upon the consent, the applicant may appeal to the Secretary of State at the Department of the Environment. Notice of appeal must be given within 6 months or such further time as the Secretary of State will allow.

Where there has been a 'breach of planning control', the local planning authority has a discretion to issue an enforcement notice on the owners and occupiers of the land and any other person who the authority considers is materially affected by the notice. The notice must specify the events complained of, the steps to be taken to remedy the breach, the date upon which the notice will take effect and the period for compliance with the notice. Breach of planning control on its own is not a criminal offence but failure to comply with a valid enforcement notice is.

In the case of operations development the notice must be served within 4 years of the breach of planning control. There is no time limit in the case of a material change of use. Any appeal against the notice should be made to the Secretary of State.

In the event of non-compliance with the notice, the local planning authority may enter the land and carry out the steps required by the enforcement notice and recover any expenses. If the owner is prosecuted, apart from any fine payable, he may well be subject to a daily penalty for as long as the breach continues. As the enforcement notice fails to take effect until the outcome of any appeal against it, the local planning authority will frequently issue a stop notice along with the enforcement notice. This prohibits the carrying on of any activity complained about in the enforcement notice.

There is no appeal against a stop notice.

AMENITY CONTROL

In certain cases, special rules apply. There is an obligation upon the Secretary of State to compile a list of buildings of special architectural or historic interest. District councils receive a copy of the list so that the owners of properties affected can be informed. Those buildings of outstanding importance are listed as Grade 1 while the rest come into Grade 2. There is also a Grade 2* which denotes the better examples in the second category. Before any alteration or extension can take place to such a building, the applicant must obtain a listed building consent. Any failure to obtain such consent may lead to a listed building enforcement notice being served on the person responsible.

The Civic Amenities Act 1967 introduced the concept of the conservation area. Subject to certain exceptions, listed building control is applicable to all buildings in such an area. Similar rules apply to trees. A tree preservation order (TPO) may prohibit the destruction of trees and secure replanting. Trees in conservation areas are protected in a similar way to those in a tree preservation order.

10.5 Housing law

The term housing law is used in connection with housing conditions and the obligations which fall to local authorities in this area of the law. It is an area of law where much legislation has been enacted on to the statute book, some of it political in character.

UNFIT HOUSING

All housing authorities (mainly district councils) have an obligation to review housing conditions within their areas at periodic intervals. If this review is not carried out, the Secretary of State may direct that it be undertaken. The underlying intention of the Housing Acts is that no person ought to be allowed to live in a house which is unfit for human habitation. In deciding whether or not a dwelling is statutorily unfit, the nine factors in section 4 of the 1957 Housing Act must be considered. If the house is 'so far defective' in one or more of the nine items so as to be 'not reasonably suitable for occupation' it is unfit. These matters include repair, stability, freedom from damp, internal arrangement, natural lighting, ventilation, water supply, drainage and sanitary convenience, and the facilities for preparation and cooking of food and for the disposal of waste water. Only these aspects are to be taken into account and it is a question of degree in each case as to whether the property is unfit. In *Summers* v. *Salford Corporation* (1943) even a defective sash cord rendered the house unfit on the particular facts of the case.

Individual unfit housing

If the authority considers that a dwelling is unfit for human habitation or it is in 'substantial disrepair' it has to consider whether the house is capable of being rendered fit for human habitation at a reasonable expense. If so, a repair notice is served upon the person who has control of the house. This notice will specify the works to be carried out. The notice is subject to a right of appeal.

If the person having control of the dwelling fails to carry out the repairs the authority themselves may do the work. If the owner fails to pay for the work carried out, the property itself is subject to the debt. Success depends to a large extent upon the attitude of the local authority in exercising its default powers. Compulsory purchase may be authorised if on appeal the court decides that the works cannot be carried out at a reasonable expense.

If the property is not capable of repair at reasonable cost, a different procedure will be followed. The authority will arrange a 'time and place' meeting at which all interested parties should meet. Unless such a party gives an undertaking to execute the necessary works within a reasonable time, the consequence will be demolition or a closing order. The closing order is preferred if the property is a terrace house and demolition would remove the support of adjoining houses or if the property can be used for a purpose other than human habitation. If necessary, a compulsory acquisition of the property may take effect. The occupants will then be rehoused and compensated by the local authority.

Groups of unfit houses

The local authority may declare an area to be a clearance area. This will be the case if all the houses in the area are unfit for human habitation and the only satisfactory method of dealing with the problem is to demolish all the dwellings in the area. Since 1974, the authority must purchase dwellings in the area by agreement or on a compulsory basis. Those displaced from their homes will be rehoused.

Where appropriate, an authority will declare an area to be a Housing Action Area. Such an area is one where housing conditions are unsatisfactory and it is considered that the problem can be dealt with effectively in a period of 5 years so as to improve the housing conditions in the area as a whole.

A General Improvement Area is a predominantly residential area in which living conditions should be improved and where the authority considers that they should carry out or assist the improvement.

10.6 Compulsory purchase

In the United Kingdom, compulsory acquisition of land can only be carried out if there is a power of acquisition granted by law. Therefore, there is a need for statutory powers. In the late eighteenth and early nineteenth centuries powers were frequently sought from parliament by private companies to enable them to provide services such as canals and railways. At the time the only method available of obtaining compulsory powers was to promote a private bill. The Land Clauses Consolidation Act 1845 improved the situation by incorporating into one act the types of provisions previously inserted into each separate act by providing a code of law covering all questions relating to the exercise of powers of compulsory acquisition. This code of compulsory purchase power could therefore be incorporated into other legislation by reference. These provisions are now consolidated in the Compulsory Purchase Act 1965. Nowadays the normal acquiring bodies are government departments and local and public authorities.

COMPULSORY POWERS

Sometimes, local authorities and public bodies acquire land by agreement instead of activating their compulsory powers. Where an authority, with the necessary statutory powers purchases land with the agreement of the vendor without having first made a compulsory purchase order, the transaction is similar to ordinary conveyancing procedures. Sometimes there is a confirmed Compulsory Purchase Order (CPO) in the background when the acquisition by agreement takes place. A variety of legislation deals with compulsory acquisition. Certain acts give a general power to acquire land such as the Local Government Act 1972, while others contain specific powers such as the Highways and Housing Acts (see 10.1 and 10.5). In the vast majority of cases authorisation to acquire is governed by the Acquisition of Land Act 1981. Under this act:

(a) The authority makes the order, advertises it in a local newspaper for two consecutive weeks and sends a copy of the notice to owners, lessees and occupiers. A plan must accompany the order.

(b) Any person on whom the notice is served may make written objections to the Secretary of State. The notice served on the occupier must specify a period of not less than 21 days in which objections may be made.

(c) If there are objections a local public enquiry will be held. This gives the 'statutory objectors' the opportunity to put their case before an inspector appointed by the minister. Such objectors may be represented by solicitor or counsel, and witnesses may be called. After the hearing, the inspector makes his report to the minister who decides as a matter of policy the decision which is to be made. The minister must give his decision in writing. As an alternative to a public enquiry, the minister may hold a less formal hearing.

(d) If no objections to the order are raised or they are not substantiated, the order will be sent to the confirming authority to be confirmed with or without modification. Every order must be confirmed before it becomes operative. The order becomes operative from the date of first publication. Notice must be given to those already served and placed in a local newspaper. In special cases such as National Trust land and ancient monuments, a draft of the order must be laid before parliament. After confirmation the order cannot be challenged apart from the standard procedure for appeal to the High Court within 6 weeks, on the ground that the order is *ultra vires* or there has been a failure to comply with a procedural requirement. The 6-week period is a rigid one, while appeal on the procedural ground will only succeed if the applicant can show that he has been substantially prejudiced by failure to observe the formalities.

(e) Notice to treat must be served after confirmation of the order. This is notification of the acquiring authority's intention to purchase the owner's interest in a particular piece of land. The notice requires persons affected to submit details of their interests and their claim for compensation. This notice fixes the nature of the interest to be acquired.

Until fairly recently, the date of service of notice to treat was the basis upon which valuation was assessed. As a consequence of the decision in *Birmingham Corporation* v. *West Midland Baptist (Trust) Association Inc.* (1970) the date for valuation is that upon which the acquiring authority takes possession or when the purchase price is agreed, whichever is earlier. When the compensation is agreed, that agreement and the notice to treat amount to an enforceable contract. Notice to treat must be served within three years of the making of the order, otherwise it will lapse. The rights given by the notice may also be lost by abandonment. In *Grice* v. *Dudley Corporation* (1958) the authority served notice to treat in 1939, but failed to proceed until 1955 when they still intended to purchase under the original notice. The court decided that the acquiring authority had clearly shown an intention to abandon the order from the delay. Consequently, the earlier notice to treat was no longer valid.

(f) Completion of the transaction is by execution of a conveyance to the acquiring authority. An acquiring authority may obtain early possession of the land as long as notice to treat has been served by giving notice of entry on to the land. The usual practice is to pay 90 per cent of the estimated compensation to the claimant and on completion to make final adjustment together with interest on the purchase price.

An alternative procedure to the service of a notice to treat is found in the use of a General Vesting Declaration (GVD). Instead of two separate transactions, the notice to treat and the conveyance to the authority are combined. Owners and occupiers are informed that the authority intends to proceed on this basis and when the vesting declaration is made it vests title to the land in the authority. The declaration must be registered as a local land charge.

ASSESSMENT OF COMPENSATION

The basis of compensation where land is compulsorily acquired is market value. Section 5 of the Land Compensation Act 1961 lays down a number of rules relating to the value of the land while retaining the right of the claimant to additional compensation for disturbance and other matters suffered in consequence of the land being taken.

The 'six rules'

1. No allowance is to be made on account of the acquisition being compulsory.

2. The value of the land shall be taken to be the amount which it might be expected to realise if sold on the open market by a willing seller. This rule is the proper basis of valuation. Such a seller is a free agent. He is not 'a person willing to sell his property without reserve for any price he can obtain for it'.

3. Where the land is specially suited or adaptable for a particular purpose, this shall not be taken into account, if the purpose is one to which the land could be applied only in pursuance of a statutory power or for which there is no market apart from the special needs of a particular purchaser or the requirements of any authority possessing compulsory purchaser powers.

4. Where the value of the land is increased by reason of the use thereof or of any premises thereon in a manner which could be constrained by a court or is contrary to law or detrimental to the health of the inmates or to the public health, the amount of that increase would not be taken into account.

5. Where the land is used for a purpose of a kind for which there is no general demand or market, compensation may be assessed on the basis of the reasonable cost of reinstatement if the Lands Tribunal is satisfied that reinstatement in some other place is bona fide intended.

   This 'equivalent reinstatement' rule is applicable where the claimant owns property for which there is no ready market. An assessment on market value basis would be unjust. Therefore the cost of acquiring property elsewhere for a specific purpose is allowed. There must be a bona fide intention to rebuild elsewhere while the cost of reinstatement must not be disproportionately high.

6. This refers back to rule and states that the provisions of rule 2 shall not affect the assessment of compensation for disturbance or other matter not directly based on the valuation of land.

Additional rules deal with market increases and decreases. Those which are not genuine are to be disregarded while an increase in the value of an owner's adjoining land which is not taken by the authority must be 'set off' against compensation if it results from the compulsory acquisition. Certain assumptions are also made by the act in respect of planning permissions.

Additional claims

In addition to market value compensation a claim may be made for disturbance. This is to compensate for the claimant having to vacate the premises. Any loss which relates to the compulsory acquisition can be recovered as long as it is not too remote and it is the direct consequence of the compulsory acquisition. In *Harvey v. Crawley Development Corporation* (1957) the plaintiff made an additional claim for disturbance and expenses arising out of an abortive purchase of a new house and the actual purchase of her new home. The claim was successful.

Disturbance compensation may sometimes be assessed on the basis of total extinguishment. This only applies if the claimant is over 60 years of age, occupies business premises with a rateable value not exceeding £2,250 and does not wish to relocate the business elsewhere. The claimant is required to undertake that he will not dispose of the goodwill or re-engage in a similar business within the area. He must also adhere to the limits imposed by the authority.

Where part of the claimant's land is taken he may claim for injurious affection. This may take a number of forms. A severance payment is claimed where the value of the claimant's land which remains after compulsory acquisition, is so reduced that its new value, taking compensation paid for the land into account, is lower than the total value before the land was severed. A good example of severance in practice would occur where farmland is severed because a new motorway is built. Injurious affection proper greatly resembles private nuisance. The claim is made where after compulsory acquisition of part of the claimant's land, that land which remains is reduced in value because of works which are carried out on the land taken. This may cause noise, dust, loss of privacy or similar discomfort. Compensation will be equal to the diminution in value of the land.

Where no land has been taken from the claimant and he is prejudicially affected by what is done on neighbouring land, much more difficulty arises. Before such a claim can be successful, the conditions laid down in *Metropolitan Board of Works* v. *McCarthy* (1874) have to be satisfied. These are as follows:

(a) The action giving rise to the depreciation of the claimant's land must be authorised by statute.
(b) The cause of depreciation must be actionable at law but for the statutory authority.

(c) Compensation can only be claimed for depreciation of rights in land.

(d) The loss must be caused by 'execution of the works' and not by the use of the land after the acquiring authority has carried out those works.

Because of the narrow basis upon which such a claim could be brought, the Land Compensation Act 1973 was enacted. This gave owners a right to compensation for depreciation to their land caused by the use as distinct from the execution of public works.

Table of Cases

Note: The following abbreviations are used:

AC – Law Reports (3rd series) Appeal Cases
All ER – All England Law Reports
App Cas – Law Reports (2nd series) Appeal Cases
BLR – Building Law Reports
Ch.D – Law Reports, Chancery Division
CL & Fin. – Clark and Finnelly Reports
CPD – Common Pleas Division
EG – Estates Gazette
H & C – Hurlstone & Coltman
H L Cas – House of Lords Cases
KB – Law Reports, King's Bench Division
LGR – Local Government Reports
LJ CP – Law Journal, Common Pleas
LR CP – Law Reports, Common Pleas
LR HL – English and Irish Appeals
LL LR – Lloyd's List Law Reports
P & CR – Planning & Compensation Reports
QB – Law Reports, Queen's Bench Division
TLR – Times Law Reports
WLR – Weekly Law Reports

Table of Statutes

Subject Index